Second Workshop on Computational Linguistics and Clinical Psychology: From Linguistic Signal to Clinical Reality 2015

Held at NAACL HLT 2015

Denver, Colorado, USA
5 June 2015

ISBN: 978-1-5108-0436-4

Printed from e-media with permission by:

Curran Associates, Inc.
57 Morehouse Lane
Red Hook, NY 12571

Some format issues inherent in the e-media version may also appear in this print version.

Printed by Curran Associates, Inc. (2015)

For permission requests, please contact the Association for Computational Linguistics at the address below.

Association for Computational Linguistics
209 N. Eighth Street
Stroudsburg, Pennsylvania 18360

Phone: 1-570-476-8006
Fax: 1-570-476-0860

acl@aclweb.org

Additional copies of this publication are available from:

Curran Associates, Inc.
57 Morehouse Lane
Red Hook, NY 12571 USA
Phone: 845-758-0400
Fax: 845-758-2634
Email: curran@proceedings.com
Web: www.proceedings.com

Introduction

In the United States, mental health problems are among the most costly challenges we face. The numbers are staggering: An estimated $57.5B was spent on mental health care in 2006. Some 25 million American adults will have an episode of major depression this year, and suicide is the third leading cause of death for people between 10 and 24 years old. The importance of clinical psychology as a problem space cannot be overstated.

For clinical psychologists, language plays a central role in diagnosis, and many clinical instruments fundamentally rely on manual coding of patient language. Applying language technology in this domain can have an enormous impact: Many individuals under-report psychiatric symptoms, such as active duty soldiers; or lack the self-awareness to report accurately, such as individuals involved in substance abuse who do not recognize their own addiction. Many people cannot even obtain access to a clinician who is qualified to perform a psychological evaluation, such as those without adequate insurance or who live in rural areas. Bringing language technology to bear on these problems could lead to inexpensive screening measures that may be administered by a wider array of healthcare professionals, suited to the realities of healthcare practice.

Researchers have begun targeting such issues, applying computational linguistic methods to clinical psychology with compelling results. Prior to this workshop series, research had looked at identifying emotion in suicide notes, analyzing the language of those with autistic spectrum disorders, aiding the diagnosis of dementia, and screening for depression.

ACL 2014 hosted the first Computational Linguistics and Clinical Psychology Workshop, which brought together the researchers in this nascent field. This workshop was a great success, with accepted papers proposing methods for predicting veteran suicide risk, aiding the diagnosis of dementia, and predicting depression and post-traumatic stress order in social media.

NAACL 2015 hosts the second Computational Linguistics and Clinical Psychology Workshop. Members of the community have come together to organize a hackathon, with a data release and shared task for detecting mental illness as part of this workshop. We hope to build the momentum towards releasing tools and data that can be used by clinical psychologists, and as such, we diverge from the conventional "mini-conference" workshop format, including practicing clinical psychologists on our program committee and as discussants in the workshop. The ability to communicate relevant computational methods and results clearly, connecting the work to clinical practice, is as important as the quality of the work itself, and more important than research novelty.

We received 15 submissions for the main workshop and 3 for the shared task. Of the main workshop submissions, 12 (80%) were accepted: 6 for oral and 6 for poster presentation. Oral presentations will be followed by discussions led by several experts on working with patients and clinical data: Shandra M. Brown Levey, Loring J. Ingraham, John P. Pestian, and Kytja K. S. Voeller. We also have an invited talk from Munmun De Choudhury, an expert in computational social science who has done pioneering work on understanding mental health in social media.

We wish to thank everyone who showed interest and submitted a paper, all of the authors for their contributions, the members of the Program Committee for their thoughtful reviews, our clinical discussants for their helpful insights, and all the attendees of the workshop. We also wish to extend thanks to the Association for Computational Linguistics for making this workshop possible, and to Microsoft Research for its generous sponsorship.

– Meg, Glen, and Kristy

Organizers:

Margaret Mitchell, Microsoft Research (MSR)
Glen Coppersmith, Qntfy
Kristy Hollingshead, Florida Institute for Human and Machine Cognition (IHMC)

Clinical Discussants:

Shandra M. Brown Levey, University of Colorado Denver
Loring J. Ingraham, George Washington University
John P. Pestian, Cincinnati Children's Hospital Medical Center
Kytja K. S. Voeller, Western Institute for Neurodevelopmental Studies and Interventions

Program Committee:

Steven Bedrick, Oregon Health & Science University
Wei Chen, Nationwide Children's Hospital
Glen Coppersmith, Qntfy
Mark Dredze, Johns Hopkins University
Michael Gamon, Microsoft Research
Kimberly Glasgow, Johns Hopkins Applied Physics Laboratory
Dan Goldwasser, University of Maryland
Graeme Hirst, University of Toronto
Christopher Homan, Rochester Institute of Technology
Loring J. Ingraham, George Washington University
William Jarrold, Nuance Communications
Yangfeng Ji, Georgia Institute of Technology
Tong Liu, Rochester Institute of Technology
Antolin Llorente, Mt. Washington Pediatric Hospital
Aimee Mooney, Oregon Health & Science University
Eric Morley, Oregon Health & Science University
Sylvester Olubolu Orimaye, Monash University Malaysia
Cecilia Ovesdotter Alm, Rochester Institute of Technology
Craig Pfeifer, The MITRE Corporation
Matthew Purver, Queen Mary University of London
Philip Resnik, University of Maryland
Rebecca Resnik, Mindwell Psychology Bethesda
Brian Roark, Google
Masoud Rouhizadeh, Oregon Health & Science University
Ronald Schouten, Harvard Medical School
H. Andrew Schwartz, University of Pennsylvania
Richard Sproat, Google
Hiroki Tanaka, NAIST
Paul Thompson, Dartmouth College
Jan van Santen, Oregon Health & Science University

Invited Speaker:

Munmun De Choudhury, Georgia Tech

Table of Contents

Workshop Program

2015/06/05

09:00–09:15 *Opening Remarks*
Margaret Mitchell, Glen Coppersmith, Kristy Hollingshead

09:15–11:00 Oral Presentations, Session 1

From ADHD to SAD: Analyzing the Language of Mental Health on Twitter through Self-Reported Diagnoses
Glen Coppersmith, Mark Dredze, Craig Harman and Kristy Hollingshead

Quantifying the Language of Schizophrenia in Social Media
Margaret Mitchell, Kristy Hollingshead and Glen Coppersmith

The role of personality, age, and gender in tweeting about mental illness
Daniel Preoţiuc-Pietro, Johannes Eichstaedt, Gregory Park, Maarten Sap, Laura Smith, Victoria Tobolsky, H. Andrew Schwartz and Lyle Ungar

11:00–11:15 Break

11:15–11:45 Shared Task

CLPsych 2015 Shared Task: Depression and PTSD on Twitter
Glen Coppersmith, Mark Dredze, Craig Harman, Kristy Hollingshead and Margaret Mitchell

Mental Illness Detection at the World Well-Being Project for the CLPsych 2015 Shared Task
Daniel Preoţiuc-Pietro, Maarten Sap, H. Andrew Schwartz and Lyle Ungar

Screening Twitter Users for Depression and PTSD with Lexical Decision Lists
Ted Pedersen

The University of Maryland CLPsych 2015 Shared Task System
Philip Resnik, William Armstrong, Leonardo Claudino and Thang Nguyen

11:35–11:45 *Discussion*
Philip Resnik

2015/06/05 (continued)

11:45–12:45 Poster Presentations

Computational cognitive modeling of inflectional verb morphology in Spanish-speakers for the characterization and diagnosis of Alzheimer's Disease
M. Dolores del Castillo, J. Ignacio Serrano and Jesús Oliva

Recursive Neural Networks for Coding Therapist and Patient Behavior in Motivational Interviewing
Michael Tanana, Kevin Hallgren, Zac Imel, David Atkins, Padhraic Smyth and Vivek Srikumar

Putting Feelings into Words: Cross-Linguistic Markers of the Referential Process
Sean Murphy, Bernard Maskit and Wilma Bucci

Towards Developing an Annotation Scheme for Depressive Disorder Symptoms: A Preliminary Study using Twitter Data
Danielle Mowery, Craig Bryan and Mike Conway

Beyond LDA: Exploring Supervised Topic Modeling for Depression-Related Language in Twitter
Philip Resnik, William Armstrong, Leonardo Claudino, Thang Nguyen, Viet-An Nguyen and Jordan Boyd-Graber

Automated morphological analysis of clinical language samples
Kyle Gorman, Steven Bedrick, Geza Kiss, Eric Morley, Rosemary Ingham, Metrah Mohammed, Katina Papadakis and Jan van Santen

12:45–14:00 Lunch

14:00–14:45 Invited Talk

14:00–14:45 *Invited Talk*
Munmun De Choudhury

2015/06/05 (continued)

14:45–15:00 Break

15:00–16:45 Oral Presentations, Session 2

Similarity Measures for Quantifying Restrictive and Repetitive Behavior in Conversations of Autistic Children
Masoud Rouhizadeh, Richard Sproat and Jan van Santen

Practical issues in developing semantic frameworks for the analysis of verbal fluency data: A Norwegian data case study
Mark Rosenstein, Peter Foltz, Anja Vaskinn and Brita Elvevåg

A Computer Program for Tracking the Evolution of a Psychotherapy Treatment
Bernard Maskit, Wilma Bucci and Sean Murphy

16:45–17:00 Closing Remarks

From ADHD to SAD: Analyzing the Language of Mental Health on Twitter through Self-Reported Diagnoses

Glen Coppersmith
Qntfy
glen@qntfy.io

Mark Dredze, Craig Harman
Human Language Technology
Center of Excellence
Johns Hopkins University
mdredze|charman@jhu.edu

Kristy Hollingshead
IHMC
kseitz@ihmc.us

Abstract

Many significant challenges exist for the mental health field, but one in particular is a lack of data available to guide research. Language provides a natural lens for studying mental health – much existing work and therapy have strong linguistic components, so the creation of a large, varied, language-centric dataset could provide significant grist for the field of mental health research. We examine a broad range of mental health conditions in Twitter data by identifying self-reported statements of diagnosis. We systematically explore language differences between ten conditions with respect to the general population, and to each other. Our aim is to provide guidance and a roadmap for where deeper exploration is likely to be fruitful.

1 Introduction

A recent study commissioned by the World Economic Forum projected that mental disorders will be the single largest health cost, with global costs increasing to $6 trillion annually by 2030 (Bloom et al., 2011). Since mental health impacts the risk for chronic, non-communicable diseases, in a sense there is "no health without mental health" (Prince et al., 2007). The importance of mental health has driven the search for new and innovative methods for obtaining reliable information and evidence about mental disorders. The WHO's Mental Health Action Plan for the next two decades calls for the strengthening of "information systems, evidence and research," which necessitates new development and improvements in global mental health surveillance capabilities (World Health Organization, 2013).

As a result, research on mental health has turned to web data sources (Ayers et al., 2013; Althouse et al., 2014; Yang et al., 2010; Hausner et al., 2008), with a particular focus on social media (De Choudhury, 2014; Schwartz et al., 2013a; De Choudhury et al., 2011). While many users discuss physical health conditions such as cancer or the flu (Paul and Dredze, 2011; Dredze, 2012; Aramaki et al., 2011; Hawn, 2009), some also discuss mental illness. There are a variety of motivations for users to share this information on social media: to offer or seek support, to fight the stigma of mental illness, or perhaps to offer an explanation for certain behaviors.

Past mental health work has largely focused on depression, with some considering post-traumatic stress disorder (Coppersmith et al., 2014b), suicide (Tong et al., 2014; Jashinsky et al., 2014), seasonal affective disorder, and bipolar disorder (Coppersmith et al., 2014a). While these represent some of the most common mental disorders, it only begins to consider the range of mental health conditions for which social media could be utilized. Yet obtaining data for many conditions can be difficult, as previous techniques required the identification of affected individuals using traditional screening methods (De Choudhury, 2013; Schwartz et al., 2013b).

Coppersmith et al. (2014a) proposed a novel way of obtaining mental health related Twitter data. Using the self-identification technique of Beller et al. (2014), they looked for statements such as "I was diagnosed with depression", automatically uncovering a large number of users with mental health conditions. They demonstrated success at both surveillance and analysis of four mental health conditions. While a promising first step, the technique's efficacy for a larger range of disorders remained untested.

Proceedings of the 2nd Workshop on Computational Linguistics and Clinical Psychology: From Linguistic Signal to Clinical Reality, pages 1–10,
Denver, Colorado, June 5, 2015.

In this paper we employ the techniques of Coppersmith et al. (2014a) to amass a large, diverse collection of social media and associated labels of diagnosed mental health conditions. We consider the broadest range of conditions to date, many significantly less prevalent than the disorders examined previously. This tests the capacity of our approach to scale to many mental health conditions, as well as its capability to analyze relationships between conditions. In total, we present results for ten conditions, including the four considered by Coppersmith et al. (2014a). To demonstrate the presence of quantifiable signals for each condition, we build machine learning classifiers capable of separating users with each condition from control users.

Furthermore, we extend previous analysis by considering approximate age- and gender-matched controls, in contrast to the randomly selected controls in most past studies. Dos Reis and Culotta (2015) found demographic controls an important baseline, as they muted the strength of the measured outcomes in social media compared to a random control group. Using demographically-matched controls allows us to clarify the analysis in conditions where age is a factor, e.g., people with PTSD tend to be older than the average user on Twitter.

Using the ten conditions and control groups, we characterize a broad range of differences between the groups. We examine differences in usage patterns of categories from the Linguistic Inquiry Word Count (LIWC), a widely used psychometrically validated tool for psychology-related analysis of language (Pennebaker et al., 2007; Pennebaker et al., 2001). Depression is the only condition for which considerable previous work on social media exists for comparison, and we largely replicate those previous results. Finally, we examine relationships between the language used by people with various conditions — a task for which comparable data has never before been available. By considering multiple conditions, we can measure similarities and differences of language usage between conditions, rather than just between a condition and the general population.

The paper is structured as follows: we begin with a description of how we gathered and curated the data, then present an analysis of the data's coherence and the quantifiable signals we can extract from it, including a broad survey of observed differences in LIWC categories. Finally, we measure language correlations between pairs of conditions. We conclude with a discussion of some possible future directions suggested by this exploratory analysis.

2 Related Work

There is rich literature on the interaction between mental health and language (Tausczik and Pennebaker, 2010; Ramirez-Esparza et al., 2008; Chung and Pennebaker, 2007; Pennebaker et al., 2007; Rude et al., 2004; Pennebaker et al., 2001). Social media's emergence has renewed interest in this topic, though gathering data has been difficult. Deriving measurable signals relevant to mental health via statistical approaches requires large quantities of data that pair a person's mental health status (e.g., diagnosed with PTSD) to their social media feed.

Successful approaches towards obtaining these data have relied on three approaches: **(1) Crowdsourced surveys**: Some mental health conditions have self-assessment questionnaires amenable to administration over the Internet. Combining this with crowdsource platforms like Amazon's Mechanical Turk or Crowdflower, a researcher can administer relevant mental health questionnaires and solicit the user's public social media data for analysis. This technique has been effectively used to examine depression (De Choudhury, 2013; De Choudhury et al., 2013c; De Choudhury et al., 2013b). **(2) Facebook**: Researchers created an application for Facebook users that administered various personality tests, and as part of the terms of service of the application, granted the researchers access to a user's public status updates. This corpus has been used in a wide range of questions from personality (Schwartz et al., 2013b; Park et al., In press), heart disease (Eichstaedt et al., 2015), depression (Schwartz et al., 2014), and psychological well-being (Schwartz et al., 2013a). **(3) Self-Stated Diagnoses**: Some social media users discuss their mental health publicly and openly, which allows researchers to create rich corpora of social media data from users who have a wide range of mental health conditions. This has been used previously to examine depression, PTSD, bipolar, and seasonal affective disorder (Coppersmith et al., 2014a; Coppersmith et al.,

2014b; Hohman et al., 2014). A similar approach has been used to identify new mothers for studying the impact of major life events (De Choudhury et al., 2013a). **(4) Affiliation**: Some rely on a user's affiliation to indicate a mental health condition, such as using posts from a depression forum as a sample of depression (Nguyen et al., 2014).

Other work on mental health and related topics have studied questions that do not rely on an explicit diagnosis, such as measuring the moods of Twitter users (De Choudhury et al., 2011) to measure their affective states (De Choudhury et al., 2012). Outside of social media, research has demonstrated how web search queries can measure population level mental health trends (Yang et al., 2010; Ayers et al., 2013; Althouse et al., 2014).

3 Data

We follow the Twitter data acquisition and curation process of Coppersmith et al. (2014a). This data collection method has been previously validated through replication of previous findings and showing predictive power for real-world phenomena (Coppersmith et al., 2014a; Coppersmith et al., 2014b; Hohman et al., 2014), though there likely is some 'selection bias' by virtue of the fact that the data is collected from social media – specifically Twitter – which may be more commonly used by a subset of the population. We summarize the main points of the data collection method here[1].

We obtain messages with self-reported diagnoses using the Twitter API. Self-reported diagnoses are tweets containing statements like "I have been diagnosed with CONDITION", where CONDITION is one of ten selected conditions (each of which has at least 100 users): Attention Deficit Hyperactivity Disorder (ADHD), Generalized Anxiety Disorder (Anx), Bipolar Disorder, Borderline Personality Disorder (Border), Depression (Dep), Eating Disorders (Eating; includes anorexia, bulimia, and eating disorders not otherwise specified [EDNOS]), obsessive compulsive disorder (OCD), post-traumatic stress disorder (PTSD), schizophrenia (Schizo; to include schizophrenia, schizotypal, schizophreniform) and seasonal affective disorder (Seasonal). We use the

[1]All uses of these data as reported in this paper have been approved by the relevant Institutional Review Board (IRB).

Condition	Users	Median	Total
ADHD	102	3273	384k
Anxiety	216	3619	1591k
Bipolar	188	3383	720k
Borderline	101	3330	321k
Depression	393	3306	546k
Eating	238	3229	724k
OCD	100	3331	314k
PTSD	403	3241	1251k
Schizophrenia	172	3236	493k
Seasonal Affective	100	3229	340k

Table 1: The number of users with a genuine statement of diagnosis (verified by a human annotator), their median number of tweets, and total tweets for each condition.

common names for these disorders, rather than adhering to a more formal one (e.g., DSM-IV or DSM-5), for two reasons: **(1)** to remain agnostic to the current discussion in clinical psychology around the standards of diagnosis; and **(2)** our classification is based on user statements. While sometimes an obvious mapping exists for user statements to more formal definitions (e.g., "shell shock" equates to today's "PTSD"), other times it is less obvious (e.g., "Anxiety" might refer to generalized anxiety disorder or social anxiety disorder).

Each self-reported diagnosis was examined by one of the authors to verify that it was a genuine statement of a diagnosis, i.e., excluding jokes, quotes, or disingenuous statements.[2] Previous work shows high inter-annotator agreement ($\kappa = 0.77$) for assessing genuine statements of diagnosis (Coppersmith et al., 2014a). For each author of a genuine diagnosis tweet we obtain a set of their **public** Twitter posts using the Twitter API (at least 100 posts per user, but usually more); we do not have access to private messages. All collected data was publicly posted to Twitter between 2008 and 2015.

3.1 Exclusion and Preprocessing

Our analyses focus on user-authored content; we exclude retweets and tweets with a URL since these often quote text from the link. The text is lower-cased and all non-standard characters (e.g., emoji) are converted to a systematic ASCII representation

[2]We did not formally analyze the disingenuous statements, but anecdotally many of the jokes seems to stem from laymens terms and understanding of a condition; for example, "The weather in Maryland is totally bipolar."

via Unidecode[3]. Users were removed if their tweets were not at least 75% English, as determined by the Google Compact Language Detector[4]. To avoid bias, we removed the tweets that were used to manually assess genuine statements of diagnosis. However, other tweets with a self-statement of diagnosis may remain in a user's data. Table 1 summarizes the number of users identified and their median number of tweets for each condition.

3.2 Age- and Gender-Matched Controls

Generally, control groups were formed via random selection of Twitter users. Yet physical and mental health conditions have different prevalence rates depending on age and gender. Dos Reis and Culotta (2015) demonstrated that failing to account for these can yield biased control groups that skew results, so we aim to form approximate age- and gender-matched control groups.

There is a rich literature investigating the influence of age and gender on language (Pennebaker, 2011). Since Twitter does not provide demographic information for users, these insights have been broadly applied to inferring demographic information from social media (Volkova et al., 2015; Fink et al., 2012; Burger et al., 2011; Rao et al., 2011; Rao et al., 2010). We use these techniques to estimate the age and gender of each user so as to select an age- and gender-matched control group. For each user in our mental health collection we obtain age and gender estimates from the tools provided by the World Well-Being Project (Sap et al., 2014)[5]. These tools use lexica derived from Facebook data to identify demographics, and have been shown successful on Twitter data. The tools provide continuous valued estimates for age and gender, so we threshold the gender values to obtain a binary label, and use the age score as is.

We draw our community controls from all the Twitter users who tweeted during a two week period in early 2014 as part of Twitter's 1% 'spritzer' stream. Each user who tweeted in English and whose tweets were public had an equal probability of being included in our pool of controls. From this pool, we identify the closest matching control user in terms of age and gender for each user in the mental health collection. We select controls without replacement so a control user can only be included once. In practice, differences between estimated age of paired users were miniscule.

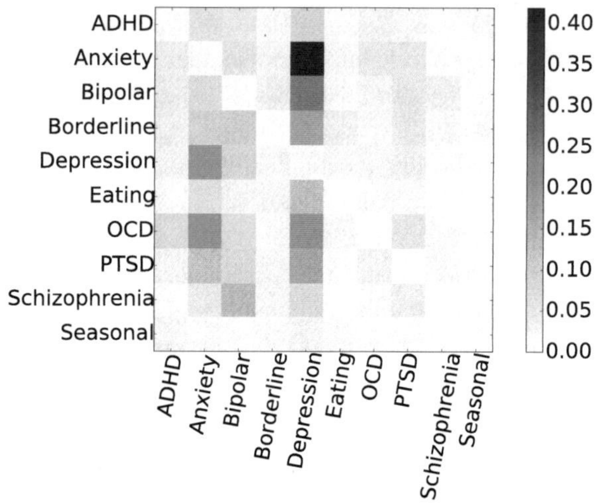

Figure 1: Concomitances or comorbidities: cell color indicates the probability that a user diagnosed with one condition (row) has a concomitant diagnosis of another condition (column). For example: ~30% of users with schizophrenia also had a diagnosis for bipolar.

3.3 Concomitance and Comorbidity

Concomitant diagnoses are somewhat common in clinical psychology; our data is no different. In cases where a user states a diagnosis for more than one condition, we include them in each condition. For most pairs of conditions, these overlaps are only a small proportion of the data, with a few noted exceptions (e.g., up to 40% of users who have anxiety also have depression, 30% for schizophrenia and bipolar). Figure 1 summarizes the concomitance in our data.

4 Methods and Results

4.1 LIWC differences

We provide a comprehensive picture of differences in usage patterns of LIWC categories between users with various mental health conditions. We measure the proportion of word tokens for each user that falls into a given LIWC category, aggregate by condition, and compare across conditions.

For each user, we calculate the proportion of their tokens that were part of each LIWC category. Thus

[3]https://pypi.python.org/pypi/Unidecode

[4]https://code.google.com/p/cld2/

[5]http://wwbp.org/data.html

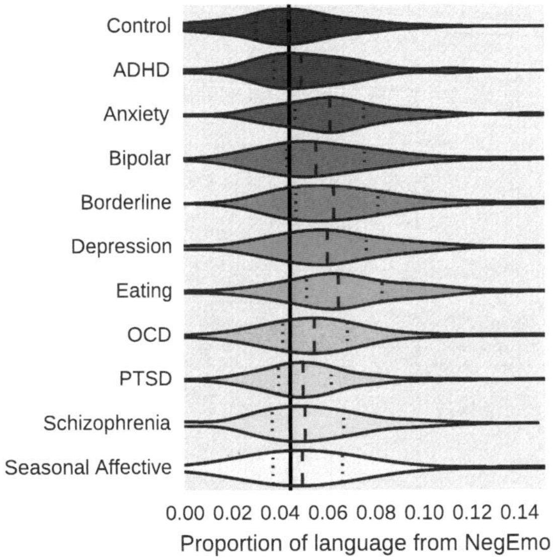

Figure 2: Violin plot showing the frequency of negative emotion LIWC category words by condition. The center dashed line is the median, the dotted line is the inter-quartile-range, and the envelope is an estimate of the distribution. The vertical line is the control group's median.

for each category and each condition, we have an empirical distribution of the proportion of language attributable to that category. The violin plots in Figure 2 show an example of how this changes across conditions as compared to controls.

Table 2 shows deviations for all categories and conditions as follows: '+++' indicates that condition users evince this category significantly more frequently[6] than control users; '+' indicates that the distribution is noticeably higher for the condition population than the control population, but not outside the inter-quartile-range; '−' indicates differences where condition users use this category less frequently than control users.

Some interesting trends emerge from this analysis. First, some categories show differences across a broad range of mental health conditions (e.g., the ANXIETY, AUXILIARY VERBS, COGNITIVE MECHANISMS, DEATH, FUNCTION, HEALTH, and TENTATIVE categories of words). This suggests that there are a subset of changes in language that may be indicative of an underlying mental health condition (without much regard for specificity), while others seem to be very specific to the conditions they are associated with (e.g., INGEST and NEGATIONS with eating disorders). Some of the connections between LIWC categories and mental health conditions have already been substantiated in the mental health literature, while others (e.g., AUXVERB) have not and are ripe for further exploration. Second, many of the conditions show similar patterns (e.g., anxiety, bipolar, borderline, and depression), while others have distinct patterns (e.g., eating disorders and seasonal affective disorder). It is worth emphasizing that a direct mapping between these and previously-reported LIWC results (in, e.g., Coppersmith et al. (2014a) and De Choudhury et al. (2013c)) is not straightforward, since previous work did not use demographically-matched control users.

4.2 Open-vocabulary Approach

Validated and accepted lexicons like LIWC cover a mere fraction of the total language usage on social media. Thus, we also use an open-vocabulary approach, which has greater coverage than LIWC, and has been shown to find quantifiable signals relevant to mental health in the past (Coppersmith et al., 2014a; Coppersmith et al., 2014b). Though many open-vocabulary approaches exist, we opt for one that provides a reasonable score even for very short text, and is robust to the creative spellings, lack of spaces, and other textual *faux pas* common on Twitter: character n-gram language models (CLMs).

In essence, rather than examining words or sequences of words, CLMs examine sequences of characters, including spaces, punctuation, and emoticons. Given a set of data from two classes (in our case, one from a given mental health condition, the other from its matched controls), the model is trained to recognize which sequences of characters are likely to be generated by either class. When these models are presented with novel text, they estimate which of the classes was more likely to have generated it. For brevity we will omit discussion of the exact score calculation and refer the interested reader to Coppersmith et al. (2014a). For all we do here, higher scores will indicate a tweet is more likely to come from a user with a given mental health condition, and lower scores are more likely to come from a control user. Since we are examining ten conditions, we have ten pairs of CLMs (for each pair,

[6] Specifically, the median of the condition distribution is outside the inter-quartile-range of the control distribution.

LIWC	**ADHD**	**Anx**	**Bipolar**	**Border**	**Dep**	**Eating**	**OCD**	**PTSD**	**Schizo**	**Seasonal**
Funct	+++	+++	+++	+++	+++	+++	+++	+	+++	+++
Pronoun		+			+	+++	+			
PPron		+					+			
I		+			+	+++	+++			
We		-	-	—	-	—				
They	+++		+	+				+	+	
IPron	+++	+		+			+++			
Article						-		+	+++	+
Verb				+	+	+++	+			
AuxVerb	+	+++	+++	+++	+++	+++	+++	+	+++	+
Past			+							+
Present					+	+++				
Adverb		+				+++	+			
Conj*	+	+++	+	+++	+++	+++	+++		+	+++
Negate						+				
Quant	+	+		+++			+	+	+++	
Swear				+		+	+			
PosEmo							-	-		-
NegEmo		+++	+	+++	+	+++				
Anxiety	+	+++	+	+++	+	+++	+++	+	+	+
Anger		+	+	+++	+	+++	+			
Sad				+		+++	+			
CogMech	+++	+++	+++	+++	+++	+++	+++	+	+++	
Insight	+++	+				+++	+++	+	+	
Cause	+++	+	+	+	+	+++	+++	+	+	
Discrep		+				+++				
Tentat	+++	+++	+	+++	+++		+++	+	+++	
Incl				+						+++
Excl	+++	+++	+	+++	+++	+++	+++			
Feel						+				
Bio		+	+	+		+++	+			
Body						+				
Health	+	+++	+++	+++	+	+++	+++	+	+	
Ingest						+				
Relativ	—						-	-	-	
Motion	-	-	-	—	-	-	—	—	—	
Space						-				+
Time	-			-				+++	+++	
Leisure				-	-	—		-	-	
Home				-					-	
Death	+	+++	+	+++	+	+	+	+	+++	
Assent	-								-	
Pro1		+			+	+++	+++			
Pro3	+							+		
LIWC	**ADHD**	**Anx**	**Bipolar**	**Border**	**Dep**	**Eating**	**OCD**	**PTSD**	**Schizo**	**Seasonal**

Table 2: Full list of deviations by LIWC category for each condition. Category names that are *'d may have been affected by our normalization and tokenization procedure. Categories for which no significant differences were observed: Achieve, Affect, Certain, Family, Filler*, Friend, Future, Hear, Humans, Inhibition, Money, Nonfluencies, Number, Perceptual, Prepositions, Pro2, Religion, See, Sexual, SheHe, Social.

one CLM is trained from the users with a given mental health condition, and one CLM is trained from their matched controls).

4.3 Quantifiable Differences

To validate that our CLMs are capturing quantifiable differences relevant to their specific conditions, we examine their accuracy on a heldout set of users. Each condition-specific CLM produces a score that roughly equates to how much more (or less) likely it is to have come from a user with the given condition (e.g., PTSD) than a control. We aggregate these scores to compute a final score for use in classification. We score each tweet with the CLM and use the score to make a binary distinction – is this tweet more likely to have been generated by someone who has PTSD or a control? We calculate the proportion of these tweets that are classified as PTSD-like (the *overall mean*), which can be thought of as how PTSD-like this user looks over all time. Given that some of these symptoms change with time, we can also compute a more localized version of this mean, and derive a score according to the "most PTSD-like period the user has". This is done by ordering these binary decisions by the time the tweet was authored, selecting a window of 50 tweets, and calculating the proportion of those tweets classified as PTSD-like. We then slide this window one tweet further (removing the oldest tweet, and adding in the next in the user's timeline) and calculate the proportion again. The highest this rolling-window mean achieves will be referred to as the *maximum local mean*. We combine these scores to yield the classifier score $\psi =$ *overall mean* $*$ *maximum local mean*, capturing how PTSD-like the user is over all time, and how PTSD-like they are at their most severe.

We estimated the performance of our classifiers for each condition on distinguishing users with a mental health condition from their community controls via 10-fold cross-validation. This differs only slightly from standard cross-fold validation in that our observations are paired; we maintain this pairing when assigning folds – each mental health condition user and their matched control are in the same fold. To assess performance, we could draw a line (a threshold) in the ranked list, and classify all users above that line as having the mental health condition, and all users below that line as controls. Those

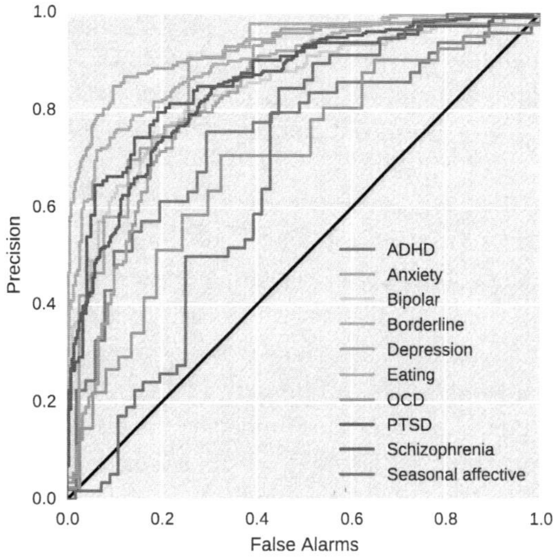

Figure 3: ROC curves for distinguishing diagnosed from control users, for each of the disorders examined. Chance performance is indicated by the black diagonal line.

Condition	Precision
ADHD	52%
Anxiety	85%
Bipolar	63%
Borderline	58%
Depression	48%
Eating	76%
OCD	27%
PTSD	55%
Schizophrenia	67%
Seasonal Affective	5 %

Table 3: Classifier precision with 10% false alarms.

with the condition above the line would be correctly classified (hits), while those controls above the line would be incorrectly classified (false alarms). Figure 3 shows performance of this classifier as Receiver Operating Characteristic (ROC) curves as we adjust this threshold, one curve per mental health condition. The x-axis shows the proportion of false alarms and the y-axis shows the proportion of true hits. All our classifiers are better than chance, but far from perfect. To aid interpretation, Table 3 shows precision at 10% false alarms.

Performance for most conditions is reasonable, except seasonal affective disorder which is very difficult (as was reported by Coppersmith et al. (2014a)). Anxiety and eating disorders have much better performance than the other conditions. Most importantly, though, for all conditions (including seasonal affective disorder), we are able to identify language usage differences from control groups.

4.4 Cross Condition Comparisons

Given the breadth of our language data, we can compare across mental health conditions, examining relationships between the conditions under investigation, rather than only how each condition differs from controls. Previous work (Coppersmith et al., 2014a) reported preliminary findings that indicated a possible relationship between the language use from different mental health conditions: similar conditions (either in concomitance and comorbidity or symptomatology) had similar language. The story found here is related, but more complicated. For this comparison, we build new CLMs that *exclude* any user with a concomitant disorder (to prevent their data from making their conditions appear artificially similar). We then score a random sample of 1 million tweets that meet our earlier filters with the CLMs from each condition. We could then examine how the language in any pair of conditions is related by calculating the Pearson's correlation (r) between the scores from these models.

More interesting, though, is how all these conditions relate to one another, rather than any given pair. To that end, we use a standard clustering algorithm[7], shown in Figure 4. Here, each condition is represented by a vector of its Pearson's r correlations, calculated as above, to each of the conditions (to include an $r = 1.0$ to itself). Each condition starts as its own cluster on the left side of the figure. Moving to the right, clusters are merged, most similar first, until all conditions merge into a single cluster. One particular clustering is highlighted by the colors: conditions with blue lines are in clusters of their own, so seasonal affective, ADHD, and borderline appear to be significantly different from the rest); and schizophrenia and OCD are clustered together, shown in red. While this is not the most obvious grouping of conditions, the patterns are far from random: the disorders in green (PTSD, bipolar, eating disorders, anxiety, and depression) have somewhat frequent concomitance in our data and elsewhere (Kessler et al., 2005) and recent research indicates links between OCD and schizophrenia (Meier et al., 2014). Notably, these data are not age- and gender-matched, so these variables also likely factor into the clustering. Thus, we leave this particular relationship between language and mental health as an open question, suggesting fertile grounds for more controlled future work.

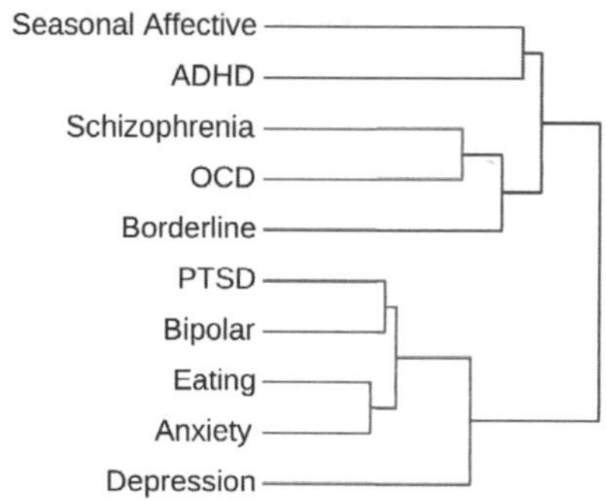

Figure 4: Hierarchical clustering dendrogram of conditions clustered according to the similarity of their users' language. Distance between merged clusters increases monotonically with the level of the merger; thus lower merges (further to the left) indicate greater similarity (e.g., language usage from Seasonal Affective and ADHD users is very different from conditions in the green cluster, given how far right the red merge-point is).

[7]Hierarchical, agglomerative clustering from Python's scipy.hierarchy.linkage (Jones et al., 2001).

5 Conclusion

We examined the language of social media from users with a wide range of mental health conditions, providing a roadmap for future work. We explored simple classifiers capable of distinguishing these users from their age- and gender-matched controls, based on signals quantified from the users' language. The classifiers also allowed us to systematically compare the language used by those with the ten conditions investigated, finding some groupings of the conditions found elsewhere in the literature, but not altogether obvious. We take this as evidence that examining mental health through the lens of language is fertile ground for advances in mental health writ large. The wealth of information encoded in continually-generated social media is ripe for analysis – data scientists, computational linguists, and clinical psychologists, together, are well positioned to drive this field forward.

Acknowledgments

The authors would like to thank Bradley Skaggs, Matthew DiFabion, and Aleksander Yelskiy for their insights throughout this endeavor.

References

Benjamin M. Althouse, Jon-Patrick Allem, Matthew A. Childers, Mark Dredze, and John W. Ayers. 2014. Population health concerns during the United States' great recession. *American Journal of Preventive Medicine*, 46(2):166–170.

Eiji Aramaki, Sachiko Maskawa, and Mizuki Morita. 2011. Twitter catches the flu: Detecting influenza epidemics using Twitter. In *Proceedings of EMNLP*.

John W. Ayers, Benjamin M. Althouse, Jon-Patrick Allem, J. Niels Rosenquist, and Daniel E. Ford. 2013. Seasonality in seeking mental health information on Google. *American Journal of Preventive Medicine*, 44(5):520–525.

Charley Beller, Rebecca Knowles, Craig Harman, Shane Bergsma, Margaret Mitchell, and Benjamin Van Durme. 2014. I'm a Belieber: Social roles via self-identification and conceptual attributes. In *Proceedings of ACL*.

David E. Bloom, Elizabeth Cafiero, Eva Jané-Llopis, Shafika Abrahams-Gessel, Lakshmi Reddy Bloom, Sana Fathima, Andrea B. Feigl, Tom Gaziano, Ali Hamandi, Mona Mowafi, Ankur Pandya, Klaus Prettner, Larry Rosenberg, Ben Seligman, Adam Z. Stein, and Cara Weinstein. 2011. The global economic burden of non-communicable diseases. Technical report, Geneva: World Economic Forum.

John D. Burger, John Henderson, George Kim, and Guido Zarrella. 2011. Discriminating gender on Twitter. In *Proceedings of EMNLP*.

Cindy Chung and James Pennebaker. 2007. The psychological functions of function words. *Social Communication*.

Glen Coppersmith, Mark Dredze, and Craig Harman. 2014a. Quantifying mental health signals in Twitter. In *Proceedings of the ACL Workshop on Computational Linguistics and Clinical Psychology*.

Glen Coppersmith, Craig Harman, and Mark Dredze. 2014b. Measuring post traumatic stress disorder in Twitter. In *Proceedings of ICWSM*.

Munmun De Choudhury, Scott Counts, and Michael Gamon. 2011. Not all moods are created equal! Exploring human emotional states in social media. In *Proceedings of ICWSM*.

Munmun De Choudhury, Michael Gamon, and Scott Counts. 2012. Happy, nervous or surprised? Classification of human affective states in social media. In *Proceedings of ICWSM*.

Munmun De Choudhury, Scott Counts, and Eric Horvitz. 2013a. Major life changes and behavioral markers in social media: Case of childbirth. In *Proceedings of the 16th ACM Conference on Computer Supported Cooperative Work and Social Computing (CSCW)*.

Munmun De Choudhury, Scott Counts, and Eric Horvitz. 2013b. Social media as a measurement tool of depression in populations. In *Proceedings of the 5th ACM International Conference on Web Science*.

Munmun De Choudhury, Michael Gamon, Scott Counts, and Eric Horvitz. 2013c. Predicting depression via social media. In *Proceedings of ICWSM*.

Munmun De Choudhury. 2013. Role of social media in tackling challenges in mental health. In *Proceedings of the 2nd International Workshop on Socially-Aware Multimedia*.

Munmun De Choudhury. 2014. Can social media help us reason about mental health? In *Proceedings of the Companion Publication of the 23rd International Conference on World Wide Web (WWW)*.

Virgile Landeiro Dos Reis and Aron Culotta. 2015. Using matched samples to estimate the effects of exercise on mental health from Twitter. In *Proceedings of AAAI*.

Mark Dredze. 2012. How social media will change public health. *IEEE Intelligent Systems*, 27(4):81–84.

Johannes C. Eichstaedt, Hansen Andrew Schwartz, Margaret L. Kern, Gregory Park, Darwin R. Labarthe, Raina M. Merchant, Sneha Jha, Megha Agrawal, Lukasz A. Dziurzynski, Maarten Sap, Christopher Weeg, Emily E. Larson, Lyle H. Ungar, and Martin E. P. Seligman. 2015. Psychological language on Twitter predicts county-level heart disease mortality. *Psychological Science*, 26(2):159–169.

Clayton Fink, Jonathon Kopecky, and Maksym Morawski. 2012. Inferring gender from the content of tweets: A region specific example. In *Proceedings of the 6th International AAAI Conference on Weblogs and Social Media (ICWSM)*.

Helmut Hausner, Göran Hajak, and Hermann Spießl. 2008. Gender differences in help-seeking behavior on two internet forums for individuals with self-reported depression. *Gender Medicine*, 5(2):181–185.

Carleen Hawn. 2009. Take two aspirin and tweet me in the morning: How Twitter, Facebook, and other social media are reshaping health care. *Health Affairs*, 28(2):361–368.

Elizabeth Hohman, David Marchette, and Glen Coppersmith. 2014. Mental health, economics, and population in social media. In *Proceedings of JSM*.

Jared Jashinsky, Scott H Burton, Carl L Hanson, Josh West, Christophe Giraud-Carrier, Michael D Barnes, and Trenton Argyle. 2014. Tracking suicide risk factors through Twitter in the U.S. *Crisis*, 35(1).

Eric Jones, Travis Oliphant, Pearu Peterson, et al. 2001. SciPy: Open source scientific tools for Python. [Online; accessed 2015-03-11].

R. C. Kessler, W. T. Chiu, O. Demler, and E. E. Walters. 2005. Prevalence, severity, and comorbidity of twelve-month DSM-IV disorders in the National Comorbidity Survey Replication (NCS-R). *Archives of General Psychiatry*, 62(6):617–627.

Sandra M. Meier, Liselotte Petersen, Marianne G. Pedersen, Mikkel C.B. Arendt, Philip R. Nielsen, Manuel Mattheisen, Ole Mors, and Preben B. Mortensen. 2014. Obsessive-compulsive disorder as a risk factor for schizophrenia: a nationwide study. *JAMA psychiatry*, 71(11):1215–1221.

Thin Nguyen, Dinh Phung, Bo Dao, Svetha Venkatesh, and Michael Berk. 2014. Affective and content analysis of online depression communities. *IEEE Transactions on Affective Computing*, 5(3):217–226.

Greg Park, H. Andrew Schwartz, Johannes C. Eichstaedt, Margaret L. Kern, David J. Stillwell, Michal Kosinski, Lyle H. Ungar, and Martin E. P. Seligman. In press. Automatic personality assessment through social media language. *Journal of Personality and Social Psychology*.

Michael J. Paul and Mark Dredze. 2011. You are what you tweet: Analyzing Twitter for public health. In *Proceedings of ICWSM*.

James W. Pennebaker, Martha E. Francis, and Roger J. Booth. 2001. *Linguistic inquiry and word count: LIWC2001*. Erlbaum Publishers, Mahwah, NJ.

James W. Pennebaker, Cindy K. Chung, Molly Ireland, Amy Gonzales, and Roger J. Booth. 2007. *The development and psychometric properties of LIWC2007*. LIWC.net, Austin, TX.

James W. Pennebaker. 2011. The secret life of pronouns. *New Scientist*, 211(2828):42–45.

Martin Prince, Vikram Patel, Shekhar Saxena, Mario Maj, Joanna Maselko, Michael R. Phillips, and Atif Rahman. 2007. No health without mental health. *The Lancet*, 370(9590):859–877.

Nairan Ramirez-Esparza, Cindy K. Chung, Ewa Kacewicz, and James W. Pennebaker. 2008. The psychology of word use in depression forums in English and in Spanish: Testing two text analytic approaches. In *Proceedings of ICWSM*.

Delip Rao, David Yarowsky, Abhishek Shreevats, and Manaswi Gupta. 2010. Classifying latent user attributes in Twitter. In *Proceedings of the 2nd International Workshop on Search and Mining User-generated Contents*.

Delip Rao, Michael J. Paul, Clayton Fink, David Yarowsky, Timothy Oates, and Glen Coppersmith. 2011. Hierarchical bayesian models for latent attribute detection in social media. In *Proceedings of ICWSM*.

Stephanie S. Rude, Eva-Maria Gortner, and James W. Pennebaker. 2004. Language use of depressed and depression-vulnerable college students. *Cognition & Emotion*, 18(8):1121–1133.

Maarten Sap, Greg Park, Johannes C. Eichstaedt, Margaret L. Kern, David J. Stillwell, Michal Kosinski, Lyle H. Ungar, and H. Andrew Schwartz. 2014. Developing age and gender predictive lexica over social media. In *Proceedings of EMNLP*, pages 1146–1151.

H. Andrew Schwartz, Johannes C. Eichstaedt, Margaret L. Kern, Lukasz Dziurzynski, Richard E. Lucas, Megha Agrawal, Gregory J. Park, Shrinidhi K. Lakshmikanth, Sneha Jha, Martin E. P. Seligman, and Lyle H. Ungar. 2013a. Characterizing geographic variation in well-being using tweets. In *Proceedings of ICWSM*.

H. Andrew Schwartz, Johannes C. Eichstaedt, Margaret L. Kern, Lukasz Dziurzynski, Stephanie M. Ramones, Megha Agrawal, Achal Shah, Michal Kosinski, David Stillwell, Martin E. P. Seligman, and Lyle H. Ungar. 2013b. Personality, gender, and age in the language of social media: The open-vocabulary approach. *PLOS ONE*, 8(9).

H. Andrew Schwartz, Johannes Eichstaedt, Margaret L. Kern, Gregory Park, Maarten Sap, David Stillwell, Michal Kosinski, and Lyle Ungar. 2014. Towards assessing changes in degree of depression through facebook. In *Proceedings of the ACL Workshop on Computational Linguistics and Clinical Psychology*.

Yla R. Tausczik and James W. Pennebaker. 2010. The psychological meaning of words: LIWC and computerized text analysis methods. *Journal of Language and Social Psychology*, 29(1):24–54.

Christopher M Homan Tong, Ravdeep Johar, Liu Cecilia, Megan Lytle, Vincent Silenzio, and Cecilia O. Alm. 2014. Toward macro-insights for suicide prevention: Analyzing fine-grained distress at scale. In *Proceedings of the ACL Workshop on Computational Linguistics and Clinical Psychology*.

Svitlana Volkova, Yoram Bachrach, Michael Armstrong, and Vijay Sharma. 2015. Inferring latent user properties from texts published in social media. In *Proceedings of AAAI*.

World Health Organization. 2013. *Mental health action plan 2013-2020*. Geneva: World Health Organization.

Albert C. Yang, Norden E. Huang, Chung-Kang Peng, and Shih-Jen Tsai. 2010. Do seasons have an influence on the incidence of depression? The use of an internet search engine query data as a proxy of human affect. *PLOS ONE*, 5(10):e13728.

Quantifying the Language of Schizophrenia in Social Media

Margaret Mitchell
Microsoft
memitc@microsoft.com

Kristy Hollingshead
IHMC
kseitz@ihmc.us

Glen Coppersmith
Qntfy
glen@qntfy.io

Abstract

Analyzing symptoms of schizophrenia has traditionally been challenging given the low prevalence of the condition, affecting around 1% of the U.S. population. We explore potential linguistic markers of schizophrenia using the tweets[1] of self-identified schizophrenia sufferers, and describe several natural language processing (NLP) methods to analyze the language of schizophrenia. We examine how these signals compare with the widely-used LIWC categories for understanding mental health (Pennebaker et al., 2007), and provide preliminary evidence of additional linguistic signals that may aid in identifying and getting help to people suffering from schizophrenia.

1 Introduction

Schizophrenia is a group of mental disorders that affect thinking and emotional responsiveness, documented throughout history (e.g., The Book of Hearts, 1550 BCE). Today it is diagnosed and monitored leveraging self-reported experiences.[2] This may be challenging to elicit from schizophrenia sufferers, as a hallmark of the disease is the sufferer's belief that he or she does not have it (Rickelman, 2004; National Alliance on Mental Illness, 2015). Schizophrenia sufferers are therefore particularly at-risk for not leveraging help (Pacific Institute of Medical Research, 2015). This suggests that techniques that leverage social language shared by schizophrenia sufferers could be greatly beneficial in treatment of the disease. Early identification and monitoring of schizophrenia can increase the chances of successful management of the condition, reducing the chance of psychotic episodes (Häfner and Maurer, 2006) and helping a schizophrenia sufferer lead a more comfortable life.

We focus on unsupervised groupings of the words used by people on the social media platform Twitter, and see how well they discriminate between matched schizophrenia sufferers and controls. We find several potential linguistic indicators of schizophrenia, including words that mark an irrealis mood ("think", "believe"), and a lack of emoticons (a potential signature of flat affect). We also demonstrate that a support vector machine (SVM) learning approach to distinguish schizophrenia sufferers from matched controls works reasonably well, reaching 82.3% classification accuracy.

To our knowledge, no previous work has sought out linguistic markers of schizophrenia that can be automatically identified. Schizophrenia is a relatively rare mental health condition, estimated to affect around 1% of the population in the U.S. (The National Institute of Mental Health, 2015; Perälä et al., 2007; Saha et al., 2005), or some 3.2 million people. Other mental health conditions with a high prevalence rate such as depression[3] have recently received increased attention (Schwartz et al., 2014; De Choudhury et al., 2013b; Resnik et al., 2013; Coppersmith et al., 2014a). However, similar studies for schizophrenia have been hard to pursue, given

[1] A posting made on the social media website Twitter, https://twitter.com/

[2] With the Diagnostic and Statistical Manual of Mental Disorders (DSM-5) (American Psychiatric Association, 2013).

[3] 16.9% lifetime prevalence rate (Kessler et al., 2005)

Proceedings of the 2nd Workshop on Computational Linguistics and Clinical Psychology: From Linguistic Signal to Clinical Reality, pages 11–20,
Denver, Colorado, June 5, 2015.

the rarity of the condition and thus the inherent difficulty in collecting data.

We follow the method from Coppersmith et al. (2014a) to create a relatively large corpus of users diagnosed with schizophrenia from publicly available Twitter data, and match them to Twitter controls. This provides a view of the social language that a schizophrenia sufferer may choose to share with a clinician or counselor, and may be used to shed light on the illness and the effect of treatments.

2 Background and Motivation

There has been a recent growth in work using language to automatically identify people who may have mental illness and quantifying its progression, including work to help people suffering from depression (Howes et al., 2014; Hohman et al., 2014; Park et al., In press; Schwartz et al., 2014; Schwartz et al., 2013; De Choudhury et al., 2013a; De Choudhury et al., 2013b; De Choudhury et al., 2011; Nguyen et al., 2014) and post-traumatic stress disorder (Coppersmith et al., 2014b). Related work has also shown it is possible to aid clinicians in identifying patients who suffer from Alzheimer's (Roark et al., 2011; Orimaye et al., 2014) and autism (Rouhizadeh et al., 2014). The time is ripe to begin exploring an illness that deeply affects an estimated 51 million people.

The term *schizophrenia*, derived from the Greek words for "split mind", was introduced in the early 1900s to categorize patients whose thoughts and emotional responses seemed disconnected. Schizophrenia is often described in terms of symptoms from three broad categories: positive, negative, and cognitive. Positive symptoms include disordered thinking, disordered moving, delusions, and hallucinations. Negative symptoms include a flat affect and lack of ability to begin and sustain planned activities. Cognitive symptoms include poor ability to understand information and make decisions, as well as trouble focusing.

Some symptoms of schizophrenia may be straightforward to detect in social media. For example, the positive symptoms of *neologisms*, or creating new words, and *word salad*, where words and sentences are strung together without a clear syntactic or semantic structure, may be expressed in the text written by some schizophrenia sufferers. Negative symptoms may also be possible to find, for example, a lack of emoticons can reflect a flat affect, or a lower proportion of commonly used terms may reflect cognitive difficulties.

As we discuss below, natural language processing (NLP) techniques can be used to produce features similar to these markers of schizophrenia. For example, *perplexity* may be useful in measuring how unexpected a user's language is, while *latent Dirichlet allocation* (Blei et al., 2003) may be useful in characterizing the difference in general themes that schizophrenia sufferers discuss vs. control users. All NLP features we describe are either automatically constructed or *unsupervised*, meaning that no manual annotation is required to create them. It is important to note that although these features are inspired by the literature on schizophrenia, they are not direct correlates of standard schizophrenia markers.

3 Data

We follow the data acquisition and curation process of Coppersmith et al. (2014a), summarizing the major points here: Social media, such as Twitter, contains frequent public statements by users reporting diagnoses for various medical conditions. Many talk about physical health conditions (e.g., cancer, flu) but some also discuss mental illness, including schizophrenia. There are a variety of motivations for users to share this information on social media: to offer or seek support, to fight the stigma of mental illness, or perhaps to offer an explanation for certain behaviors.[4]

We obtain messages with these self-reported diagnoses using the Twitter API, and filtered via (case-insensitive) regular expression to require "schizo" or a close phonetic approximation to be present; our expression matched "schizophrenia", its subtypes, and various approximations: "schizo", "skitzo", "skitso", "schizotypal", "schizoid", etc. All data we collect are public posts made between 2008 and 2015, and exclude any message marked as 'private' by the author. All use of the data reported in this

[4] Anecdotally, many of the users in this study tend to be talking about a recent diagnosis (looking for information or support) or fighting the stigma of mental illness (by sharing their struggles).

paper has been approved by the appropriate Institutional Review Board (IRB).

Each self-stated diagnosis included in this study was examined by a human annotator (one of the authors) to verify that it appeared to be a genuine statement of a schizophrenia diagnosis, excluding jokes, quotes, or disingenuous statements. We obtained 174 users with an apparently genuine self-stated diagnosis of a schizophrenia-related condition. Note that we cannot be certain that the Twitter user was actually diagnosed with schizophrenia, only that their statement of being diagnosed appears to be genuine. Previous work indicates that inter-annotator agreement for this task is good: $\kappa = 0.77$ (Coppersmith et al., 2014a).

For each user, we obtained a set of their public Twitter posts via the Twitter API, collecting up to 3200 tweets.[5] As we wish to focus on user-authored content, we exclude from analysis all retweets and any tweets that contain a URL (which often contain text that the user did not author). We lowercase all words and convert any non-standard characters (including emoji) to a systematic ASCII representation via Unidecode.[6]

For our community controls, we used randomly-selected Twitter users who primarily tweet in English. Specifically, during a two week period in early 2014, each Twitter user who was included in Twitter's 1% "spritzer" sample had an equal chance for inclusion in our pool of community controls. We then collected some of their historic tweets and assessed the language(s) they tweeted in according to the Chromium Compact Language Detector.[7] Users were excluded from our community controls if their tweets were less than 75% English.[8]

3.1 Age- and Gender-Matched Controls

Since mental health conditions, including schizophrenia, have different prevalence rates depending on age and gender (among other demographic variables), controlling for these will be important when examining systematic differences between schizophrenic users and community controls. In particular, we would like to be able to attribute any quantifiable signals we observe to the presence or absence of schizophrenia, rather than to a confounding age or gender divergence between the populations (Dos Reis and Culotta, 2015). To that end, we estimated the age and gender of all our users (from their language usage) via the tools graciously made available by the World Well-Being Project (Sap et al., 2014). For each user, we applied a hard threshold to the gender prediction to obtain a binary 'Female' or 'Male' label. Then, in order to select the best match for each schizophrenia user, we selected the community control that had the same gender label and was closest in age (without replacement).

3.2 Drawbacks of a Balanced Dataset

We use a balanced dataset here for our analysis (an equal number of schizophrenia users and community controls). This 50/50 split makes the machine learning and analysis easier, and will allow us to focus more on emergent linguistics that are related to schizophrenia than if we had examined a dataset more representative of the population (more like 1/99). Moreover, we have not factored in the cost of false negatives or false positives (how should the consequences of misclassifying a schizophrenia user as non-schizophrenic be weighed against the consequences of misclassifying a non-schizophrenic user as schizophrenic?). All our classification results should be taken as validation that the differences in language we observe are relevant to schizophrenia, but only one step towards applying something derived from this technology in a real world scenario.

3.3 Concomitance

Often, people suffering from mental illness have a diagnosis for more than one disorder, and schizophrenia is no exception. Of our 174 users with a genuine self-statement of diagnosis of a schizophrenia-related condition, 41 also state a diagnosis of at least one other mental illness (30%), while 15 of those state that they have a diagnosis of more than one other mental illness (11%). The vast majority of these concomitances are with bipolar (25 users), followed by depression (14), post traumatic stress disorder (8) and generalized anxi-

[5]This is the maximum number of historic tweets permitted by the API.

[6]https://pypi.python.org/pypi/Unidecode

[7]https://code.google.com/p/cld2/

[8]A similar exclusion was applied to the schizophrenia users, but in practice none fell below the 75% threshold.

ety disorder (6). These comorbidity rates are notably lower than the generally accepted prevalence rates, which may be due to one of several factors. First, we rely on stated diagnoses to calculate comorbidity, and the users may not be stating each of their diagnosed conditions, either because they have not been diagnosed as such, or they choose to identify most strongly with the stated diagnosed conditions, or they simply ran out of space (given Twitter's 140-character limit). Second, we are analyzing Twitter users, which consists of only a subset of the population, and the users that choose to state, publicly, on Twitter, their schizophrenia diagnosis, may not be an accurate representation of the population of schizophrenia sufferers. The noted concomitance of schizophrenia and bipolar disorder is frequently labeled as "schizoaffective disorder with a bipolar subtype", with some recent research indicating shared impairments in functional connectivity across patients with schizophrenia and bipolar disorders (Meda et al., 2012). It is worth keeping in mind throughout this paper that we examine all subtypes of schizophrenia together here, and further in-depth analysis between subtypes is warranted.

4 Methods

We first define features relevant to mental health in general and schizophrenia in particular, and explore how well each feature distinguishes between schizophrenia-positive users and community controls. We then design and describe classifiers capable of separating the two groups based on the values for these features in their tweets. We reflect on and analyze the signals extracted by these automatic NLP methods and find some interesting patterns relevant to schizophrenia.

4.1 Lexicon-based Approaches

We used the Linguistic Inquiry Word Count (LIWC, Pennebaker et al. (2007)) to analyze the systematic language differences between our schizophrenia-positive users and their matched community controls. LIWC is a psychometrically validated lexicon mapping words to psychological concepts, and has been used extensively to examine language (and even social media language) to understand mental health. LIWC provides lists of words for categories such as FUTURE, ANGER, ARTICLES, etc. We treat each category as a feature; the feature values for a user are then the proportion of words in each category (e.g., the number of times a user writes "I" or "me", divided by the total number of words they have written is encoded as the LIWC "first person pronoun" category).

4.2 Open-vocabulary Approaches

In addition to the manually defined lexicon-based features described above, we also investigate some open-vocabulary approaches. This includes latent Dirichlet allocation (LDA) (Blei et al., 2003), Brown clustering (Brown et al., 1992), character n-gram language modeling (McNamee and Mayfield, 2004), and perplexity.[9] We now turn to a brief discussion of each approach.

Latent Dirichlet Allocation LDA operates on data represented as "documents" to infer "topics". The idea behind LDA is that each document can be viewed as a mixture of topics, where each topic uses words with different probabilities (e.g., "health" would be likely to come from a *psychology* topic or an *oncology* topic, but "schizophrenia" is more common from the former). LDA infers these topics automatically from the text – they do not have labels to start with, but often a human reading the most frequent words in the topic can see the semantic relationship and assign one.

In our case, all tweets from a user make up a "document", and we use collapsed Gibbs sampling to learn the distribution over topics for each document. In other words, given a specific number of topics k (in our work, k=20), LDA estimates the probability of each word given a topic and the probability of each topic given a document. Tweets from a user can then be featurized as a distribution over the topics: Each topic is a feature, whose feature value is the probability of that topic in the user's tweets.

The LDA implementation we use is available in the MALLET package (McCallum, 2002).

Brown Clustering Words in context often provide more meaning than the words in isolation, so we use methods for grouping together words that occur in similar linguistic constructions. Brown clustering is

[9] `http://en.wikipedia.org/wiki/Perplexity`

a greedy hierarchical algorithm that finds a clustering of words that maximizes the mutual information between adjacent clusters; in other words, words that are preceded by similar words are grouped together to form clusters, and then these clusters are merged based on having similar preceding words, and then these clusters are further merged, etc. Each word is therefore associated to clusters of increasing granularity. We define all leaf clusters[10] as features, and the feature value of each for a user is the proportion of words from the user in that cluster. The Brown clustering implementation we use is currently available on github,[11] and is used with default parameter settings, including a limit of 100 clusters.

Character n-grams Character n-gram language models are models built on sequences (n-grams) of characters. Here, we use 5-grams: for all the tweets a user authored, we count the number of times each sequence of 5 characters is observed. For example, for this sentence we would observe the sequences: "for e", "or ex", "r exa", " exam", and so on. The general approach is to examine how likely a sequence of characters is to be generated by a given type of user (schizophrenic or non-schizophrenic).

To featurize character n-grams, for each character 5-gram in the training data, we calculate its probability in schizophrenic users and its probability in control users. At test time, we search for sets of 50 sequential tweets that look "most schizophrenic" by comparing the schizophrenic and control probabilities estimated from the training data for all the 5-grams in those tweets. We experimented with different window sizes for the number of tweets and different n for n-grams; for brevity, we report only the highest performing parameter settings at low false alarm rates: 5-grams and a window size of 50 tweets. An example of this can be found in Figure 1, where one schizophrenic and one control user's score over time is plotted (top). To show the overall trend, we plot the same for all users in this study (bottom), where separation between the schizophrenics (in red) and control users (in blue) is apparent. The highest score from this windowed analysis becomes the feature value.

Note that this feature corresponds to only a subset of a user's timeline. For schizophrenia sufferers, this is perhaps when their symptoms were most severe, a subtle but critical distinction when one considers that many of these people are receiving treatment of some sort, and thus may have their symptoms change or subside over the course of our data.

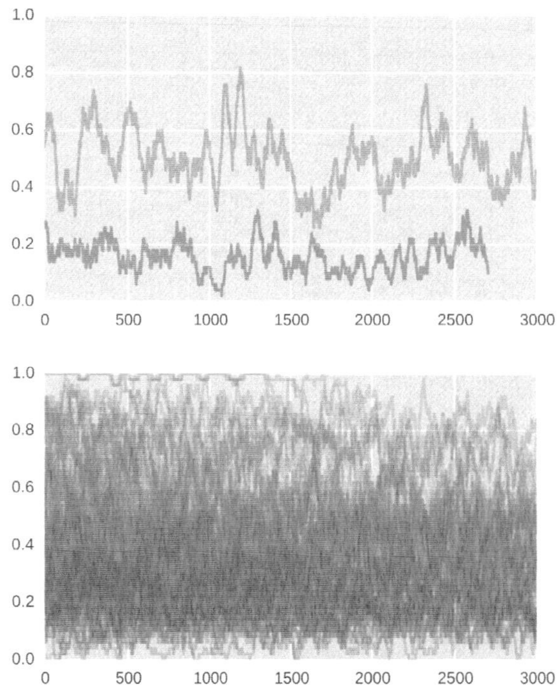

Figure 1: Timeseries of schizophrenia-like tweets for each user, x-axis is the tweets in order, y-axis denotes the proportion of tweets in a window of 50 tweets that are classified as *schizophrenia-like* by the CLMs. Top: Example plots of one schizophrenia (red) and one control user (blue). Bottom: All users.

Perplexity The breadth of language used (to include vocabulary, topic areas, and syntactic construction) can be measured via perplexity – a measurement based on entropy, and roughly interpreted as a measurement of how predictable the language is. We train a trigram language model on one million randomly selected tweets from the 2014 1% feed, and then use this model to score the perplexity on all the tweets for each user. If a user's language wanders broadly (and potentially has the *word salad* effect sometimes a symptom of schizophrenia), we would expect a high perplexity score for the user. This gives us a single feature value for the perplexity feature for each user.

[10] I.e., the most granular clusters for each word.

[11] https://github.com/percyliang/brown-cluster

Cond.	Topic	Top Words
Sch	2	don('t) (I')ve (I')ll feel people doesn('t) thing didn('t) time twitter won('t) make kind woman things isn('t) bad cat makes
Sch	9	don('t) love fuck fucking shit people life hell hate stop gonna god wanna die feel make kill time anymore
Sch	12	people don('t) lc world mental schizophrenia (I')ve god jesus schizophrenic illness health care paranoid medical truth time life read
Sch	18	people work today good years time make call long find made point thought free twitter back thing days job
Con	6	lol shit nigga im tho fuck ass ain('t) lmao don('t) good niggas gotta bitch smh damn ya man back
Con	7	game rochester football girls basketball final boys billsmafia win rt valley team season sectional north play miami st soccer
Con	11	great love time hope today day rt support custserv big happy awesome amazing easy trip toronto forward orleans hear
Con	19	lol dd love don('t) today day good happy time ddd miss hate work night back (I')ll birthday tomorrow tonight

Table 1: LDA topics with statistically significant differences between groups. The condition with the highest mean proportion is given in column 1, where Sch=schizophrenia and Con=control.

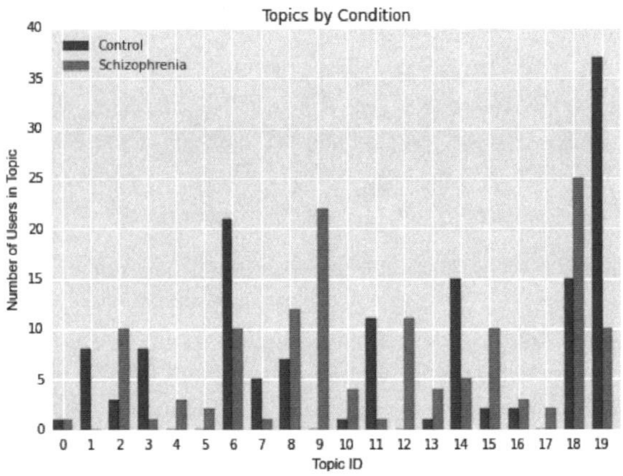

Figure 2: LDA topic prevalence by condition, shown by the number of users with each identified topic as their maximum estimated probability topic (t).

5 Results

5.1 Isolated Features

We examine differences in the language between schizophrenia sufferers and matched controls by mapping the words they use to broader categories, as discussed above, and measuring the relative frequencies of these categories in their tweets. Different approaches produce different word categories: We focus on LIWC vectors, topics from latent Dirichlet allocation (LDA), and clusters from Brown clustering. We compare whether the difference in the relative frequencies of each category is significant using an independent sample t-test,[12] Bonferroni-corrected.

[12]We assume a normal distribution; future work may examine how well this assumption holds.

Cond.	Topic	Top Words
Sch	01011111111	but because cause since maybe bc until cuz hopefully plus especially except
Sch	01011111110	if when sometimes unless whenever everytime someday
Sch	010000	i
Sch	010100111	know think thought care believe guess remember understand forget swear knew matter wonder forgot realize worry imagine exist doubt kno realized decide complain
Sch	010111010	of
Con	0001001	lol haha omg lmao idk hahaha wtf smh ugh o bruh lmfao ha #askemma tbh exactly k bye omfg hahahaha fr hahah btw jk
Con	01011011010	today
Con	0010111	! << >>
Con	01011010100	back home away checked forward asleep stuck button stream rewards closer messages anywhere apart swimming inspired dong tricks spree cv delivered tuned increased
Con	00001	" rt #nowplaying

Table 2: Example Brown clusters with statistically significant differences between groups. The condition with the highest mean proportion is given in column 1, where Sch=schizophrenia and Con=control.

LIWC vectors We did not make predictions about which LIWC categories might show deviations between our schizophrenia and control users, but instead examine all the LIWC categories (72 categories, corrected $\alpha = 0.0007$). We find that the language of schizophrenia users had significantly more words from the following major categories: COGNITIVE MECHANISMS, DEATH, FUNCTION WORDS, NEGATIVE EMOTION, and in the following subcategories: ARTICLE, AUXILIARY VERBS, CONJUGATIONS, DISCREPANCIES, EXCL, HEALTH, I, INCL, INSIGHT, IPRON, PPRON, PRO1, PRONOUN, TENTATIVE, and THEY. Schizophrenia users had significantly fewer words in the major categories of HOME, LEISURE, and POSITIVE EMOTION, and in the subcategories of ASSENT, MOTION, RELATIVE, SEE, and TIME.

Latent Dirichlet Allocation We find that the difference between the two groups is statistically significant for 8 of the 20 topics, i.e., the relative frequency of the topic per user is significantly different between groups (corrected $\alpha = 0.0025$). Significant topics and top words are shown in Table 1, with the condition with the highest mean proportion shown in the leftmost column and indicated by color: red for schizophrenia (Sch) and blue for control (Con) topics. We then find the topic t with the maximum estimated probability for each user. To see the prevalence of each topic for each condition, see Figure 2, where each user is represented only by their LDA topic t.

Brown Clustering To narrow in on a set of Brown clusters that may distinguish between schizophrenia sufferers and controls, we sum the relative frequency of each cluster per user, and extract those clusters with at least a 20% difference between groups. This yields 29 clusters. From these, we find that the difference between most of the clusters is statistically significant (corrected $\alpha = 0.0017$). Example significant clusters and top words are shown in Table 2.

Perplexity We find this to be only marginally different between groups (p-value = 0.07872), suggesting that a more in-depth and rigorous analysis of this measure and its relationship to the *word salad* effect is warranted.

5.2 Machine Learning

In Section 4, we discussed how we featurized LIWC categories, LDA topics, Brown clusters, Character Language Models, and perplexity. We now report machine learning experiments using these features. We compare two machine learning methods: Support Vector Machines (SVM) and Maximum Entropy (MaxEnt). All methods are imported with default parameter settings from python's scikit-learn (Pedregosa et al., 2011).

As shown in Table 3, the character language model ('CLM') method performs reasonably well at classifying users in isolation, and the features based on the distribution over Brown clusters ('BDist') performs well in a maximum entropy model. An SVM model with features created from LIWC categories and a distribution over LDA topics ('LIWC+TDist') works best at discovering schizophrenia sufferers in our experiments, reaching 82.3% classification accuracy on our balanced test set. Featurizing the distribution over topics provided by LDA increases classification accuracy over using linguistically-informed LIWC categories alone by 13.5 percentage points.

The CLM method performed surprisingly well, given its relative simplicity, and outperformed the LIWC features by nearly ten percentage points when used in isolation, perhaps indicating that the open-vocabulary approach made possible by the CLM is more robust to the type of data we see in Twitter. Combining the LIWC and CLM features, though, only gives a small bump in performance over CLMs alone. Given the fairly distinct distribution of LDA topics by condition as shown in Figure 2, we expected that the ID of the LDA topic t would serve well as a feature, but found that we needed to use the distribution over topics (TDist) in order to perform above chance. This topic distribution feature was the best-performing individual feature, and also performed well in combination with other features, thus seeming to provide a complementary signal. Interestingly, while the CLM model out-performed the LIWC model, the combination of LIWC and TDist features outperformed the combination of CLM and TDist features, yielding our best-performing model.

5.3 Analysis of Language-Based Signals: LDA and Brown Clustering

In the previous section, we examined how well the signals we define discriminate between schizophrenia sufferers and controls in a balanced dataset. We now turn to an exploratory discussion of the language markers discovered with the unsupervised NLP techniques of LDA and Brown clustering, in the hopes of shedding some light on language-based differences between the two groups.

Features	SVM	MAXENT
Perplexity (ppl)	52.0	51.4
Brown-Cluster Dist (BDist)	53.3	72.3
LIWC	68.8	70.8
CLM	77.1	77.2
LIWC+CLM	78.2	77.2
LDA Topic Dist (TDist)	80.4	80.4
CLM+TDist+BDist+ppl	81.2	79.7
CLM+TDist	81.5	81.8
LIWC+TDist	**82.3**	**81.9**

Table 3: Feature ablation results on 10-fold cross-validation. We find that LIWC categories combined with the distribution over automatically inferred LDA topics (TDist) works well for this classification task.

Refer to Tables 1 and 2. Both LDA and Brown clustering produce groups of related words, with different views of the data. We find that both methods group together words for laughing – "haha", "lol", etc. – and these discriminate between schizophrenia sufferers and controls. In LDA, this is Topic 6; in Brown clustering, this is Cluster 0001001.[13] Controls are much more likely to ask someone to retweet ("rt"), pulled out in both methods as well (Topics 7 and 11; Cluster 00001). The two approaches produce word groups with time words like "today" and "tonight" that discriminate between schizophrenia sufferers and controls differently; the word "today" in particular is found in a topic and in a cluster that is more common for controls (Topic 19 and Cluster 01011011010).

LDA pulls out positive sentiment words such as "love", "awesome", "amazing", "happy", "good", etc. (Topics 11 and 19), and topics with these words are significantly more common in controls. It also finds groups for negated words like "don't", "didn't", "won't", etc. (Topic 2), and this is significantly more common in the language of schizophrenia sufferers. Both decreased occurrence of positive sentiment topics and increase of negated word topics is suggestive of the *flat affect* common to schizophrenics. Topic 12 contains a group of words specific to mental health, including the words "mental", "health", and "medical", as well as, interestingly, "schizophrenia" and "schizophrenic" – unsurprisingly occurring significantly more under the schizophre-

[13]Brown clustering is an unsupervised learning process, so the labels just indicate the hierarchical structure of the clusters; for example, Cluster 01 is the parent of Clusters 010 and 011.

nia condition. Recall that we remove the original diagnosis tweet from our analysis, but this topic indicates much more talk about the condition. One wonders whether this might extend to other mental health conditions, and whether the stigma of discussing mental health is reduced within the anonymity provided by the Internet and social media. Figure 2 furthermore indicates that only schizophrenia sufferers have this Topic 12 as their LDA topic t.

Brown clustering pulls out the first person pronoun 'I' as a main cluster, and we find that this is significantly more frequent in schizophrenia sufferers than in controls. This is comparable to the LIWC category 'I', which we also find to be proportionally higher in the language of schizophrenia sufferers. Interestingly, Brown clustering pulls out words that mark *hedging* and *irrealis moods* in English (Cluster 010100111). This is found in phrases such as "I think", "I believe", "I guess", etc. We find that this cluster is significantly more common in the language of schizophrenia sufferers, perhaps related to the dissociation from reality common to the disorder. We also find a Brown cluster for *connectives* (words like "but", "because", "except") in Cluster 01011111111; and this is also significantly more common in schizophrenia sufferers. The use of an exclamation point (Cluster 0010111) also differs between schizophrenia sufferers and controls. Note that markers << and >> are also common in this cluster. This is an artifact of our text processing of emojis; in other words, both emojis and exclamation points are significantly less likely in the language of schizophrenics. This is potentially another reflection of the *flat affect* negative symptom of schizophrenia.

6 Conclusion

Given its relative rarity compared to other mental health conditions like depression or anxiety disorders, schizophrenia has been harder to obtain enough data to leverage state-of-the-art natural language processing techniques. Many such techniques depend on large amounts of text data for adequate training, and such data has largely been unavailable. However, we can discover a sufficient amount of schizophrenia sufferers via publicly available social media data, and from here we can begin to explore text-based markers of the illness. This comes with a notable caveat: These users battling schizophrenia may be different in some systematic ways from the schizophrenic population as a whole – they are Twitter users, and they are speaking publicly about their condition. This suggests that replication of these findings in more controlled settings is warranted before hard conclusions are drawn.

By applying a wide range of natural language processing techniques to users who state a diagnosis of schizophrenia, age- and gender-matched to community controls, we discovered several significant signals for schizophrenia. We demonstrated that character n-grams featurized over specific tweets in a user's history performs reasonably well at separating schizophrenia sufferers from controls, and further, featurizing the distribution over topics provided by latent Dirichlet allocation increases classification accuracy over using linguistically-informed LIWC categories alone by 13.5 percentage points in an SVM machine learning approach. Moreover, the features produced by these unsupervised NLP methods provided some known, some intuitive, and some novel linguistic differences between schizophrenia and control users.

Our cursory inspection here is only capturing a fraction of the insights into schizophrenia from text-based analysis, and we see great potential from future analyses of this sort. Identifying quantifiable signals and classifying users is a step towards a deeper understanding of language differences associated with schizophrenia, and hopefully, an advancement in available technology to help those battling with the illness.

References

American Psychiatric Association. 2013. *Diagnostic and Statistical Manual of Mental Disorders (5th Edition)*. Arlington, VA: American Psychiatric Publishing.

David M. Blei, Andrew Y. Ng, and Michael I. Jordan. 2003. Latent Dirichlet allocation. *Journal of Machine Learning Research*, 3:993–1022, March.

Peter F. Brown, Peter V. deSouza, Robert L. Mercer, Vincent J. Della Pietra, and Jenifer C. Lai. 1992. Class-based n-gram models of natural language. *Computational Linguistics*, 18(4):467–479, December.

Glen Coppersmith, Mark Dredze, and Craig Harman. 2014a. Quantifying mental health signals in Twitter. In *Proceedings of the ACL Workshop on Computational Linguistics and Clinical Psychology*.

Glen Coppersmith, Craig Harman, and Mark Dredze. 2014b. Measuring post traumatic stress disorder in Twitter. In *Proceedings of the 8th International AAAI Conference on Weblogs and Social Media (ICWSM)*.

Munmun De Choudhury, Scott Counts, and Michael Gamon. 2011. Not all moods are created equal! Exploring human emotional states in social media. In *Proceedings of the 5th International AAAI Conference on Weblogs and Social Media (ICWSM)*.

Munmun De Choudhury, Scott Counts, and Eric Horvitz. 2013a. Social media as a measurement tool of depression in populations. In *Proceedings of the 5th ACM International Conference on Web Science*.

Munmun De Choudhury, Michael Gamon, Scott Counts, and Eric Horvitz. 2013b. Predicting depression via social media. In *Proceedings of the 7th International AAAI Conference on Weblogs and Social Media (ICWSM)*.

Virgile Landeiro Dos Reis and Aron Culotta. 2015. Using matched samples to estimate the effects of exercise on mental health from Twitter. In *Proceedings of the Twenty-Ninth AAAI Conference on Artificial Intelligence*.

H. Häfner and K. Maurer. 2006. Early detection of schizophrenia: current evidence and future perspectives. *World Psychiatry*, 5(3):130–138.

Elizabeth Hohman, David Marchette, and Glen Coppersmith. 2014. Mental health, economics, and population in social media. In *Proceedings of the Joint Statistical Meetings*.

Christine Howes, Matthew Purver, and Rose McCabe. 2014. Linguistic indicators of severity and progress in online text-based therapy for depression. In *Proceedings of the ACL Workshop on Computational Linguistics and Clinical Psychology*.

Ronald C. Kessler, Olga Demler, Richard G. Frank, Mark Olfson, Harold Alan Pincus, Ellen E. Walters, Philip Wang, Kenneth B. Wells, and Alan M. Zaslavsky. 2005. Prevalence and treatment of mental disorders, 1990 to 2003. *New England Journal of Medicine*, 352(24):2515–2523.

Andrew Kachites McCallum. 2002. MALLET: A machine learning for language toolkit. http://mallet.cs.umass.edu. [Online; accessed 2015-03-02].

Paul McNamee and James Mayfield. 2004. Character n-gram tokenization for European language text retrieval. *Information Retrieval*, 7(1-2):73–97.

Shashwath A. Meda, Adrienne Gill, Michael C. Stevens, Raymond P. Lorenzoni, David C. Glahn, Vince D. Calhoun, John A. Sweeney, Carol A. Tamminga, Matcheri S. Keshavan, Gunvant Thaker, et al. 2012. Differences in resting-state functional magnetic resonance imaging functional network connectivity between schizophrenia and psychotic bipolar probands and their unaffected first-degree relatives. *Biological Psychiatry*, 71(10):881–889.

National Alliance on Mental Illness. 2015. Schizophrenia. http://www.nami.org/Learn-More/Mental-Health-Conditions/Schizophrenia. [Online; accessed 2015-03-10].

Thin Nguyen, Dinh Phung, Bo Dao, Svetha Venkatesh, and Michael Berk. 2014. Affective and content analysis of online depression communities. *IEEE Transactions on Affective Computing*, 5(3):217–226.

Sylvester Olubolu Orimaye, Jojo Sze-Meng Wong, and Karen Jennifer Golden. 2014. Learning predictive linguistic features for Alzheimer's disease and related dementias using verbal utterances. In *Proceedings of the ACL Workshop on Computational Linguistics and Clinical Psychology*.

Pacific Institute of Medical Research. 2015. Common schizophrenia symptoms. http://www.pacificmedresearch.com/common-schizophrenia-symptoms/. [Online; accessed 2015-03-10].

Greg Park, H. Andrew Schwartz, Johannes C. Eichstaedt, Margaret L. Kern, David J. Stillwell, Michal Kosinski, Lyle H. Ungar, and Martin E. P. Seligman. In press. Automatic personality assessment through social media language. *Journal of Personality and Social Psychology*.

Fabian Pedregosa, Gaël Varoquaux, Alexandre Gramfort, Vincent Michel, Bertrand Thirion, Olivier Grisel, Mathieu Blondel, Peter Prettenhofer, Ron Weiss, Vincent Dubourg, Jake Vanderplas, Alexandre Passos, David Cournapeau, Matthieu Brucher, and Matthieu Perrot Édouard Duchesnay. 2011. scikit-learn: Machine learning in Python. *The Journal of Machine Learning Research*, 12:2825–2830.

James W. Pennebaker, Cindy K. Chung, Molly Ireland, Amy Gonzales, and Roger J. Booth. 2007. *The development and psychometric properties of LIWC2007*. LIWC.net, Austin, TX.

Jonna Perälä, Jaana Suvisaari, Samuli I. Saarni, Kimmo Kuoppasalmi, Erkki Isometsä, Sami Pirkola, Timo Partonen, Annamari Tuulio-Henriksson, Jukka Hintikka, Tuula Kieseppä, et al. 2007. Lifetime prevalence of psychotic and bipolar I disorders in a general population. *Archives of General Psychiatry*, 64(1):19–28.

Philip Resnik, Anderson Garron, and Rebecca Resnik. 2013. Using topic modeling to improve prediction of neuroticism and depression. In *Proceedings of the 2013 Conference on Empirical Methods in Natural*, pages 1348–1353.

Bonnie L. Rickelman. 2004. Anosognosia in individuals with schizophrenia: Toward recovery of insight. *Issues in Mental Health Nursing*, 25:227–242.

Brian Roark, Margaret Mitchell, John-Paul Hosom, Kristy Hollingshead, and Jeffrey A. Kaye. 2011. Spoken language derived measures for detecting mild cognitive impairment. *IEEE Transactions on Audio, Speech & Language Processing*, 19(7):2081–2090.

Masoud Rouhizadeh, Emily Prud'hommeaux, Jan van Santen, and Richard Sproat. 2014. Detecting linguistic idiosyncratic interests in autism using distributional semantic models. In *Proceedings of the ACL Workshop on Computational Linguistics and Clinical Psychology*.

Sukanta Saha, David Chant, Joy Welham, and John McGrath. 2005. A systematic review of the prevalence of schizophrenia. *PLoS medicine*, 2(5):e141.

Maarten Sap, Greg Park, Johannes C. Eichstaedt, Margaret L. Kern, David J. Stillwell, Michal Kosinski, Lyle H. Ungar, and H. Andrew Schwartz. 2014. Developing age and gender predictive lexica over social media. In *Proceedings of the Conference on Empirical Methods in Natural Language Processing (EMNLP)*, pages 1146–1151.

H. Andrew Schwartz, Johannes C. Eichstaedt, Margaret L. Kern, Lukasz Dziurzynski, Richard E. Lucas, Megha Agrawal, Gregory J. Park, Shrinidhi K. Lakshmikanth, Sneha Jha, Martin E. P. Seligman, and Lyle H. Ungar. 2013. Characterizing geographic variation in well-being using tweets. In *Proceedings of the 8th International AAAI Conference on Weblogs and Social Media (ICWSM)*.

H. Andrew Schwartz, Johannes Eichstaedt, Margaret L. Kern, Gregory Park, Maarten Sap, David Stillwell, Michal Kosinski, and Lyle Ungar. 2014. Towards assessing changes in degree of depression through Facebook. In *Proceedings of the ACL Workshop on Computational Linguistics and Clinical Psychology*.

The National Institute of Mental Health. 2015. Schizophrenia. http://www.nimh.nih.gov/health/topics/schizophrenia. [Online; accessed 2015-03-04].

The Role of Personality, Age and Gender in Tweeting about Mental Illnesses

Daniel Preoţiuc-Pietro[1,2], **Johannes Eichstaedt**[1], **Gregory Park**[1], **Maarten Sap**[1]
Laura Smith[1], **Victoria Tobolsky**[1], **H. Andrew Schwartz**[2,3] and **Lyle Ungar**[1,2]
[1]Department of Psychology, University of Pennsylvania
[2]Computer & Information Science, University of Pennsylvania
[3]Computer Science, Stony Brook University
danielpr@sas.upenn.edu

Abstract

Mental illnesses, such as depression and post traumatic stress disorder (PTSD), are highly underdiagnosed globally. Populations sharing similar demographics and personality traits are known to be more at risk than others. In this study, we characterise the language use of users disclosing their mental illness on Twitter. Language-derived personality and demographic estimates show surprisingly strong performance in distinguishing users that tweet a diagnosis of depression or PTSD from random controls, reaching an area under the receiver-operating characteristic curve – AUC – of around .8 in all our binary classification tasks. In fact, when distinguishing users disclosing depression from those disclosing PTSD, the single feature of estimated age shows nearly as strong performance (AUC = .806) as using thousands of topics (AUC = .819) or tens of thousands of n-grams (AUC = .812). We also find that differential language analyses, controlled for demographics, recover many symptoms associated with the mental illnesses in the clinical literature.

1 Introduction

Mental illnesses, such as depression and post traumatic stress disorder (PTSD) represent a large share of the global burden of disease (Üstün et al., 2004; Mathers and Loncar, 2006), but are underdiagnosed and undertreated around the world (Prince et al., 2007). Previous research has demonstrated the important role of demographic factors in depression risk. For example, while clinically-assessed depression is estimated at 6.6% in a 12-month interval for U.S. adults (Kessler et al., 2003), the prevalence in males is 3-5%, while the prevalence is 8-10% in females (Andrade et al., 2003). Similarly, prevalence of PTSD among U.S. adults in any 12-month period is estimated at 3.5% (Kessler et al., 2005b) – 1.8% in males and 5.2% in females – yet this risk is not distributed evenly across age groups; prevalence of PTSD increases throughout the majority of the lifespan to reach a peak of 9.2% between the ages of 49-59, before dropping sharply to 2.5% past the age of 60. (Kessler et al., 2005a).

Large scale user-generated content provides the opportunity to extract information not only about events, but also about the person posting them. Using automatic methods, a wide set of user characteristics, such as age, gender, personality, location and income have been shown to be predictable from shared social media text. The same holds for mental illnesses, from users expressing symptoms of their illness (e.g. low mood, focus on the self, high anxiety) to talking about effects of their illness (e.g. mentioning medications and therapy) and to even self-disclosing the illness.

This study represents an analysis of language use in users who share their mental illness though social media, in this case depression and PTSD. We advocate adjusting for important underlying demographic factors, such as age and gender, to avoid confounding by language specific to these underlying characteristics. The age and gender trends from the U.S. population are present in our dataset, although imperfectly, given the biases of self-reports and social media sampling. Our differential language analyses show symptoms associated with these illnesses congruent with existing clinical theory and consequences of diagnoses.

In addition to age and gender, we focus on the important role of inferred personality in predicting

Proceedings of the 2nd Workshop on Computational Linguistics and Clinical Psychology: From Linguistic Signal to Clinical Reality, pages 21–30,
Denver, Colorado, June 5, 2015.

mental illness. We show that a model which uses only the text-predicted user level 'Big Five' personality dimensions plus age and gender perform with high accuracy, comparable to methods that use standard dictionaries of psychology as features. Users who self-report a diagnosis appear more neurotic and more introverted when compared to average users.

2 Data

We use a dataset of Twitter users reported to suffer from a mental illness, specifically depression and post traumatic stress disorder (PTSD). This dataset was first introduced in (Coppersmith et al., 2014a). The self-reports are collected by searching a large Twitter archive for disclosures using a regular expression (e.g. 'I have been diagnosed with depression'). Candidate users were filtered manually and then all their most recent tweets have been continuously crawled using the Twitter Search API. The self-disclosure messages were excluded from the dataset and from the estimation of user inferred demographics and personality scores. The control users were selected at random from Twitter.

In total there are 370 users diagnosed only with PTSD, 483 only with depression and 1104 control users. On average, each user has 3400.8 messages. As Coppersmith et al. (2014b) acknowledge, this method of collection is susceptible to multiple biases, but represents a simple way to build a large dataset of users and their textual information.

3 Features

We use the Twitter posts of a user to infer several user traits which we expect to be relevant to mental illnesses based on standard clinical criteria (American Psychiatric Association, 2013). Recently, automatic user profiling methods have used on user-generated text and complementary features in order to predict different user traits such as: age (Nguyen et al., 2011), gender (Sap et al., 2014), location (Cheng et al., 2010), impact (Lampos et al., 2014), political preference (Volkova et al., 2014), temporal orientation (Schwartz et al., 2015) or personality (Schwartz et al., 2013).

3.1 Age, Gender and Personality

We use the methods developed in (Schwartz et al., 2013) to assign each user scores for age, gender and personality from the popular five factor model of personality – 'Big Five' – (McCrae and John, 1992), which consists of five dimensions: extraversion, agreeableness, conscientiousness, neuroticism and openness to experience.

The model was trained on a large sample of around 70,000 Facebook users who have taken Big Five personality tests and shared their posts using a model using 1-3 grams and topics as features (Park et al., 2014; Schwartz et al., 2013). This model achieves $R > .3$ predictive performance for all five traits. This dataset is also used to obtain age and gender adjusted personality and topic distributions.

3.2 Affect and Intensity

Emotions play an important role in the diagnosis of mental illness (American Psychiatric Association, 2013). We aim to capture the expression of users' emotions through their generated posts. We characterize expressions along the dimensions of *affect* (from positive to negative) and *intensity* (from low to high), which correspond to the two primary axes of the circumplex model, a well-established system for describing emotional states (Posner et al., 2005).

Machine learning approaches perform significantly better at quantifying emotion/sentiment from text compared to lexicon-based methods (Pang and Lee, 2008). Emotions are expressed at message-level. Consequently, we trained a text classification model on 3,000 Facebook posts labeled by affect and intensity using unigrams as features. We applied this model on each user's posts and aggregated over them to obtain a user score for both dimensions.

3.3 Textual Features

For our qualitative text analysis we extract textual features from all of a user's Twitter posts. Traditional psychological studies use a closed-vocabulary approach to modelling text. The most popular method is based on Linguistic Inquiry and Word Count (LIWC) (Pennebaker et al., 2001). In LIWC, psychological theory was used to build 64 different categories. These include different parts-of-speech, topical categories and emotions. Each user is thereby represented as a distribution over these categories. We also use all frequent 1-3 grams (used by more than 10% of users in our dataset), where we use point-wise mutual information (PMI) to filter infrequent 2-3 grams.

For a better qualitative assessment and to reduce risk of overfitting, we use a set of topics as a form of dimensionality reduction. We use the 2,000 clusters introduced in (Schwartz et al., 2013) obtained by applying Latent Dirichlet Allocation (Blei et al., 2003), the most popular topic model, to a large set of Facebook posts.

4 Prediction

In this section we present an analysis of the predictive power of inferred user-level features. We use the methods introduced in Section 3 to predict nine user level scores: age, gender, affect, intensity and the Big Five personality traits.

The three populations in our dataset are used to formulate three binary classification problems in order to analyse specific pairwise group peculiarities. Users having both PTSD and depression are held-out when classifying between these two classes. To assess the power of our text-derived features, we use as features broader textual features such as the LIWC categories, the LDA inferred topics and frequent 1-3 grams.

We train binary logistic regression classifiers (Pedregosa et al., 2011) with Elastic Net regularisation (Zou and Hastie, 2005). In Table 1 we report the performance using 10-fold cross-validation. Performance is measured using ROC area under the curve (ROC AUC), an adequate measure when the classes are imbalanced. A more thorough study of predictive performance for identifying PTSD and depressed users is presented in (Preoţiuc-Pietro et al., 2015).

Our results show the following:

- Age alone improves over chance and is highly predictive when classifying PTSD users. To visualise the effect of age, Figure 1 shows the probability density function in our three populations. This highlights that PTSD users are consistently predicted older than both controls and depressed users. This is in line with findings from the National Comorbidity Survey and replications (Kessler et al., 2005a; Kessler et al., 2005b). As a consequence, factoring in age in downstream analysis is necessary, as language changes with age on social media.

Feature	No.feat	C–D	C–P	D–P
Random	-	.5	.5	.5
Age	1	.557	.742	.801
Gender	1	.559	.513	.522
Age + Gender	2	.590	.747	.8
Big5	5	.784	.813	.777
Age + Gender + Big5	7	.783	.844	.806
Affect + Intensity	2	.583	.519	.559
LIWC	64	.824	.854	.781
Topics	2000	.851	.901	**.819**
Unigrams	5432	.858	.911	.809
1-3 grams	12677	**.859**	**.917**	.812

Table 1: Predictive performance using Logistic Regression in ROC area under the curve (AUC) between controls (**C**), depressed (**D**) and PTSD (**P**).

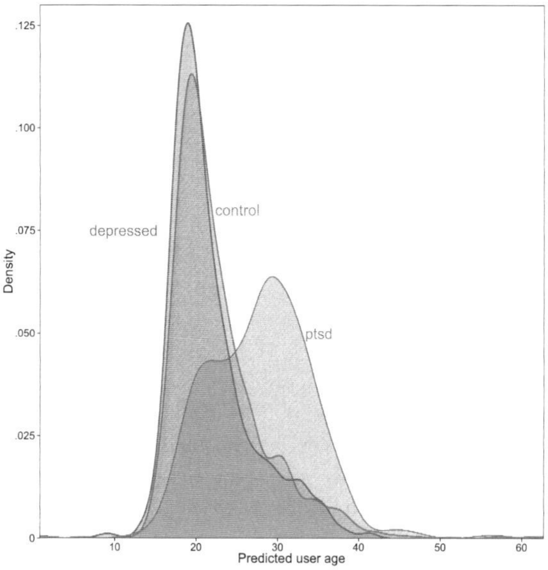

Figure 1: Age density functions for each group.

- Gender is only weakly predictive of any mental illness, although significantly above chance in depressed vs. controls ($p < .01$, DeLong test[1]). Interestingly, in this task age and gender combined improve significantly above each individual prediction, illustrating they contain complementary information. Consequently, at least when analysing depression, gender should

[1] A non-parametric test for identifying significant differences in ROC curves (DeLong et al., 1988)

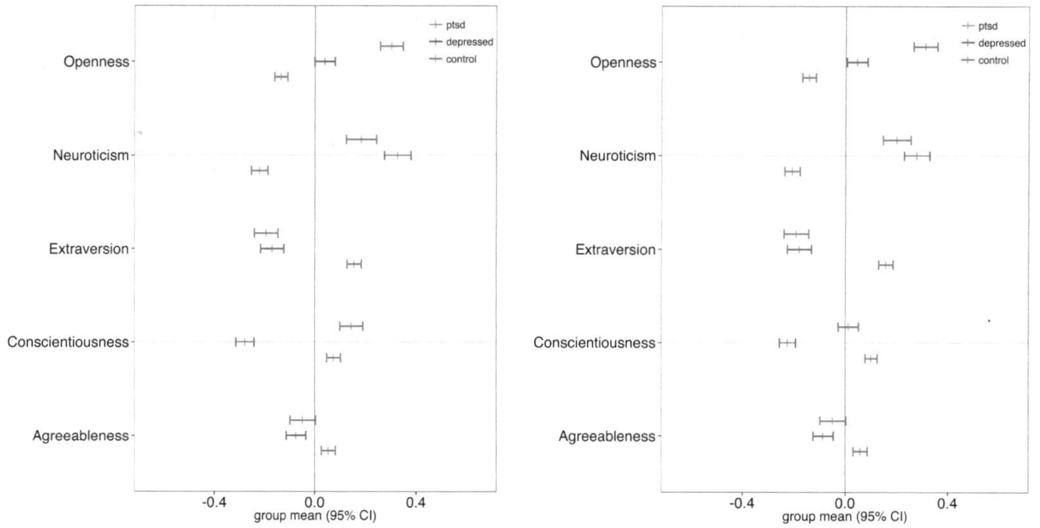

(a) Not controlled for age and gender. (b) Controlled for age and gender.

Figure 2: Big Five personality means (grand mean centered) and confidence intervals for each group.

be accounted for in addition to age.

- Personality alone obtains very good predictive accuracies, reaching over .8 ROC AUC for classifying depressed vs. PTSD. In general, personality features alone perform with strong predictive accuracy, within .1 of >5000 unigram features or 2000 topics. Adding age and gender information further improves predictive power (C–P $p < .01$, D–P $p < .01$, DeLong test) when PTSD is one of the compared groups.

In Figure 2 we show the mean personality scores across the three groups. In this dataset, PTSD users score highest on average in openness with depressed users scoring lowest. However, neuroticism is the largest separator between mentally ill users and the controls, with depressed having slightly higher levels of neuroticism than PTSD. Neuroticism alone has an ROC AUC of .732 in prediction depression vs. control and .674 in predicting PTSD vs. control. Controls score higher on extraversion, a trait related to the frequency and intensity of positive emotions (Smillie et al., 2012). Controlling for age (Figure 2b) significantly reduces the initial association between PTSD and higher conscientiousness, because PTSD users are likely to be older, and conscientiousness tends to increase with age (Soto et al., 2011). After controlling, depressed users score lowest on conscientiousness, while PTSD and controls are close to each other.

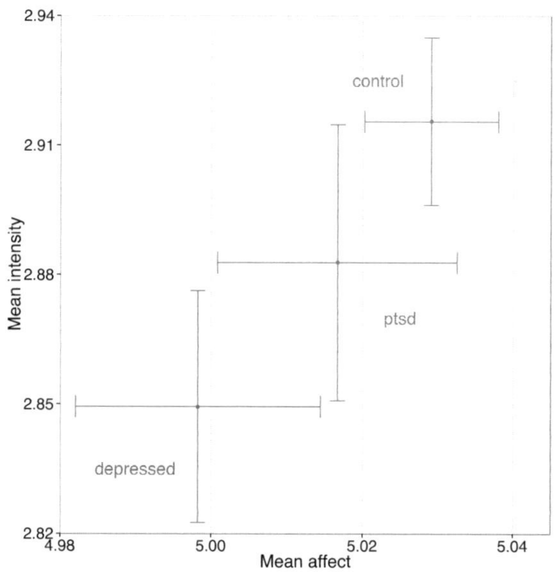

Figure 3: Users mapped on the emotion circumplex, consisting of affect (valence) and intensity (arousal).

- Average affect and intensity achieve modest predictive performance, although significant (C–D $p < .001$, D–P $p < .001$, DeLong test) when one of the compared groups are depressed. We use the two features to map users to the emotion circumplex in Figure 3. On average, control users expressed both higher intensity and higher (i.e. more positive) affect, while depressed users were lowest on both. This is consistent with the lowered (i.e. more negative) affect typically seen in both PTSD and depressed patients, and the increased intensity/arousal among PTSD users may correspond to more frequent expressions of anxiety, which is characterized by high arousal and lower/negative affect (American Psychiatric Association, 2013).

- Textual features obtain high predictive performance. Out of these, LIWC performs the worst, while the topics, unigrams and 1-3 grams have similarly high performance.

In addition to ROC AUC scores, we present ROC curves for all three binary prediction tasks in Figures 4a, 4b and 4c. ROC curves are specifically useful for medical practitioners because the classification threshold can be adjusted to choose an application-appropriate level of false positives. For comparison, we display methods using only age and gender; age, gender and personality combined, as well as LIWC and the LDA topics.

For classifying depressed users from controls, a true positive rate of ~ 0.6 can be achieved at a false positive rate of ~ 0.2 using personality, age and gender alone, with an increase to up to ~ 0.7 when PTSD users are one of the groups. When classifying PTSD users, age is the most important factor. Separating between depressed and PTSD is almost exclusively a factor of age. This suggests that a application in a real life scenario will likely overpredict older users to have PTSD.

5 Language Analysis

The very high predictive power of the user-level features and textual features motivates us to analyse the linguistic features associated with each group, taking into account age and gender.

We study differences in language between groups using differential language analysis – DLA (Schwartz et al., 2013). This method aims to find all the most discriminative features between two groups by correlating each individual feature (1-3 gram or topic) to the class label. In our case, age and gender are included as covariates in order to control for the effect they may have on the outcome. Since a large number of features are explored, we consider coefficients significant if they meet a Bonferroni-corrected two-tailed p-value of less than 0.001.

5.1 Language of Depression

The word cloud in Figure 5a displays the 1-3 grams that most distinguish the depressed users from the set of control users.

Many features show face validity (e.g. 'depressed'), but also appear to represent a number of the cognitive and emotional processes implicated in depression in the literature (American Psychiatric Association, 2013). 1-3 grams seem to disclose information relating to illness and illness management (e.g. 'depressed', 'illness', 'meds', 'pills', 'therapy'). In some of the most strongly correlated features we also observe an increased focus on the self (e.g. 'I', 'I am', 'I have', 'I haven't', 'I was', 'myself') which has been found to accompany depression in many studies and often accompanies states of psychological distress (Rude et al., 2004; Stirman and Pennebaker, 2001; Bucci and Freedman, 1981).

Depression classically relies on the presence of two sets of core symptoms: sustained periods of low mood (dysphoria) and low interest (anhedonia) (American Psychiatric Association, 2013). Phrases such as 'cry' and 'crying' suggest low mood, while 'anymore' and 'I used to' may suggest a discontinuation of activities. Suicidal ideations or more general thoughts of death and dying are symptoms used in the diagnosis of depression, and even though they are relatively rarely mentioned (grey color), are identified in the differential language analysis (e.g. 'suicide', 'to die').

Beyond what is generally thought of as the key symptoms of depression discussed above, the differential language analysis also suggests that anger and interpersonal hostility ('fucking') feature significantly in the language use of depressed users.

The 10 topics most associated with depression (correlation values ranging from $R = .282$ to $R = .229$) suggest similar themes, including dysphoria (e.g. 'lonely', 'sad', 'crying' – Figures 6b, 6c, 6f) and thoughts of death (e.g. 'suicide' – Figure 6h).

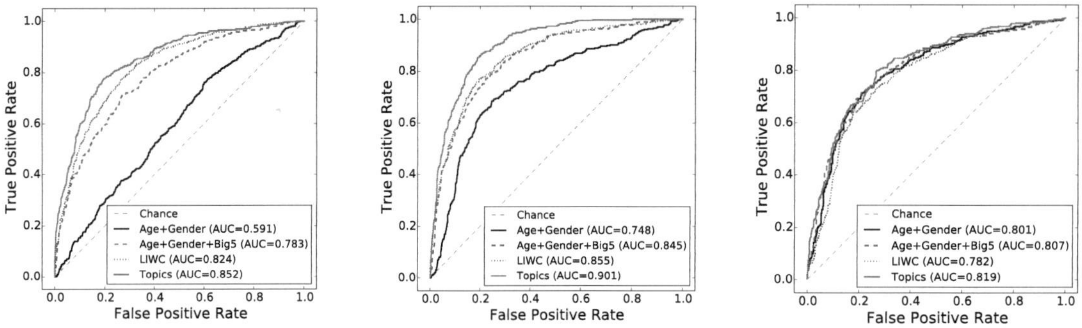

(a) Controls vs. Depressed. (b) Controls vs. PTSD. (c) Depressed vs. PTSD.

Figure 4: ROC curves for prediction using different types of features.

(a) Depression. (b) PTSD.

Figure 5: The word clouds show the 1-3 grams most correlated with each group having a mental illness, with the set of control users serving as the contrastive set in both cases. The size of the 1-3 gram is scaled by the correlation to binary depression label (point-biserial correlation). The color indexes relative frequency, from grey (rarely used) through blue (moderately used) to red (frequently used). Correlations are controlled for age and gender.

5.2 Language of PTSD

The word cloud in Figure 5b and topic clouds in Figure 7 display the 1-3 grams and topics most correlated with PTSD, with topic correlation values ranging from $R = .280$ to $R = .237$. On the whole, the language most predictive of PTSD does not map as cleanly onto the symptoms and criteria for diagnosis of PTSD as was the case with depression. Across topics and 1-3 grams, the language most correlated with PTSD suggests 'depression', disease management (e.g. 'pain', 'pills', 'meds' – Figure 7c) and a focus on the self (e.g. 'I had', 'I was', 'I am', 'I would'). Similarly, language is suggestive of death (e.g. 'suicide', 'suicidal'). Compared to the language of depressed users, themes within the language of users with PTSD appear to reference traumatic experiences that are required for a diagnosis of PTSD (e.g. 'murdered', 'died'), as well as the resultant states of fear-like psychological distress (e.g. 'terrified', 'anxiety').

5.3 PTSD and Depression

From our predictive experiments and Figure 4c, we see that language-predicted age almost completely differentiates between PTSD and depressed users. Consequently, we find only a few features that distinguish between the two groups when controlling for age. To visualise differences between the diseases we visualize topic usage in both groups in Figure 8. This shows standardised usage in both groups for each topic. As an additional factor (color), we include

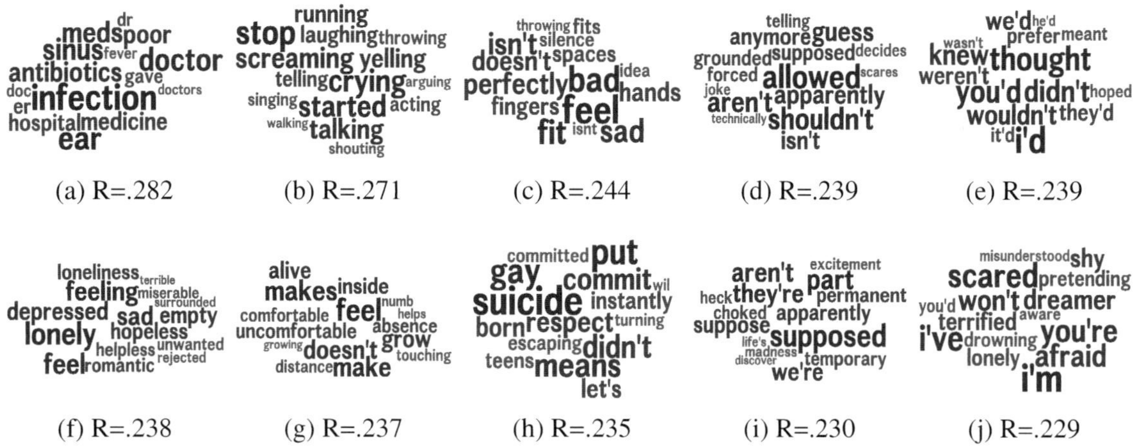

Figure 6: The LDA topics most correlated with depression controlling for age and gender, with the set of control users serving as the contrastive set. Word size is proportional to the probability of the word within the topics. Color is for display only.

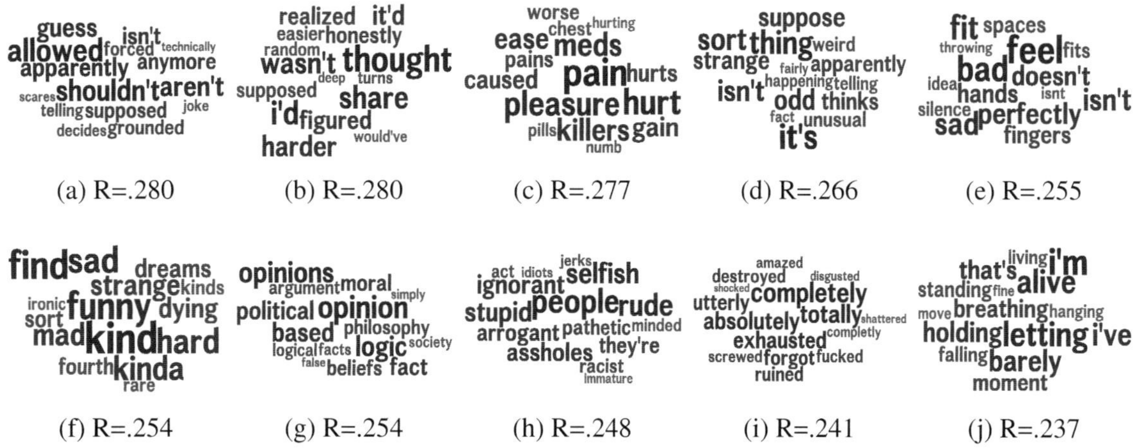

Figure 7: The LDA topics most correlated with PTSD controlling for age and gender, with the set of control users serving as the contrastive set. Word size is proportional to the probability of the word within the topics. Color is for display only.

the personality trait of neuroticism. This plays the most important role in separating between mentally ill users and controls.

The topics marked by arrows in Figure 8 are some of the topics most used by users with depression and PTSD shown above in Figures 6-7. Of the three topics, the topic shown in Figure 6h has 'suicide' as the most prevalent word. This topic's use is elevated for both depression and PTSD. Figure 6f shows a topic used mostly by depressed users, while Figure 7c highlights a topic used mainly by users with PTSD.

6 Related Work

Prior studies have similarly examined the efficacy of utilising social media data, like Facebook and Twitter, to ascertain the presence of both depression and PTSD. For instance, Coppersmith et al. (2014b) analyse differences in patterns of language use. They report that individuals with PTSD were significantly more likely to use third person pronouns and significantly less likely to use second person pronouns, without mentioning differences in the use of first person pronouns. This is in contrast to the strong differences in first person pronoun use among depressed individuals documented in the literature

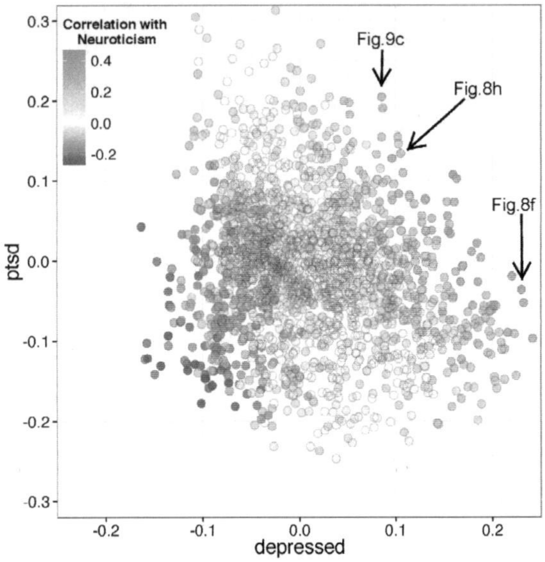

Figure 8: Topic usage (z-scored) for depressed and PTSD users. Color shows correlation of each topic to neuroticism. Labeled topics can be found in Figures 6- 7.

(Rude et al., 2004; Stirman and Pennebaker, 2001), confirmed in prior Twitter studies (Coppersmith et al., 2014a; De Choudhury et al., 2013) and replicated here. De Choudhury et al. (2013) explore the relationships between social media postings and depressive status, finding that geographic variables can alter one's risk. They show that cities for which the highest numbers of depressive Twitter users are predicted correlate with the cities with the known highest depression rates nationwide; depressive tweets follow an expected diurnal and annual rhythm (peaking at night and during winter); and women exhibit an increased risk of depression relative to men, consistent with known psychological trends. These studies thus demonstrate the utility of using social media outlets to capture nuanced data about an individual's daily psychological affect to predict pathology, and suggest that geographic and demographic factors may alter the prevalence of psychological ill-being. The present study is unique in its efforts to control for some of these demographic factors, such as personality and age, that demonstrably influence an individual's pattern of language use. Further, these demographic characteristics are known to significantly alter patterns e.g. pronoun use (Pennebaker, 2011). This highlights the utility of controlling for these factors when analysing pathological states like depression or PTSD.

7 Conclusions

This study presented a qualitative analysis of mental illness language use in users who disclosed their diagnoses. For users diagnosed with depression or PTSD, we have identified both symptoms and effects of their mental condition from user-generated content. The majority of our results map to clinical theory, confirming the validity of our methodology and the relevance of the dataset.

In our experiments, we accounted for text-derived user features, such as demographics (e.g. age, gender) and personality. Text-derived personality alone showed high predictive performance, in one case reaching similar performance to using orders of magnitude more textual features.

Our study further demonstrated the potential for using social media as a means for predicting and analysing the linguistic markers of mental illnesses. However, it also raises a few questions. First, although apparently easily predictable, the difference between depressed and PTSD users is largely only due to predicted age. Sample demographics also appear to be different than the general population, making predictive models fitted on this data to be susceptible to over-predicting certain demographics.

Secondly, the language associated with a self-reported diagnosis of depression and PTSD has a large overlap with the language predictive of personality. This suggests that personality may be explanatory of a particular kind of behavior: posting about mental illness diagnoses online. The mental illness labels thus acquired likely have personality confounds 'baked into them', stressing the need for using stronger ground truth such as given by clinicians.

Further, based on the scope of the applications – whether screening or analysis of psychological risk factors – user-generated data should at minimum be temporally partitioned to encompass content shared before and after the diagnosis. This allows one to separate mentions of symptoms from discussions of and consequences of their diagnosis, such as the use of medications.

References

American Psychiatric Association. 2013. *Diagnostic and statistical manual of mental disorders: DSM-5*. American Psychiatric Association, 5 edition.

Laura Andrade, Jorge J Caraveo-anduaga, Patricia Berglund, Rob V Bijl, Ron De Graaf, Wilma Vollebergh, Eva Dragomirecka, Robert Kohn, Martin Keller, Ronald C Kessler, et al. 2003. The epidemiology of major depressive episodes: results from the International Consortium of Psychiatric Epidemiology (ICPE) Surveys. *International Journal of Methods in Psychiatric Research*, 12(1):3–21.

David M. Blei, Andrew Y. Ng, and Michael I. Jordan. 2003. Latent Dirichlet Allocation. *Journal of Machine Learning Research*, 3:993–1022.

Wilma Bucci and Norbert Freedman. 1981. The language of depression. *Bulletin of the Menninger Clinic*.

Zhiyuan Cheng, James Caverlee, and Kyumin Lee. 2010. You are where you tweet: a content-based approach to geo-locating twitter users. In *Proceedings of the 19th ACM Conference on Information and Knowledge Management*, CIKM, pages 759–768.

Glen Coppersmith, Mark Dredze, and Craig Harman. 2014a. Quantifying mental health signals in twitter. In *Proceedings of the Workshop on Computational Linguistics and Clinical Psychology: From Linguistic Signal to Clinical Reality*, ACL.

Glen Coppersmith, Craig Harman, and Mark Dredze. 2014b. Measuring post traumatic stress disorder in twitter.

Munmun De Choudhury, Scott Counts, and Eric Horvitz. 2013. Social media as a measurement tool of depression in populations. In *Proceedings of the 5th Annual ACM Web Science Conference*, pages 47–56. ACM.

Elizabeth R. DeLong, David M. DeLong, and Daniel L. Clarke-Pearson. 1988. Comparing the Areas under Two or More Correlated Receiver Operating Characteristic Curves: A Nonparametric Approach. *Biometrics*, 44(3):837–845.

Ronald C Kessler, Patricia Berglund, Olga Demler, Robert Jin, Doreen Koretz, Kathleen R Merikangas, A John Rush, Ellen E Walters, and Philip S Wang. 2003. The epidemiology of major depressive disorder: results from the National Comorbidity Survey Replication (NCS-R). *Journal of the American Medical Association*, 289(23):3095–3105.

Ronald C Kessler, Patricia Berglund, Olga Demler, Robert Jin, Kathleen R Merikangas, and Ellen E Walters. 2005a. Lifetime prevalence and age-of-onset distributions of dsm-iv disorders in the national comorbidity survey replication. *Archives of General Psychiatry*, 62(6):593–602.

Ronald C Kessler, Wai Tat Chiu, Olga Demler, and Ellen E Walters. 2005b. Prevalence, severity, and comorbidity of 12-month dsm-iv disorders in the national comorbidity survey replication. *Archives of General Psychiatry*, 62(6):617–627.

Vasileios Lampos, Nikolaos Aletras, Daniel Preoţiuc-Pietro, and Trevor Cohn. 2014. Predicting and characterising user impact on Twitter. In *Proceedings of the 14th Conference of the European Chapter of the Association for Computational Linguistics*, EACL, pages 405–413.

Colin D Mathers and Dejan Loncar. 2006. Projections of global mortality and burden of disease from 2002 to 2030. *PLoS medicine*, 3(11):e442.

Robert R McCrae and Oliver P John. 1992. An introduction to the five-factor model and its applications. *Journal of Personality*, 60:175–215.

Dong Nguyen, Noah A. Smith, and Carolyn P. Rosé. 2011. Author Age Prediction from Text Using Linear Regression. In *Proceedings of the 5th ACL-HLT Workshop on Language Technology for Cultural Heritage, Social Sciences, and Humanities*, ACL.

Bo Pang and Lillian Lee. 2008. Opinion Mining and Sentiment Analysis. *Foundations and Trends Information Retrieval*, 2(1-2):1–135, January.

Gregory Park, H Andrew Schwartz, Johannes C Eichstaedt, Margaret L Kern, Michal Kosinski, David J Stillwell, Lyle H Ungar, and Martin EP Seligman. 2014. Automatic personality assessment Through Social Media language. *Journal of Personality and Social Psychology*.

Fabian Pedregosa, Gael Varoquaux, Alexandre Gramfort, Vincent Michel, Bertrand Thirion, Olivier Grisel, Mathieu Blondel, Peter Prettenhofer, Ron Weiss, Vincent Dubourg, Jake Vanderplas, Alexandre Passos, David Cournapeau, Matthieu Brucher, Matthieu Perrot, and Edouard Duchesnay. 2011. Scikit-learn: Machine Learning in Python. *Journal of Machine Learning Research*, 12:2825–2830.

James W. Pennebaker, Martha E. Francis, and Roger J. Booth. 2001. *Linguistic Inquiry and Word Count*. Lawerence Erlbaum Associates.

James W Pennebaker. 2011. The secret life of pronouns. *New Scientist*, 211(2828):42–45.

Jonathan Posner, James A Russell, and Bradley S Peterson. 2005. The circumplex model of affect: An integrative approach to affective neuroscience, cognitive development, and psychopathology. *Development and Psychopathology*, 17(03):715–734.

Daniel Preoţiuc-Pietro, Maarten Sap, H Andrew Schwartz, and Lyle Ungar. 2015. Mental Illness Detection at the World Well-Being Project for the CLPsych 2015

Shared Task. In *Proceedings of the Workshop on Computational Linguistics and Clinical Psychology: From Linguistic Signal to Clinical Reality*, NAACL.

Martin Prince, Vikram Patel, Shekhar Saxena, Mario Maj, Joanna Maselko, Michael R Phillips, and Atif Rahman. 2007. No health without mental health. *The Lancet*, 370(9590):859–877.

Stephanie Rude, Eva-Maria Gortner, and James Pennebaker. 2004. Language use of depressed and depression-vulnerable college students. *Cognition & Emotion*, 18(8):1121–1133.

Maarten Sap, Gregory Park, Johannes Eichstaedt, Margaret Kern, Lyle Ungar, and H Andrew Schwartz. 2014. Developing Age and Gender Predictive Lexica over Social Media. In *Proceedings of the 2014 Conference on Empirical Methods in Natural Language Processing*, EMNLP, pages 1146–1151.

H Andrew Schwartz, Johannes C Eichstaedt, Margaret L Kern, Lukasz Dziurzynski, Stephanie M Ramones, Megha Agrawal, Achal Shah, Michal Kosinski, David Stillwell, Martin EP Seligman, and Lyle H Ungar. 2013. Personality, Gender, and Age in the Language of Social Media: The Open-Vocabulary Approach. *PLOS ONE.*

H Andrew Schwartz, Greg Park, Maarten Sap, Evan Weingarten, Johannes Eichstaedt, Margaret Kern, Jonah Berger, Martin Seligman, and Lyle Ungar. 2015. Extracting Human Temporal Orientation in Facebook Language. In *Proceedings of the The 2015 Conference of the North American Chapter of the Association for Computational Linguistics - Human Language Technologies*, NAACL.

Luke D Smillie, Andrew J Cooper, Joshua Wilt, and William Revelle. 2012. Do extraverts get more bang for the buck? Refining the affective-reactivity hypothesis of extraversion. *Journal of Personality and Social Psychology*, 103(2):306.

Christopher J Soto, Oliver P John, Samuel D Gosling, and Jeff Potter. 2011. Age differences in personality traits from 10 to 65: Big Five domains and facets in a large cross-sectional sample. *Journal of Personality and Social Psychology*, 100(2):330.

Shannon Wiltsey Stirman and James W Pennebaker. 2001. Word use in the poetry of suicidal and nonsuicidal poets. *Psychosomatic Medicine*, 63(4):517–522.

TB Üstün, Joseph L Ayuso-Mateos, Somnath Chatterji, Colin Mathers, and Christopher JL Murray. 2004. Global burden of depressive disorders in the year 2000. *The British Journal of Psychiatry*, 184(5):386–392.

Svitlana Volkova, Glen Coppersmith, and Benjamin Van Durme. 2014. Inferring User Political Preferences from Streaming Communications. In *Proceedings of the 52nd Annual Meeting of the Association for Computational Linguistics*, ACL.

Hui Zou and Trevor Hastie. 2005. Regularization and variable selection via the Elastic Net. *Journal of the Royal Statistical Society, Series B*, 67:301–320.

CLPsych 2015 Shared Task: Depression and PTSD on Twitter

Glen Coppersmith
Qntfy
glen@qntfy.io

Mark Dredze
Johns Hopkins University
mdredze@cs.jhu.edu

Craig Harman
Johns Hopkins University
charman@jhu.edu

Kristy Hollingshead
IHMC
kseitz@ihmc.us

Margaret Mitchell
Microsoft Research
memitc@microsoft.com

Abstract

This paper presents a summary of the Computational Linguistics and Clinical Psychology (CLPsych) 2015 shared and unshared tasks. These tasks aimed to provide apples-to-apples comparisons of various approaches to modeling language relevant to mental health from social media. The data used for these tasks is from Twitter users who state a diagnosis of depression or post traumatic stress disorder (PTSD) and demographically-matched community controls. The unshared task was a hackathon held at Johns Hopkins University in November 2014 to explore the data, and the shared task was conducted remotely, with each participating team submitted scores for a held-back test set of users. The shared task consisted of three binary classification experiments: (1) depression versus control, (2) PTSD versus control, and (3) depression versus PTSD. Classifiers were compared primarily via their average precision, though a number of other metrics are used along with this to allow a more nuanced interpretation of the performance measures.

1 Introduction

Language is a major component of mental health assessment and treatment, and thus a useful lens for mental health analysis. The psychology literature has a long history of studying the impact of various mental health conditions on a person's language use. More recently, the computational linguistics community has sought to develop technologies to address clinical psychology challenges. Some of this work has appeared at the Computational Linguistics and Clinical Psychology workshops (Resnik et al., 2014; Mitchell et al., 2015).

The 2015 workshop hosted a shared and unshared task. These tasks focused on fundamental computational linguistics technologies that hold promise to improve mental health-related applications; in particular, detecting signals relevant to mental health in language data and associated metadata. Specifically, technologies that can demonstrably separate community controls from those with mental-health conditions are extracting signals relevant to mental health. Examining the signals those techniques extract and depend on for classification can yield insights into how aspects of mental health are manifested in language usage. To that end, the shared and unshared tasks examined Twitter users who publicly stated a diagnosis of depression or PTSD (and age- and gender-matched controls).

Shared tasks are tools for fostering research communities and organizing research efforts around shared goals. They provide a forum to explore new ideas and evaluate the best-of-breed, emerging, and wild technologies. The 2015 CLPsych Shared Task consisted of three user-level binary classification tasks: PTSD vs. control, depression vs. control, and PTSD vs. depression. The first two have been addressed in a number of settings (Coppersmith et al., 2015; Coppersmith et al., 2014b; Coppersmith et al., 2014a; Resnik et al., 2013; De Choudhury et al., 2013; Rosenquist et al., 2010; Ramirez-Esparza et al., 2008), while the third task is novel. Organizing this shared task brought together many teams to consider the same problem, which had the benefit of establishing a solid foundational understanding, common standards, and a shared deep understanding of both task and data.

Proceedings of the 2nd Workshop on Computational Linguistics and Clinical Psychology: From Linguistic Signal to Clinical Reality, pages 31–39, Denver, Colorado, June 5, 2015.

The unshared task (affectionately the "hackathon") was a weekend-long event in November 2014 hosted by Johns Hopkins University. The hackathon provided data similar to the shared task data and encouraged participants to explore new ideas. In addition to starting new research projects, some of which were subsequently published in the CLPsych workshop, the event laid the foundation for the shared task by refining task definitions and data setup.

This paper summarizes both the shared and unshared tasks at the 2015 Computational Linguistics and Clinical Psychology workshop. We outline the data used for these tasks, and summarize the methods and common themes of the shared task participants. We also present results for system combination using the shared task submissions.

2 Shared Task Data

Data for the shared task are comprised of public tweets collected according to the procedures of Coppersmith et al. (2014a). We briefly describe the procedure here, and refer interested readers to Coppersmith et al. (2014a). for details.

Users of social media may publicly discuss their health for a variety of reasons, such as to seek treatment or health advice. More specifically to mental health, users may choose a public forum to fight the societal stigma associated with mental illness, or to explain certain behaviors to friends. Many users tweet statements of diagnosis, such as "I was just diagnosed with *X* and ...", where *X* is a mental health condition. While this can include a large variety of mental health conditions (Coppersmith et al., 2015), the shared task considered two conditions: depression or PTSD. We chose these conditions since they are among the most common found in Twitter and have relatively high prevalence compared to other conditions. A human annotator evaluates each such statement of diagnosis to remove jokes, quotes, or any other disingenuous statements. For each user, up to their most recent 3000 public tweets were included in the dataset. Importantly, we removed the tweet in which the genuine statement of diagnosis was found, to prevent any artifact or bias created from our data sampling technique. However, some of these users do mention their condition in other tweets, and some approaches may be influenced by this phenomenon. To ensure that each included user has a sufficient amount of data, we ensured that each user has at least 25 tweets and that the majority of them are English (75% according to the Compact Language Detector[1]).

2.1 Age- and Gender-Matched Controls

A goal of the shared task is to differentiate users with a mental health diagnosis from those who do not. To that end, the shared task data included a set of randomly selected Twitter users.

Age and gender play a significant role in many mental health conditions, making certain segments of the population more or less likely to be affected or diagnosed with them. When possible, demographic variables such as age and gender are controlled for when doing clinical psychology or mental health research. Few studies looking at social media and clinical psychology have done analysis with explicit matched samples, though some have done this implicitly by examining a segment of the population, (e.g., college students (Rude et al., 2004)). Some work in social media analysis has considered the effect of matched samples (Dos Reis and Culotta, 2015).

To create age- and gender-matched community controls, we estimated the age and gender of each user in our sample through analysis of their language. We used the demographic classification tool from the World Well-Being Project (Sap et al., 2014)[2]. For each depression and PTSD user we estimated their gender, forcing the classifier to make a binary decision as to whether the user was 'Female' or 'Male', and used the age estimate as-is (an ostensibly continuous variable). We did the same for a pool of control users who tweeted during a two week time period in early 2013 and met the criteria set out above (at least 25 Tweets and their tweets were labeled as at least 75% English). To obtain our final data set, for each user in the depression or PTSD class, we sampled (without replacement) a paired community control user of the same estimated gender with the closest estimate age.

We expect (and have some anecdotal evidence)

[1]`https://code.google.com/p/cld2/`
[2]`http://wwbp.org/`

that some of the community controls suffer from depression or PTSD, and made no attempt to remove them from our dataset. If we assume that the rate of contamination in the control users is commensurate with the expected rate in the population, that would mean that this contamination makes up a small minority of the data (though a nontrivial portion of the data, especially in the case of depression).

2.2 Anonymization

Per research protocols approved by the Johns Hopkins University Institutional Review Board, the data was anonymized to protect the identity of all users in the dataset. We used a whitelist approach to allow only certain kinds of information to be maintained, as they posed minimal risk of inadvertently exposing the identity of the user. We kept unedited the timestamp and the language identification of the text. For metadata about the user, we kept the number of friends, followers, and favorites the user has, the time zone the user has set in their profile, and the time their account was created. Screen names and URLs were anonymized (via salted hash), so they were replaced with a seemingly-random set of characters. This procedure was applied to the text content and all the metadata fields (to include embedded tweets such as retweets and replies). This was done systematically so the same set of random characters was used each time a given screen name or URL was used. This effectively enabled statistics such as term frequency or inverse document frequency to be computed without revealing the identity of the user or URL (which sometimes provided a link to an identifiable account name, within or outside of Twitter). Some of Twitter's metadata uses character offsets into the text to note positions, so our anonymized hashes were truncated to be the same number of characters as the original text (e.g., `@username` became `@lkms23sO`). For URLs, we left the domain name, but masked everything beyond that: (e.g., `http://clpsych.org/shared_task/` became `http://clpsych.org/sijx0832aKxP`). Any other metadata that did not match the whitelisted entries or the fields subject to anonymization was removed altogether – this includes, for example, any geolocation information and any information about what devices the user tweets from.

Shared task participants each signed a privacy agreement and instituted security and protective measures on their copy of the data. Participants were responsible for obtaining ethics board approval for their work in order to obtain the shared task data. Data was distributed in compliance with the Twitter terms of service.

3 Shared Task Guidelines

The shared task focused on three binary classification tasks.

1. Identify depression users versus control users.
2. Identify PTSD users versus control users.
3. Identify depression users versus PTSD users.

Twitter users were divided into a train and test partition that was used consistently across the three tasks. The train partition consisted of 327 depression users, 246 PTSD users, and for each an age- and gender-matched control user, for a total of 1,146 users. The test data contained 150 depression users, 150 PTSD users, and an age- and gender-matched control for each, for a total of 600 users. Shared task participants were provided with user data and associated labels (depression, PTSD, or control) for the users contained in the train partition. Participants were given user data without labels for the test partition.

Participants were asked to produce systems using only the training data that could provide labels for each of the three tasks for the test data. Participants used their systems to assign a numeric real-valued score for each test user for each of the three tasks. Each participating team submitted three ranked lists of the 600 test users, one list for each task. Given that machine-learning models often have a number of parameters that alter their behavior, sometimes in unexpected ways, participants were encouraged to submit multiple parameter settings of their approaches, as separate ranked lists, and the best-performing of these for each task would be taken as the "official" figure of merit.

Evaluation was conducted by the shared task organizers using the (undistributed) labels for the test users. During evaluation, irrelevant users were removed; i.e., for PTSD versus control, only 300 users were relevant for this condition: the 150 PTSD users and their demographically matched controls. The depression users and their demographically matched controls were removed from the ranked list prior to evaluation.

Each submission was evaluated using several metrics. Our primary metric was average precision, which balances precision with false alarms, though this only tells a single story about the methods examined. We also evaluated precision at various false alarm rates (5%, 10%, and 20%) to provide a different view of performance. The reader will note that the highest-performing technique varied according to the evaluation measure chosen – a cautionary tale about the importance of matching evaluation measure to the envisioned task.

3.1 Data Balance

We decided to distribute data that reflected a balanced distribution between the classes, rather than a balance that accurately reflects the user population, i.e., one that has a larger number of controls. This decision was motivated by the need for creating a dataset maximally relevant to the task, as well as limitations on data distribution from Twitter's terms of service. A balanced dataset made some aspects of the shared task easier, such as classifier creation and interpretation. However, it also means that results need to be examined with this caveat in mind. In particular, the number of false alarms expected in the general population is much larger than in our test sample (7-15 times as frequent). In effect, this means that when examining these numbers, one must remember that each false alarm could count for 7-15 false alarms in a more realistic setting. Unfortunately, when this fact is combined with the contamination of the training data by users diagnosed (but not publicly stating a diagnosis of) depression or PTSD, it quickly becomes difficult or impossible to reliably estimate the false alarm rates in practice. A more controlled study is required to estimate these numbers more accurately. That said, the relative rankings of techniques and approaches is not subject to this particular bias: each system would be affected by the false alarm rates equally, so the relative ranking of approaches (by any of the metrics investigated) does provide a fair comparison of the techniques.

4 Shared Task Submissions

We briefly describe the approaches taken by each of the participants, but encourage the reader to examine participant papers for a more thorough treatment of the approaches.

4.1 University of Maryland

UMD examined a range of supervised topic models, computed on subsets of the documents for each user. Particularly, they used a variety of supervised topic-modeling approaches to find groups of words that had maximal power to differentiate between the users for each classification task. Moreover, rather than computing topics over two (typical) extreme cases – treating each tweet as an individual document or treating each users's tweets collectively as a single document (concatenating all tweets together) – they opted for a sensible middle ground of concatenating all tweets from a given week together as a single document (Resnik et al., 2015).

4.2 University of Pennsylvania, World Well-Being Project

The WWBP examined a wide variety of methods for inferring topics automatically, combined with binary unigram vectors (i.e., "did this user ever use this word?"), and scored using straightforward regression methods. Each of these topic-modeling techniques provided a different interpretation on modeling what groups of words belonged together, and ultimately may provide some useful insight as to which approaches are best at capturing mental health related signals (Preotiuc-Pietro et al., 2015).

4.3 University of Minnesota, Duluth

The Duluth submission took a well-reasoned rule-based approach to these tasks, and as such provides a point to examine how powerful simple, raw language features are in this context. Importantly, the Duluth systems allow one to decouple the power of an open vocabulary approach, quite independent of any complex machine learning or complex weighting schemes applied to the open vocabulary (Pedersen, 2015).

4.4 MIQ – Microsoft, IHMC, Qntfy

We include a small system developed by the organizers for this shared task to examine the effect of providing qualitatively different information from the other system submissions. In this system, which we will refer to as the MIQ[3] (pronounced 'Mike') submission, we use character language models (CLMs) to assign scores to individual tweets. These scores indicate whether the user may be suffering from PTSD, depression, or neither.

The general approach is to examine how likely a sequence of characters is to be generated by a given type of user (PTSD, depression, or control). This provides a score even for very short text (e.g., a tweet) and captures local information about creative spellings, abbreviations, lack of spaces, and other textual phenomena resulting from the 140-character limit of tweets (McNamee and Mayfield, 2004). At test time, we search for sequences of tweets that look "most like" the condition being tested (PTSD or depression) by comparing the condition and control probabilities estimated from the training data for all the n-grams in those tweets.

In more detail, we build a CLM for each condition using the training data. For each user at test time, we score each tweet based on the character n-grams in the tweet C with the CLMs for conditions A and B as $\frac{\sum_C \log p(c_A) - \log p(c_b)}{|C|}$, where $p(c_A)$ is the probability of the given n-gram c according to the CLM model for condition A, and $p(c_B)$ is the probability according to the CLM for condition B. We then compute a set of aggregate scores from a sliding window of 10 tweets at a time, where the aggregate score is either the mean, median, or the proportion of tweets with the highest probability from the CLM for condition A ('proppos'). To compute a single score for a single user, we take the median of the aggregate scores. This follows previous work on predicting depression and PTSD in social media (Coppersmith et al., 2014a; Coppersmith et al., 2014b). We also experimented with excluding or including tweets that heuristically may not have been authored by the Twitter account holder – specifically, this exclusion removes all tweets with URLs (as they are frequently prepopulated by the website hosting the link) and retweets (as they were authored by another Twitter user). We created 12 system submissions using: n-grams of length 5 and 6 (two approaches) crossed with the mean, median, and proppos aggregation approaches (three approaches), and with or without exclusion applied (two approaches).

[3]M-I-Q for the three authors' three institutions. Interestingly and coincidentally, 'MIQ' is also Albanian for 'Friends.'

The top systems for Depression versus Control used 5-grams, proppos and 5-grams, mean. The top system for PTSD versus Control used 5-grams, median, no exclusion. And the top systems for Depression versus PTSD used 6-grams, mean and 6-grams, proppos.

5 Results

We examine only the best-performing of each of the individual system submissions for each binary classification task, but again encourage the reader to examine the individual system papers for a more detailed analysis and interpretation for what each of the teams did for their submission.

5.1 Individual Systems

The results from the four submitted systems are summarized in Figure 1. The top two rows show the performance of all the parameter settings for all the submitted systems, while the bottom two rows show receiver operating characteristic (ROC) curves for only the best-performing parameter settings from each team. Each column in the figure denotes a different task: 'Depression versus Control' on the left, 'PTSD versus Control' in the middle and 'Depression versus PTSD' on the right. Chance performance is noted by a black dotted line in all plots, and all systems performed better than chance (with the exception of a system with deliberately random performance submitted by Duluth).

In the panels in the top two rows of Figure 1, each dot indicates a submitted parameter setting, arranged by team. From left to right, the dots represent Duluth (goldenrod), MIQ (black), UMD (red), and WWBP (blue). The best-performing system for each team is denoted by a solid horizontal line, for ease of comparison. The top row shows performance by the "official metric" of average precision, while the second row shows performance on precision at 10% false alarms.

The bottom two rows of Figure 1 show the results of each team's top-performing system (according to average-precision) across the full space of false alarms. The third row shows precision over the

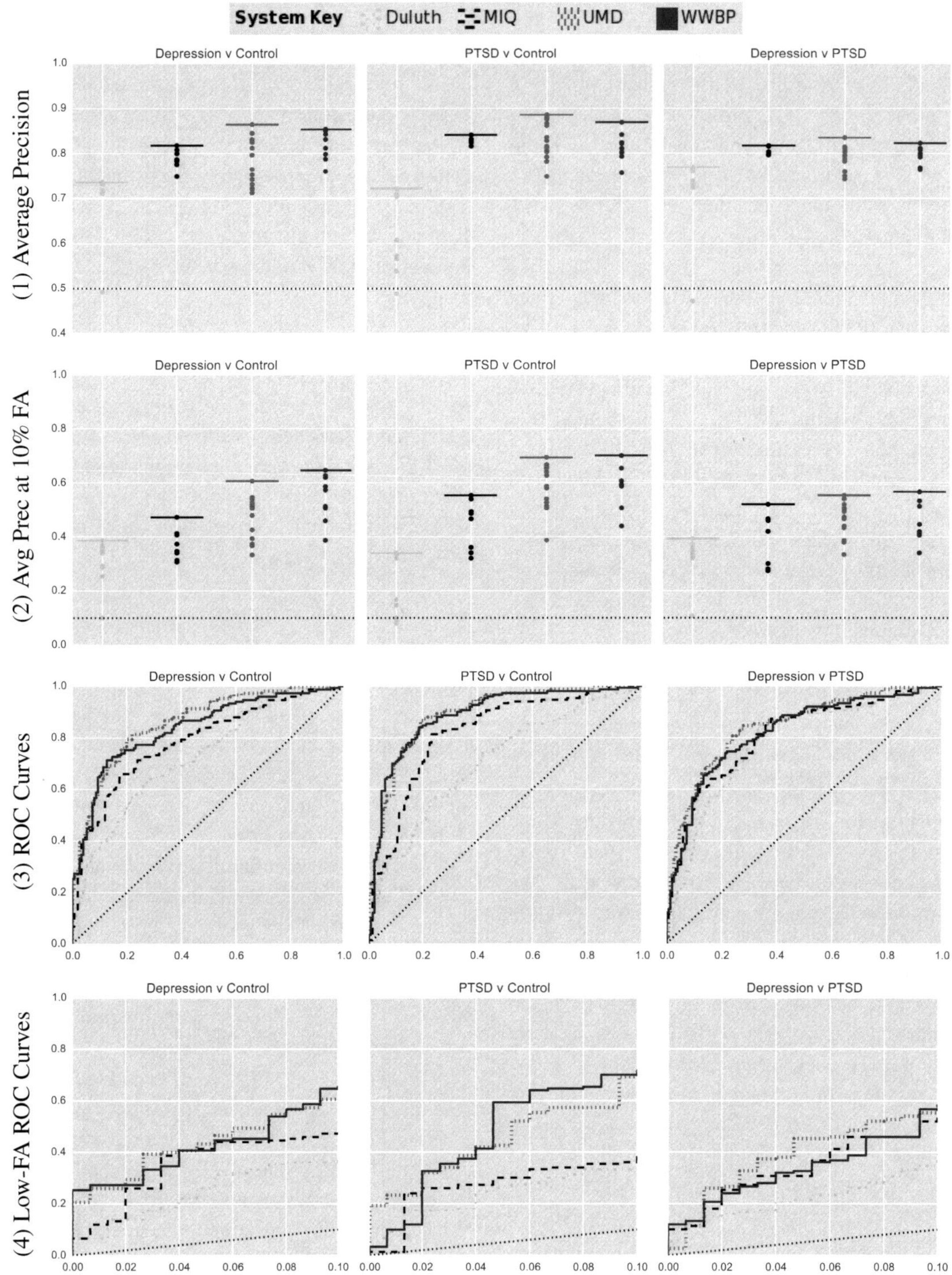

Figure 1: From top to bottom: (1) average precision and (2) precision at 10% false alarms (3) the ROC curve for each institution with the highest average precision, (4) same ROC curves, focused on the low false alarm range. For (1) and (2) the submissions are collected and colored by group. Each submitted parameter setting is represented with a single dot, with the top-scoring submission for each group in each experiment denoted with a horizontal line. The best ROC curve (according to average precision) for each institution, colored by group are shown in (3) and (4). (3) covers the range of all false alarms, while (4) is the same ROCs focused on the low false alarm range. Chance in all plots is denoted by the dotted line.

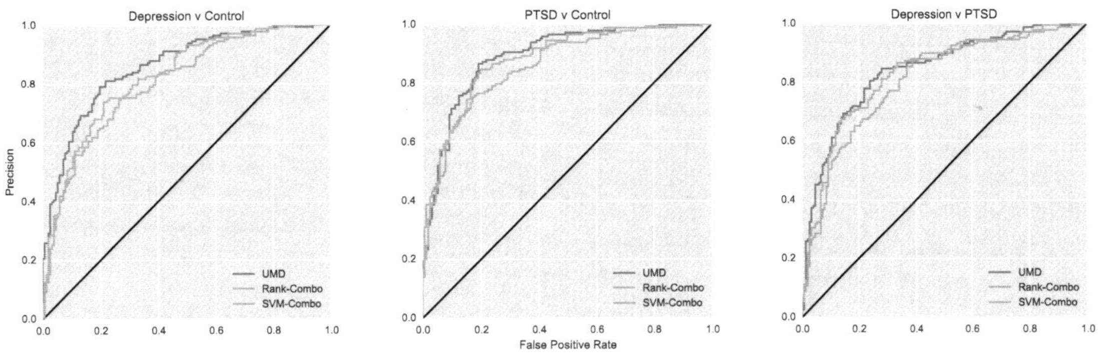

Figure 2: ROC curves for system combination results.

whole space of false alarms, while the bottom row "zooms in" to show the precision at low (0-10%) false alarm rates. These bottom two rows are shown as ROC curves, with the the false alarm rate on the x-axis and the precision on the y-axis. Performance at areas of low false alarms are particularly important to the envisioned applications, since the number of control users vastly outnumber the users with each mental health condition.

5.2 System Combination

As each of the submitted systems used what appeared to be very complementary feature sets, we performed several system combination experiments. However, as can be seen in Figure 2, system combination failed to outperform the best-performing system submitted for the shared task (UMD).

As features for system combination, we used either system ranks or scores. For each system combination experiment, we included all scores from each of the submitted systems, for a total of 47 systems (9 from Duluth, 12 from MIQ, 16 from UMD, and 10 from WWBP), without regard for how well that system performed on the classification task; future work may examine subsetting these scores for improved combination results. Since the range of the scores output by each system varied significantly, we applied a softmax normalization sigmoid function to bring all scores for each system to range from zero to one.

We explored a simple 'voting' scheme as well as a machine learning method, using Support Vector Machines (SVM). For the SVM, shown in Figure 2 as the lower blue 'SVM-Combo' curve, we experimented with using raw scores or normalized scores as features, and found the normalized scores performed much better. The SVM model is the result of training ten SVMs on system output using 10-fold cross-validation, then normalizing the SVM output prediction scores and concatenating to obtain the final result. For the voted model, which can be seen in Figure 2 as the middle green 'Rank-Combo' curve, we simply took the rank of each Twitter user according to each system output, and averaged the result. Future work will examine other methods for system combination and analysis.

6 Discussion & Conclusion

This shared task served as an opportunity for a variety of teams to come together and compare techniques and approaches for extracting linguistic signals relevant to mental health from social media data. Perhaps more importantly, though, it established a test set upon which all participating groups are now familiar, which will enable a deeper level of conversation.

Two of the classification tasks examined were previously attempted, and the techniques indicate improvement over previously-published findings. Past results did differ in a number of important factors, most notably in not examining age- and gender-matched controls, so direct comparisons are unfortunately not possible.

From these submitted systems we can take away a few lessons about classes of techniques and their relative power. There are clear benefits to using topic-modeling approaches, as demonstrated by two of the groups (UMD and WWBP) – these provide strong signals relevant to mental health, and some intuitive and interpretable groupings of words without significant manual intervention. Simple linguistic features, even without complicated machine learning techniques, provide some classification power for these tasks (as demonstrated by Duluth and MIQ). Looking forward, there is strong evidence that techniques can provide signals at a finer-grained temporal resolution than previously explored (as demonstrated by UMD and MIQ). This may open up new avenues for applying these approaches to clinical settings.

Finally, the results leave open room for future work; none of these tasks were solved. This suggests both improvements to techniques as well as more work on dataset construction. However, even at this nascent stage, insight from the mental health signals these techniques extract from language is providing new directions for mental health research.

References

Glen Coppersmith, Mark Dredze, and Craig Harman. 2014a. Quantifying mental health signals in Twitter. In *Proceedings of the ACL Workshop on Computational Linguistics and Clinical Psychology*.

Glen Coppersmith, Craig Harman, and Mark Dredze. 2014b. Measuring post traumatic stress disorder in Twitter. In *Proceedings of the 8th International AAAI Conference on Weblogs and Social Media (ICWSM)*.

Glen Coppersmith, Mark Dredze, Craig Harman, and Kristy Hollingshead. 2015. From ADHD to SAD: Analyzing the language of mental health on Twitter through self-reported diagnoses. In *Proceedings of the Workshop on Computational Linguistics and Clinical Psychology: From Linguistic Signal to Clinical Reality*, Denver, Colorado, USA, June. North American Chapter of the Association for Computational Linguistics.

Munmun De Choudhury, Michael Gamon, Scott Counts, and Eric Horvitz. 2013. Predicting depression via social media. In *Proceedings of the 7th International AAAI Conference on Weblogs and Social Media (ICWSM)*.

Virgile Landeiro Dos Reis and Aron Culotta. 2015. Using matched samples to estimate the effects of exercise on mental health from Twitter. In *Proceedings of the Twenty-Ninth AAAI Conference on Artificial Intelligence*.

Paul McNamee and James Mayfield. 2004. Character n-gram tokenization for European language text retrieval. *Information Retrieval*, 7(1-2):73–97.

Margaret Mitchell, Glen Coppersmith, and Kristy Hollingshead, editors. 2015. *Proceedings of the Workshop on Computational Linguistics and Clinical Psychology: From Linguistic Signal to Clinical Reality*. North American Association for Computational Linguistics, Denver, Colorado, USA, June.

Ted Pedersen. 2015. Screening Twitter users for depression and PTSD with lexical decision lists. In *Proceedings of the Workshop on Computational Linguistics and Clinical Psychology: From Linguistic Signal to Clinical Reality*, Denver, Colorado, USA, June. North American Chapter of the Association for Computational Linguistics.

Daniel Preotiuc-Pietro, Maarten Sap, H. Andrew Schwartz Schwartz, and Lyle Ungar. 2015. Mental illness detection at the World Well-Being Project for the CLPsych 2015 shared task. In *Proceedings of the Workshop on Computational Linguistics and Clinical Psychology: From Linguistic Signal to Clinical Reality*, Denver, Colorado, USA, June. North American Chapter of the Association for Computational Linguistics.

Nairan Ramirez-Esparza, Cindy K. Chung, Ewa Kacewicz, and James W. Pennebaker. 2008. The psychology of word use in depression forums in English and in Spanish: Testing two text analytic approaches. In *Proceedings of the 2nd International AAAI Conference on Weblogs and Social Media (ICWSM)*.

Philip Resnik, Anderson Garron, and Rebecca Resnik. 2013. Using topic modeling to improve prediction of neuroticism and depression. In *Proceedings of the Conference on Empirical Methods in Natural Language Processing (EMNLP)*, pages 1348–1353.

Philip Resnik, Rebecca Resnik, and Margaret Mitchell, editors. 2014. *Proceedings of the Workshop on Computational Linguistics and Clinical Psychology: From Linguistic Signal to Clinical Reality*. Association for Computational Linguistics, Baltimore, Maryland, USA, June.

Philip Resnik, William Armstrong, Leonardo Claudino, Thang Nguyen, Viet-An Nguyen, and Jordan Boyd-Graber. 2015. The University of Maryland CLPsych 2015 shared task system. In *Proceedings of the Workshop on Computational Linguistics and Clinical Psychology: From Linguistic Signal to Clinical Reality*, Denver, Colorado, USA, June. North American Chapter of the Association for Computational Linguistics.

J. Niels Rosenquist, James H. Fowler, and Nicholas A. Christakis. 2010. Social network determinants of depression. *Molecular psychiatry*, 16(3):273–281.

Stephanie S. Rude, Eva-Maria Gortner, and James W. Pennebaker. 2004. Language use of depressed and depression-vulnerable college students. *Cognition & Emotion*, 18(8):1121–1133.

Maarten Sap, Greg Park, Johannes C. Eichstaedt, Margaret L. Kern, David J. Stillwell, Michal Kosinski, Lyle H. Ungar, and H. Andrew Schwartz. 2014. Developing age and gender predictive lexica over social media. In *Proceedings of the Conference on Empirical Methods in Natural Language Processing (EMNLP)*, pages 1146–1151.

Mental Illness Detection at the World Well-Being Project for the CLPsych 2015 Shared Task

Daniel Preoţiuc-Pietro[1,2] **Maarten Sap**[1] **H. Andrew Schwartz**[1,2] **and Lyle Ungar**[1,2]
[1]Department of Psychology, University of Pennsylvania
[2]Computer & Information Science, University of Pennsylvania
danielpr@sas.upenn.edu

Abstract

This article is a system description and report on the submission of the World Well-Being Project from the University of Pennsylvania in the 'CLPsych 2015' shared task. The goal of the shared task was to automatically determine Twitter users who self-reported having one of two mental illnesses: post traumatic stress disorder (PTSD) and depression. Our system employs user metadata and textual features derived from Twitter posts. To reduce the feature space and avoid data sparsity, we consider several word clustering approaches. We explore the use of linear classifiers based on different feature sets as well as a combination use a linear ensemble. This method is agnostic of illness specific features, such as lists of medicines, thus making it readily applicable in other scenarios. Our approach ranked second in all tasks on average precision and showed best results at .1 false positive rates.

1 Introduction

Mental illnesses are widespread globally (Üstün et al., 2004); for instance, 18.6% of US adults were suffering from a mental illness in 2012 (Abuse and Administration, 2012). Depression and post traumatic stress disorder (PTSD) are some of the most common disorders, reaching up to 6.6% and 3.5% prevalence respectively in a 12 month period in the US (Kessler et al., 2003; Kessler et al., 2005). However, these are often argued to be under-estimates of the true prevalence (Prince et al., 2007). This is in part because those suffering from depression and PTSD do not typically seek help for their symptoms and partially due to imperfect screening methods currently employed. Social media offers us an alternative window into an individual's psyche, allowing us to investigate how changes in posting behaviour may reflect changes in mental state.

The CLPsych 2015 shared task is the first evaluation to address the problem of automatically identifying users with diagnosis of mental illnesses, here PTSD or depression. The competition uses a corpus of users who self-disclosed their mental illness diagnoses on Twitter, a method first introduced in (Coppersmith et al., 2014). The shared task aims to distinguish between: (a) control users and users with depression, (b) control users and users with PTSD and (c) users with depression and users with PTSD.

For our participation in this shared task, we treat the task as binary classification using standard regularised linear classifiers (i.e. Logistic Regression and Linear Support Vector Machines). We use a wide range of automatically derived word clusters to obtain different representations of the topics mentioned by users. We assume the information captured by these clusters is complimentary (e.g. semantic vs. syntactic, local context vs. broader context) and combine them using a linear ensemble to reduce classifier variance and improve accuracy. Our classifier returns for each binary task a score for each user. This enables us to create a ranked list of use in our analysis.

The results are measured on average precision, as we are interested in evaluating the entire ranking. On the official testing data, our best models achieve over .80 average precision (AP) for all three binary tasks, with the best model reaching .869 AP on predicting PTSD from controls in the official evaluation. A complementary qualitative analysis is presented in (Preoţiuc-Pietro et al., 2015).

Proceedings of the 2nd Workshop on Computational Linguistics and Clinical Psychology: From Linguistic Signal to Clinical Reality, pages 40–45, Denver, Colorado, June 5, 2015.

2 System Overview

In our approach, we aggregate the word counts in all of a user's posts, irrespective of their timestamp and the word order within (a bag-of-words approach). Each user in the dataset is thus represented by a distribution over words. In addition, we used automatically derived groups of related words (or 'topics') to obtain a lower dimensional distribution for each user. These topics, built using automatic clustering methods from separate large datasets, capture a set of semantic and syntactic relationships (e.g. words reflecting boredom, pronouns). In addition, we use metadata from the Twitter profile of the user, such as number of followers or number of tweets posted. A detailed list is presented in the next section. We trained three standard machine learning binary classifiers using these user features and known labels for Controls, Depressed and PTSD users.

Data

The data used for training consisted of 1,145 Twitter users, labeled as Controls, Depressed and PTSD. This dataset was provided by the shared task organisers (Coppersmith et al., 2015). From training and testing we removed 2 users as they had posted less than 500 words and thus their feature vectors were very sparse and uninformative. Dataset statistics are presented in Table 1. Age and gender were provided by the task organisers and were automatically derived by the method from (Sap et al., 2014).

	Control	**Depressed**	**PTSD**
Number of users	572	327	246
Avg. age	24.4	21.7	27.9
% female	74.3%	69.9%	67.5%
Avg. # followers	1,733	1,448	1,784
Avg. # friends	620	836	1,148
Avg. # times listed	22	17	29
Avg. # favourites	1,195	3,271	5,297
Avg. # statuses	10,772	17,762	16,735
Avg. # unigrams	31,083	32,938	38,337

Table 1: Descriptive statistics for each of the three categories of users.

3 Features and Methods

3.1 Features

We briefly summarise the features used in our prediction task. We divide them into user features and textual features.

Metadata Features (Metadata) The metadata features are derived from the user information available from each tweet that were not anonymised by the organizers. Table 2 introduces the eight features in this category.

m_1	log number of followers
m_2	log number of friends
m_3	follower/friend ratio
m_4	log number of times listed
m_5	no. of favourites the account made
m_6	total number of tweets
m_7	age
m_8	gender

Table 2: Metadata features for a Twitter user.

Unigram Features (Unigram) We use unigrams as features in order to capture a broad range of textual information. First, we tokenised the Twitter posts into unigrams using our tailored version[1] of Chris Potts' emoticon-aware *HappyFunTokenizer*. We use the unigrams mentioned by at least 1% of users in the training set, resulting in a total of 41,687 features.

Brown Clusters (Brown) Using all unigrams may cause different problems in classification. The feature set in this case is an order of magnitude larger than the number of samples ($\sim 40,000 \gg \sim 1000$), which leads to sparse features and may cause overfitting. To alleviate this problem, we use as features different sets of words which are semantically or syntactically related i.e. 'topics'. These are computed on large corpora unrelated to our dataset in order to confer generality to our methods.

The first method is based on Brown clustering (Brown et al., 1992). Brown clustering is a HMM-based algorithm that partitions words hierarchically into clusters, building on the intuition that

[1] Available for download at `http://www.wwbp.org/data.html`

the probability of a word's occurrence is based on the cluster of word directly preceding it. We use the clusters introduced by Owoputi et al. (2013) which use the method of Liang (2005) to cluster 216,856 tokens into a base set of 1000 clusters using a dataset of 56 million English tweets evenly distributed from 9/10/2008 to 8/14/2012.

NPMI Word Clusters (NPMI) Another set of clusters is determined using the method presented in (Lampos et al., 2014). This uses a word to word similarity matrix computed over a large reference corpus of 400 million tweets collected from 1/2/2011 to 2/28/2011. The word similarity is measured using Normalised Pointwise Mutual Information (NPMI). This information-theoretic measure indicates which words co-occur in the same context (Bouma, 2009) where the context is the entire tweet. To obtain hard clusters of words we use spectral clustering (Shi and Malik, 2000; Ng et al., 2002). This methods was shown to deal well with high-dimensional and non-convex data (von Luxburg, 2007). In our experiments we used 1000 clusters from 54,592 tokens.

Word2Vec Word Clusters (W2V) Neural methods have recently been gaining popularity in order to obtain low-rank word embeddings and obtained state-of-the-art results for a number of semantic tasks (Mikolov et al., 2013b).

These methods, like many recent word embeddings, also allow to capture local context order rather than just 'bag-of-words' relatedness, which leads to also capture syntactic information. We use the skip-gram model with negative sampling (Mikolov et al., 2013a) to learn word embeddings from a corpus of 400 million tweets also used in (Lampos et al., 2014). We use a hidden layer size of 50 with the Gensim implementation.[2] We then apply spectral clustering on these embeddings to obtain hard clusters of words. We create 2000 clusters from 46,245 tokens.

GloVe Word Clusters (GloVe) A different type of word embeddings was introduced by (Pennington et al., 2014). This is uses matrix factorisation on a word-context matrix which preserves word order and claims to significantly outperform previous neural embeddings on semantic tasks. We use the pre-trained Twitter model from the author's website[3] built from 2 billion tweets. In addition to the largest layer size (200), we also use spectral clustering as explained above to create 2000 word clusters from 38,773 tokens.

LDA Word Clusters (LDA) A different type of clustering is obtained by using topic models, most popular of which is Latent Dirichlet Allocation (Blei et al., 2003). LDA models each post as being a mixture of different topics, each topic representing a distribution over words, thus obtaining soft clusters of words. We use the 2000 clusters introduced in (Schwartz et al., 2013), which were computed over a large dataset of posts from 70,000 Facebook users. These soft clusters should have a slight disadvantage in that they were obtained from Facebook data, rather than Twitter as all previously mentioned clusters and our dataset.

LDA ER Word Clusters (ER) We also use a different set of 500 topics. These were obtained by performing LDA on a dataset of $\sim$ 700 Facebook user's posts who reported to the emergency room and opted in a research study.

3.2 Methods

We build binary classifiers to separate users being controls, depressed or having PTSD. As classifiers, we use linear methods as non-linear methods haven't shown improvements over linear methods in our preliminary experiments. We use both logistic regression (**LR**) (Freedman, 2009) with Elastic Net regularisation (Zou and Hastie, 2005) and Support Vector Machines (**LinSVM**) with a linear kernel (Vapnik, 1998). We used the implementations of both classifiers from ScikitLearn (Pedregosa et al., 2011) which use Stochastic Gradient Descent for inference.

A vital role for good performance in both classifiers is parameter tuning. We measure mean average precision on our training set using 10 cross-fold validation and 10 random restarts and optimise parameters using grid search for each feature set individually.

Different feature sets are expected to contribute

[2] https://radimrehurek.com/gensim/

[3] http://nlp.stanford.edu/projects/glove/

Feature type	Features	CvD-LR	CvD-LinSVM	CvP-LR	CvP-LinSVM	DvP-LR	DvP-LinSVM
Metadata	8	.576	.567	.588	.585	.816	.817
Unigram	41687	.838	**.843**	**.850**	.845	.831	.820
Brown	1000	.790	.784	.770	.770	.830	.834
NPMI	1000	.789	.770	.785	.774	.825	.822
W2V	2000	.808	.791	.786	.775	**.850**	.845
GloVe	2000	.788	.784	.780	.761	.844	.839
LDA	2000	.820	.812	.807	.794	.841	.835
LDA ER	500	.785	.787	.740	.736	.850	.834
Ensemble-Avg.	8	.854	.862	.850	**.860**	.856	.839
Ensemble-Lin.	8	.856	**.867**	.856	.840	.862	**.866**

Table 3: Average precision for each individual set of features and both classifiers. The three binary classification tasks are Controls vs. Depressed (CvD), Controls vs. PTSD (CvP) and Depressed vs. PTSD (DvP).

to the general classification results with different insights. A combination of features is thus preferable in order to boost performance and also reduce variance or increase robustness.

We create an ensemble of classifiers, each of which uses the different textual feature sets described in the previous section. The predicted scores for each model are used to train a logistic regression classifier in order to identify the weights assigned to each classifier before their output is combined (**Ensemble-Lin.**). We also experimented with a non-weighted combination of classifiers (**Ensemble-Avg.**).

4 Results

The results of our methods on cross-validation are presented in Table 3. Results using different feature sets show similar values, with all unigram features showing overall best results. However, we expect that each set of features will contribute with distinctive and complimentary information.

The ensemble methods show minor, but consistent improvement over the scores of each individual user set. The linear combination of different classifiers shows better performance compared to the average by appropriately down-weighting less informative sets of features.

Figure 1 shows the three ROC (Receiver Operator Characteristic) curves for our binary classification tasks. These curves are specifically useful for medical practitioners as the classification threshold can be adjusted to obtain an application specific level of false positives.

For example, we highlight that at a false positive rate of 0.1, we reach a true positive rate of 0.8 for separating Controls from users with PTSD and of 0.75 for separating Controls from depressed users. Distinguishing PTSD from depressed users is harder at small false positive rates, with only ~ 0.4 true positive rate.

5 Discussion and Conclusions

This paper reported on the participation of the World Well-Being Project in the CLPsych 2015 shared task on identifying users having PTSD or depression.

Our methods were based on combining linear classifiers each using different types of word clusters. The methods we presented were designed to be as task agnostic as possible, aiming not to use medical condition specific keywords or data. We thus expect similar methods to perform well in identifying other illnesses or conditions.

This generalised approach yielded results ranking second in the shared task, scoring above 0.80 on all tasks and reaching up to 0.87 for one of the binary tasks. Further analysis shows that our models perform especially well at small false positive rates (up to 0.8 true positive rate at 0.1 false positive rate) where it ranked first.

Our perspective for future improvements is to use other datasets with similar labels for illnesses in a domain adaptation scenario, as more observations is likely to lead to better prediction quality. Another direction for possible improvement to our methods is to use a 'learning to rank' algorithm in place of classifiers.

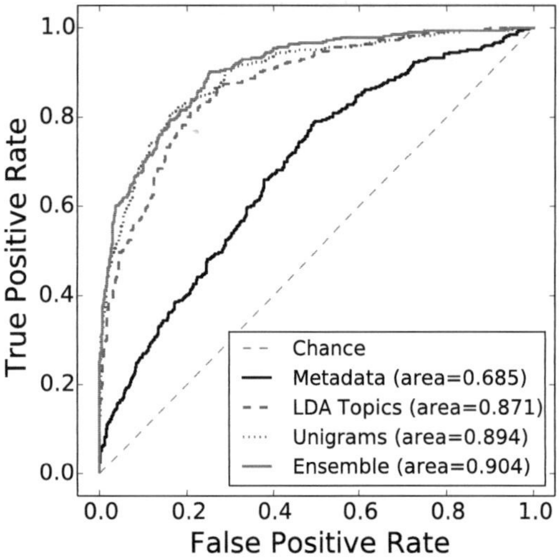

(a) Controls vs. Depression(+).

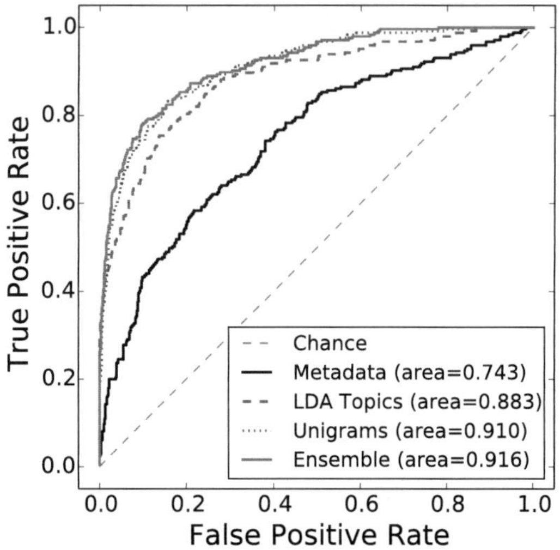

(b) Controls vs. PTSD(+).

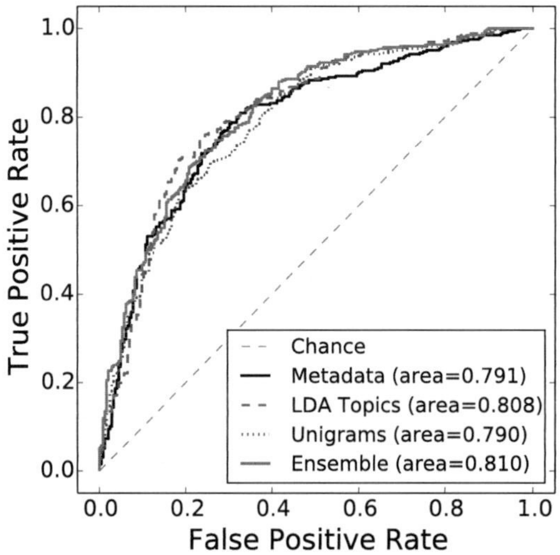

(c) Depression vs. PTSD(+).

Figure 1: ROC curves and area under the curve for a selected set of features using Linear Support Vector Classification. (+) denotes positive class.

References

Substance Abuse and Mental Health Services Administration. 2012. Results from the 2010 National Survey on Drug use and Health: Mental Health Findings. *NSDUH series H-42, HHS publication no.(SMA) 11-4667*.

David M. Blei, Andrew Y. Ng, and Michael I. Jordan. 2003. Latent Dirichlet Allocation. *Journal of Machine Learning Research*, 3:993–1022.

Gerlof Bouma. 2009. Normalized (pointwise) Mutual Information in collocation extraction. In *Biennial GSCL Conference*, pages 31–40.

Peter F. Brown, Peter V. deSouza, Robert L. Mercer, Vincent J. Della Pietra, and Jenifer C. Lai. 1992. Class-based N-gram Models of Natural Language. *Computational Linguistics*, 18(4):467–479.

Glen Coppersmith, Mark Dredze, and Craig Harman. 2014. Quantifying Mental Health Signals in Twitter. In *52nd Annual Meeting of the Association for Computational Linguistics*, ACL.

Glen Coppersmith, Mark Dredze, Craig Harman, Kristy Hollingshead, and Margaret Mitchell. 2015. CLPsych 2015 shared task: Depression and PTSD on Twitter. In *Proceedings of the Workshop on Computational Lin-*

guistics and Clinical Psychology: From Linguistic Signal to Clinical Reality, NAACL.

David Freedman. 2009. *Statistical models: theory and practice*. Cambridge University Press.

Ronald C Kessler, Patricia Berglund, Olga Demler, Robert Jin, Doreen Koretz, Kathleen R Merikangas, A John Rush, Ellen E Walters, and Philip S Wang. 2003. The epidemiology of major depressive disorder: results from the National Comorbidity Survey Replication (NCS-R). *Journal of the American Medical Association*, 289(23):3095–3105.

Ronald C Kessler, Wai Tat Chiu, Olga Demler, and Ellen E Walters. 2005. Prevalence, severity, and comorbidity of 12-month dsm-iv disorders in the national comorbidity survey replication. *Archives of general psychiatry*, 62(6):617–627.

Vasileios Lampos, Nikolaos Aletras, Daniel Preoţiuc-Pietro, and Trevor Cohn. 2014. Predicting and characterising user impact on Twitter. In *Proceedings of the 14th Conference of the European Chapter of the Association for Computational Linguistics*, EACL.

Percy Liang. 2005. Semi-supervised Learning for Natural Language. In *Master's Thesis*, MIT.

Tomas Mikolov, Kai Chen, Greg Corrado, and Jeffrey Dean. 2013a. Efficient estimation of word representations in vector space. In *Proceedings of Workshop at the International Conference on Learning Representations*, ICLR.

Tomas Mikolov, Wen tau Yih, and Geoffrey Zweig. 2013b. Linguistic Regularities in Continuous Space Word Representations. In *Proceedings of the 2010 annual Conference of the North American Chapter of the Association for Computational Linguistics*, NAACL, pages 746–751.

Andrew Y. Ng, Michael I. Jordan, and Yair Weiss. 2002. On Spectral Clustering: Analysis and an algorithm. In *Advances in Neural Information Processing Systems*, NIPS, pages 849–856.

Olutobi Owoputi, Brendan O'Connor, Chris Dyer, Kevin Gimpel, Nathan Schneider, and A. Noah Smith. 2013. Improved Part-of-Speech Tagging for Online Conversational Text with Word Clusters. In *Proceedings of the 2013 Conference of the North American Chapter of the Association for Computational Linguistics: Human Language Technologies*, NAACL.

Fabian Pedregosa, Gael Varoquaux, Alexandre Gramfort, Vincent Michel, Bertrand Thirion, Olivier Grisel, Mathieu Blondel, Peter Prettenhofer, Ron Weiss, Vincent Dubourg, Jake Vanderplas, Alexandre Passos, David Cournapeau, Matthieu Brucher, Matthieu Perrot, and Edouard Duchesnay. 2011. Scikit-learn: Machine Learning in Python. *Journal of Machine Learning Research*, 12:2825–2830.

Jeffrey Pennington, Richard Socher, and Christopher D. Manning. 2014. GloVe: Global Vectors for Word Representation. In *Proceedings of the 2014 Conference on Empirical Methods in Natural Language Processing*, EMNLP.

Daniel Preoţiuc-Pietro, Johannes Eichstaedt, Gregory Park, Maarten Sap, Laura Smith, Victoria Tobolsky, H. Andrew Schwartz, and Lyle Ungar. 2015. The Role of Personality, Age and Gender in Tweeting about Mental Illnesses. In *Proceedings of the Workshop on Computational Linguistics and Clinical Psychology: From Linguistic Signal to Clinical Reality*, NAACL.

Martin Prince, Vikram Patel, Shekhar Saxena, Mario Maj, Joanna Maselko, Michael R Phillips, and Atif Rahman. 2007. No health without mental health. *The Lancet*, 370(9590):859–877.

Maarten Sap, Gregory Park, Johannes Eichstaedt, Margaret Kern, Lyle Ungar, and H Andrew Schwartz. 2014. Developing Age and Gender Predictive Lexica over Social Media. In *Proceedings of the 2014 Conference on Empirical Methods in Natural Language Processing*, EMNLP, pages 1146–1151.

H Andrew Schwartz, Johannes C Eichstaedt, Margaret L Kern, Lukasz Dziurzynski, Stephanie M Ramones, Megha Agrawal, Achal Shah, Michal Kosinski, David Stillwell, Martin EP Seligman, and Lyle H Ungar. 2013. Personality, Gender, and Age in the Language of Social Media: The Open-Vocabulary Approach. *PLoS ONE*.

Jianbo Shi and Jitendra Malik. 2000. Normalized cuts and image segmentation. *Transactions on Pattern Analysis and Machine Intelligence*, 22(8):888–905.

TB Üstün, Joseph L Ayuso-Mateos, Somnath Chatterji, Colin Mathers, and Christopher JL Murray. 2004. Global burden of depressive disorders in the year 2000. *The British journal of psychiatry*, 184(5):386–392.

Vladimir N Vapnik. 1998. *Statistical learning theory*. Wiley, New York.

Ulrike von Luxburg. 2007. A tutorial on Spectral Clustering. *Statistics and computing*, 17(4):395–416.

Hui Zou and Trevor Hastie. 2005. Regularization and variable selection via the Elastic Net. *Journal of the Royal Statistical Society, Series B*, 67:301–320.

Screening Twitter Users for Depression and PTSD with Lexical Decision Lists

Ted Pedersen
Department of Computer Science
University of Minnesota
Duluth, MN, 55812, USA
tpederse@d.umn.edu

Abstract

This paper describes various systems from the University of Minnesota, Duluth that participated in the CLPsych 2015 shared task. These systems learned decision lists based on lexical features found in training data. These systems typically had average precision in the range of .70 – .76, whereas a random baseline attained .47 – .49.

1 Introduction

The Duluth systems that participated in the CLPsych Shared Task (Coppersmith et al., 2015) explore the degree to which a simple Machine Learning method can successfully identify Twitter users who suffer from Depression or Post Traumatic Stress Disorder (PTSD).

Our approach was to build decision lists of Ngrams found in training Tweets that had been authored by users who had disclosed a diagnosis of Depression or PTSD. The resulting lists were applied to the Tweets of other Twitter users who served as a held–out test sample. The test users were then ranked based on the likelihood that they suffered from Depression or PTSD. This ranking depends on the number of Ngrams found in their Tweets that were associated with either condition.

There were eight different systems that learned decision lists plus one random baseline. The resulting lists are referred to as DecisionList_1 – DecisionList_9, where the system that produced the list is identified by the associated integer. Note that system 9 is a random baseline and not a decision list.

2 Data Preparation

The organizers provided training data that consisted of Tweets from 327 Twitter users who self–reported a diagnosis of Depression, and 246 users who reported a PTSD diagnosis. Each of these users had at least 25 Tweets. There were also Control users identified who were of the same gender and similar age, but who did not have a diagnosis of Depression or PTSD. While each control was paired with a specific user with Depression or PTSD, we did not make any effort to identify or use these pairings.

If a Twitter user has been judged to suffer from either Depression or PTSD, then all the Tweets associated with that user belong to the training data for that condition. This is true regardless of the contents of the Tweets. Thus for many users relatively few Tweets pertain to mental illness, and the rest focus on more general topics. All of the Tweets from the Control users are also collected in their own training set as well.

Our systems only used the text portions of the Tweets, no other information such as location, date, number of retweets, etc. was incorporated. The text was converted to lower case, and any non–alphanumeric characters were replaced with spaces. Thus, hashtags became indistinguishable from text, and emoticons were somewhat fragmented (since they include special characters) but still included as features. We did not carry out any spell checking, stemming, or other forms of normalization.

Then, the Tweets associated with each of the conditions was randomly sorted. The first eight million words of Tweets for each condition were included

Proceedings of the 2nd Workshop on Computational Linguistics and Clinical Psychology: From Linguistic Signal to Clinical Reality, pages 46–53,
Denver, Colorado, June 5, 2015.

in the training data for each condition. Any Tweets beyond that were discarded. This cut–off was selected since after pre-processing the smallest portion of the training data (PTSD) included approximately 8,000,000 words. We wanted to have the same amount of training data for each condition so as to simplify the process of feature selection.

3 Feature Identification

The decision lists were made up of Ngrams. Ngrams are defined as sequences of N contiguous words that occur within a single tweet.

Decision lists 3, 6, 7, and 8 used bigram (N == 2) features, while 1, 2, 4, and 5 used all Ngrams in size between 1 and 6. All of the Tweets in the training data for each condition were processed separately by the Ngram Statistics Package (Banerjee and Pedersen, 2003). All Ngrams of the desired size were identified and counted. An Ngram must have occurred at least 50 times more in one condition than the other to be included as a feature. Any Ngram made up entirely of stop words was removed from decision lists 2, 5, 6, and 8. The stoplist comes from the Ngram Statistics Package and consists of 392 common words, as well as single character words.

The task was to rank Twitter users based on how likely they are to suffer from Depression or PTSD. In two cases this ranking is relative to the Control group (DvC and PvC), and in the third case the ranking is between Depression and PTSD (DvP). A separate decision list is constructed for each of these cases as follows. For the condition DvC, the frequencies of the Ngrams from the Depression training data are given positive values, and the Ngrams from the Control data are given negative values. Then, the decision list is constructed by simply adding those values for each Ngram and recording the sum as the weight of the Ngram feature.

For example, if *feel tired* occurred 4000 times in the Depression training data, and 1000 times in the Control data, the final weight of this feature would be 3000. Ngrams with positive values are then indicative of Depression, whereas those with negative values point towards the Control group. An Ngram with a value of 0 would have occurred exactly the same number of times in both the Depression and Control group and would not be indicative of either condition. The same process is followed to create decision lists for PvC and DvP.

system	stoplist?	Ngrams	weights
3	N	2	binary
7	N	2	frequency
1	N	1–6	binary
4	N	1–6	frequency
6	Y	2	binary
8	Y	2	frequency
2	Y	1–6	binary
5	Y	1–6	frequency

Table 1: System Overviews.

Four of the systems limited the Ngrams in the decision lists to bigrams, while four systems used the Ngrams 1–6 as features. In the latter case, the smaller Ngrams that are also included in a longer Ngram are counted both as a part of that longer Ngram, and individually as smaller Ngrams. For example, if the trigram *I am tired* is a feature, then the bigrams *I am* and *am tired* are also features, as are *I*, *am*, *tired*.

4 Running the Decision List

After a decision list is constructed, a held out sample of test users can be evaluated and ranked for the likelihood of Depression and PTSD. The Tweets for an individual user are all processed by the Ngram Statistics Package to identify the Ngrams. Then the Ngrams in a user's Tweets are compared to the decision list and any time a user's Ngram matches the Decision List the frequency associated with that Ngram is added to a running total. Keep in mind that features for one class (e.g., Depression) will add positive values, while features for the other (e.g., Control) will add negative values. This sum is kept as all of an individual user's Tweets are processed, and in the end this sum will have either a positive or negative value that will determine the the class of the user. The raw score is used to rank the different users relative to each other.

There is also a binary weighting variation. In this case when a user's Ngram is encountered in the Decision list, if the frequency is positive a value of 1 is added to the running together, and if it is negative a value of -1 is added. This is done for all of a user's

	DvP		DvC		PvC	
rank	id	prec	id	prec	id	prec
1	2	.769	2	.736	1	.721
2	5	.764	1	.731	2	.720
3	4	.761	3	.718	3	.708
4	1	.760	8	.718	6	.704
5	8	.738	6	.718	7	.607
6	7	.731	7	.713	8	.572
7	6	.730	4	.713	4	.570
8	3	.724	5	.710	5	.539
9	9	.471	9	.492	9	.489

Table 2: System Precision per Condition.

system	DvC	DvP	PvC
1	20,788	23,552	19,973
4	20,788	23,552	19,973
2	18,617	21,145	17,936
5	18,617	21,145	17,936
3	5,704	6,385	6,068
7	5,704	6,385	6,068
6	4,442	4,998	4,747
8	4,442	4,998	4,747

Table 3: Number of Features per Decision List.

Tweets, and then whether this value is positive or negative indicates the class of the user.

Table 1 briefly summarizes the eight decision list systems. These systems vary in three respects :

- Whether the stoplist is used (Y or N),
- the length of the Ngrams used (2 or 1–6), and
- the type of weighting (binary or frequency).

All eight possible combinations of these settings were utilized.

5 Results

Table 2 shows the average precision per system for each of the three conditions.

Table 4 shows the average rank and precision attained by each system across all three conditions. It also lists the characteristics of each decision list.

When taken together, Tables 2 and 4 clearly show that systems 2 and 1 are the most effective across the three conditions. These two systems are identical, except that 2 uses a stoplist and 1 does not. They both use the binary weighting scheme and Ngrams of size 1–6.

Table 3 shows the number of features per decision list. The systems that use the ngram 1–6 features (1, 2, 4, 5) have a much larger number of features than the bigram systems (3, 6, 7, 8). Note however that in Table 2 there is not a strong correlation between a larger number of features and improved precision. While systems 1 and 2 have the highest precision (and the largest number of features) systems 4 and 5 have exactly the same features and yet attain average precision that is quite a bit lower than systems with smaller numbers of features, such as 3 or 6.

Note that the pairs of systems that have the same number of features in the decision list only differ in their weighting scheme (bigram versus frequency) and so the number of features would be expected to be the same. Also note that the number of features per condition for a given system is approximately the same – this was our intention when selecting the same number of words (8,000,000) per condition from the training data.

6 Decision Lists

Below we show the top 100 entries in each decision list created by system 2, which had overall the highest precision of our runs.

System 2 uses Ngrams of size 1–6 with stop words removed and binary weighting of features. The decision lists below show the Ngram feature and the frequency in the training data. Note that Ngrams that begin with u and are followed by numeric values (e.g., u2764, u201d, etc.) are emoticon encodings.

All of the decision lists include a mixture of standard English features and more Web specific features, such as portions of URLs and more notably emoticons. Our systems treated these like any other Ngram, and so a series of emoticons will appear as an Ngram, and URLs are broken into fragments which appears as Ngrams.

6.1 Decision List system 2, DvC

This decision list has 18,617 entries, the first 100 of which are shown below. This decision list attained average precision of 77%.

Features and positive counts in **bold** indicate De-

system	avg rank	ranks DvP, DvC, PvC	avg precision	stoplist?	Ngrams	weights
2	1.3	1, 1, 2	.742	Y	1–6	binary
1	2.3	4, 2, 1	.737	N	1–6	binary
3	4.7	8, 3, 3	.717	N	2	binary
6	5.3	7, 5, 4	.717	Y	2	binary
7	5.7	6, 6, 5	.684	N	2	frequency
4	5.7	3, 7, 7	.681	N	1–6	frequency
8	5.0	5, 4, 6	.676	Y	2	frequency
5	6.0	2, 8, 8	.671	Y	1–6	frequency
9	9.0	9, 9, 9	.484			

Table 4: Average Rank and Precision over all Conditions.

pression, while those in *italics* are negative counts that are associated with the Control.

http -26084; http t co -23935; http t -23906; co -22388; t co -22210; ud83d -20341; **ud83c 15764;** *lol -9429;* **please 8166;** *u2764 u2764 -8127; u2764 u2764 u2764 -8017; u2764 u2764 u2764 u2764 -7947; u2764 u2764 u2764 u2764 u2764 -7852; u2764 -7769; u2764 u2764 u2764 u2764 u2764 u2764 -7767; gt -7078;* **love 6041;** *u201c -5815; u201d -5635;* **follow 5578;** *amp -5420; gt gt -5237;* **ufe0f 5138; re 4875;** *ud83d ude02 -4841; ude02 -4839; photo -4791;* **fucking 4616; love you 4603; im 4542;** *u0627 -4412; rt -4132;* **udf38 4046; ud83c udf38 4046; udc95 4033; ud83d udc95 4033; u043e 3879; you re 3681; u0430 3666; ve 3624; pj3l408vwlgs3 3606; don t 3563; udf41 3543; ud83c udf41 3542; u0435 3530;** *ud83d ude02 ud83d -3529; ude02 ud83d -3528; gt gt gt -3459;* **fuck 3372; please follow 3359;** *check -3357; ud83d ude02 ud83d ude02 -3355; ude02 ud83d ude02 -3354;* **don 3298; i love 3284; u2661 3088; udf38 ud83c 3058; ud83c udf38 ud83c 3058; i don 3020; i don t 2976; i ve 2962; udc95 ud83d 2922; ud83d udc95 ud83d 2922; u0438 2905; feel 2818;** *u0644 -2733; check out -2703;* **udc95 ud83d udc95 2687; ud83d udc95 ud83d udc95 2687;** *photo http t co -2684; photo http -2684; photo http t -2683;* **u043d 2581; follow me 2517; udc95 ud83d udc95 ud83d 2511; ud83d udc95 ud83d udc95 ud83d 2511; udc95 ud83d udc95 ud83d udc95 2464; ud83d udc95 ud83d udc95 ud83d udc95 2464; u0442 2405;** *lt lt -2376;* **i love you 2371;** *today -2365;* **udc95 ud83d udc95 ud83d udc95 ud83d 2322; u0440 2289; b4a7lkokrkpq 2260; udf38 ud83c udf38 2236; ud83c udf38 ud83c udf38 2236; inbox 2218; mean 2172; udf0c 2148; ud83c udf0c 2148;** *ud83d ude02 ud83d ude02 ud83d -2147; ude02 ud83d ude02 ud83d -2146;* **ni 2142; oh 2114;** *ud83d ude02 ud83d ude02 ud83d ude02 -2101; ude02 ud83d ude02 ud83d ude02 -2100;* **u0441 2075; udf41 ud83c 2074; ud83c udf41 ud83c 2074;**

6.2 Decision List system 2, PvC

This decision list has 17,936 entries, the first 100 of which are shown below. This decision list attained average precision of 74%.

Features and positive counts in **bold** indicate PTSD, while those in *italics* are negative counts that are associated with the Control.

ud83d -82824; rt -20230; ude02 -14516; ud83d ude02 -14516; **u2026 12941;** *gt -12727; u2764 -10630; lol -9932; u201c -9736; ude02 ud83d -9112; ud83d ude02 ud83d -9112; u201d -8962; gt gt -8947; u2764 u2764 -8753; u2764 u2764 u2764 -8425; u2764 u2764 u2764 u2764 -8217; u2764 u2764 u2764 u2764 u2764 -8064; u2764 u2764 u2764 u2764 u2764 u2764 -7940; ude02 ud83d ude02 -7932; ud83d ude02 ud83d ude02 -7932;* **co 7291; t co 7140;** *ud83c -6306; gt gt gt -6171; love -5322; ude02 ud83d ude02 ud83d -5165; ud83d ude02 ud83d ude02 ud83d -5165; ude0d -5058; ud83d ude0d -5056; ude02 ud83d ude02 ud83d ude02 -4901; ud83d ude02 ud83d ude02 ud83d ude02 -4901;* **u043e 4877; u0430 4485;** *u0627 -4251;* **u0435 4241; thank 4109; thank you 4079;**

gt gt gt gt -3936; im -3843; ude18 -3617; ud83d ude18 -3617; **please 3533; u0438 3526;** *shit -3337; don -3288;* **health 3277;** *don t -3262; lt -3259; haha -3175; lt lt -3172; ude02 ud83d ude02 ud83d ude02 ud83d -3094;* **u043d 3074; u0442 3065; answer 2998; my answer 2963; http 2937;** *ude29 -2932; ud83d ude29 -2932;* **answer on 2930; tgtz to 2929; tgtz 2929; on tgtz to 2929; on tgtz 2929; my answer on tgtz to 2929; my answer on tgtz 2929; my answer on 2929; answer on tgtz to 2929; answer on tgtz 2929;** *ude2d -2911; ud83d ude2d -2911; wanna -2873; day -2869; miss -2868;* **u0440 2855;** *nigga -2798; gt gt gt gt gt -2673; u0644 -2632; udc4c -2607; ud83d udc4c -2607;* **u0441 2581;** *ude0d ud83d -2574; ud83d ude0d ud83d -2572;* **ptsd 2550; amp 2534; bqtn0bi 2510; help 2459;** *ude12 -2438; ud83d ude12 -2438; bitch -2433; girl -2398; school -2395; ass -2355; lmao -2288;* **u0432 2274;** *hate -2267; ain -2259; ain t -2258; i love -2256; lt lt lt -2242;* **nhttp 2226;**

6.3 Decision List system 2, DvP

This decision list has 21,145 entries, the first 100 of which are shown below. This decision list attained average precision of 72%.

Features and positive counts in **bold** indicate Depression, while those in *italics* are negative counts that are associated with PTSD.

ud83d 62483; *co -29679; t co -29350; http -29021; http t -26110; http t co -24404;* **ud83c 22070; rt 16098;** *u2026 -13855;* **love 11363; ude02 9677; ud83d ude02 9675; im 8385;** *amp -7954;* **follow 6927; don t 6825; don 6586; love you 6330; gt 5649; ude02 ud83d 5584; ud83d ude02 ud83d 5583; i love 5540; ufe0f 5069; pj3l408vwlgs3 4806; please 4633; ude02 ud83d ude02 4578; udc95 4577; ud83d ude02 ud83d ude02 4577; ud83d udc95 4577; ude0d 4564; ud83d ude0d 4564; fuck 4474; re 4247; udf38 4112; ud83c udf38 4112; i don t 3939; u201c 3921; i don 3882; you re 3770; gt gt 3710; shit 3695; udf41 3604; ud83c udf41 3603; follow me 3547; please follow 3506;** *news -3499;* **fucking 3499; hate 3491; u2661 3483; wanna 3410;** *thanks -3370;* **u201d 3327; i love you 3276; school 3262;** *answer -3108;* **udc95 ud83d 3104; ud83d udc95 ud83d 3104; gonna 3103; udf38 ud83c 3068; ud83c udf38 ud83c 3068;** *health -3025;* **ude02 ud83d ude02 ud83d 3019; ud83d ude02 ud83d ude02 ud83d 3018; feel 2987;** *my answer -2977;* **people 2932;** *answer on -2930; tgtz to -2929; tgtz -2929; on tgtz to -2929; on tgtz -2929; my answer on tgtz to -2929; my answer on tgtz -2929; my answer on -2929; answer on tgtz to -2929; answer on tgtz -2929;* **b4a7lkokrkpq 2875; u2764 2861; omg 2852; ude02 ud83d ude02 ud83d ude02 2801; ud83d ude02 ud83d ude02 ud83d ude02 2800; udc95 ud83d udc95 2782; ud83d udc95 ud83d udc95 2782;** *thank -2759; photo -2749;* **gt gt gt 2712;** *great -2623;* **ude2d 2618; ud83d ude2d 2616; udc95 ud83d udc95 ud83d 2590; ud83d udc95 ud83d udc95 ud83d 2590;** *thank you -2587;* **ude0d ud83d 2541; ud83d ude0d ud83d 2541; udc95 ud83d udc95 ud83d udc95 2535; ud83d udc95 ud83d udc95 ud83d udc95 2535;** *bqtn0bi -2533; nhttp -2525;* **harry 2506;** *ptsd -2502;*

7 Indicative Features

The following results show the top 100 most frequent Ngram features from the training data that were also used in the Tweets of the user with the highest score for each of the conditions. Recall that for system 2 the weighting scheme used was binary, so these features did not have any more or less value than others that may have been less frequent in the training data. However, given that each decision list had thousands of features 3, this seemed like a reasonable way to give a flavor for the kinds of features that appeared both in the training data and in users' Tweets. While not definitive, this will hopefully provide some insight into which of the decision list features play a role in determining if a user may have a particular underlying condition. Note that the very long random alpha strings are anonymized Twitter user ids.

7.1 Decision List system 2, DvC

This user used 3,267 features found in our decision list, where 2,360 of those were indicative of Depression, and 907 for Control. This gives this user a score of 1,453 which was the highest among all users for Depression. What follows are the 100 most frequent features from the training data that are indicative of Depression that this user also employed in a tweet at least one time.

ud83c; please; love; follow; re; fucking; love you; im; udf38; ud83c udf38; udc95; ud83d udc95; you re; ve; don t; fuck; please follow; don; i love; u2661; udf38 ud83c; ud83c udf38 ud83c; i don; i don t; i ve; udc95 ud83d; ud83d udc95 ud83d; feel; i love you; udf38 ud83c udf38; ud83c udf38 ud83c udf38; mean; ni; oh; think; why; actually; guys; i ll; omg; ll; lt 3; n ud83c; people; hi; 3; udf38 ud83c udf38 ud83c; ud83c udf38 ud83c udf38 ud83c; https; https t; https t co; udf38 ud83c udf38 ud83c udf38; ud83c udf38 ud83c udf38 ud83c udf38; sorry; okay; gonna; love you so; thank you; i feel; bc; this please; otygg6_yrurxouh; would mean; i hope; loves; thank; love you so much; pretty; friend; u2022; xx; cute; hope; hate; boys; depression; life; udf38 ud83c udf38 ud83c udf38 ud83c; a lot; she loves; perfect; u2014; oh my; lot; i think; thing; help; literally; u2661 u2661; the world; ve been; yeah; they re; still; it would mean; my life; friends; the fuck; crying; nplease

7.2 Decision List system 2, PvC

This user used 3,896 features found in our decision list, where 2,698 of those were indicative of PTSD, and 1,198 of Control. This gives this user a score of 1,500 which was the highest among all users for PTSD. What follows are the 100 most frequent features from the training data that are indicative of PTSD that this user also employed in a tweet at least one time.

u2026; co; t co; thank; thank you; please; health; answer; http; ptsd; amp; bqtn0bi; help; nhttp; ve; http t; https; nhttp t; https t; nhttp t co; https t co; read; medical; thanks; women; obama; i ve; ebola; oxmljtykruvsnpd; tcot; think; http u2026; curp4uo6ffzn2x1qckyok78w2hl u2026; news; thanks for; fbi; ferguson; children; support; mental; mentalhealth; story; curp4uo6ffzn2x1qckyok78w2hl; fucking; hope; living; http http t co; http http t; http http; auspol; sign; war; veterans; police; freemarinea; i think; bbc; god; woman; men; 2014; white; great; found; child; ago; drugs; kind; book; report; thank you for; n nhttp; agree; healthy; military; ppl; sure; n nhttp t; dvfrpdjwn4z; n nhttp t co; please check; care; writing; please check out; america; israel; tcot http; law; please check out my; bqtn0bi tcot; lot; son; kids; tcot http t; uk; isis; homeless; petition; the fbi; daughter

7.3 Decision List system 2, DvP (Depression)

This user used 3,797 features found in our decision list, where 2,945 of those were indicative of Depression, and 852 for PTSD. This gives this user a score of 2,093 which was the highest among all users for Depression when gauged against PTSD. Note that this is a different user than scored highest in DvC. What follows are the 100 most frequent features from the training data that are indicative of Depression as opposed to PTSD that this user also employed in a tweet at least one time.

ud83d; ud83c; rt; love; ude02; ud83d ude02; im; follow; don t; don; love you; gt; ude02 ud83d; ud83d ude02 ud83d; i love; ufe0f; please; ude02 ud83d ude02; udc95; ud83d ude02 ud83d ude02; ud83d udc95; ude0d; ud83d ude0d; fuck; re; udf38; ud83c udf38; i don t; u201c; i don; you re; gt gt; shit; udf41; ud83c udf41; follow me; fucking; hate; u2661; wanna; u201d; i love you; school; udc95 ud83d; ud83d udc95 ud83d; gonna; ude02 ud83d ude02 ud83d; ud83d ude02 ud83d ude02 ud83d; feel; people; u2764; omg; ude02 ud83d ude02 ud83d ude02; ud83d ude02 ud83d ude02 ud83d ude02; gt gt gt; ude2d; ud83d ude2d; ude0d ud83d; ud83d ude0d ud83d; happy; guys; oh; girl; mean; cute; i hate; girls; okay; why; ude18; ud83d ude18; udf41 ud83c; ud83c udf41 ud83c; n ud83c; boys; udf42; ud83c udf42; ude02 ud83d ude02 ud83d ude02 ud83d; bitch; bc; gt gt gt gt; perfect; miss; love you so; sleep; ude0d ud83d ude0d; ud83d ude0d ud83d ude0d; ude12; ud83d ude12; night; ni; u2022; life; i feel; wait; my life; ur; day; u263a; hi

7.4 Decision List system 2, DvP (PTSD)

This user used 4,167 features found in our decision list, where 2,885 of those were indicative of PTSD, and 1,282 for Depression. This gives this user a score of 1,603 which was the highest among all users for Depression when gauged against PTSD. Note that this is the same user that scored highest in PvC. What follows are the 100 most frequent features from the training data that are indicative of PTSD as opposed to Depression that this user also employed in a tweet at least one time.

co; t co; http; http t; http t co; u2026; amp; news; thanks; answer; health; thank; photo; great; thank you; bqtn0bi; nhttp; ptsd; obama;

nhttp t; nhttp t co; thanks for; medical; u2019s; read; women; tcot; curp4uo6ffzn2x1qckyok78w2hl; curp4uo6ffzn2x1qckyok78w2hl u2026; oxmljtykru-vsnpd; check; fbi; http u2026; ebola; today; ppl; help; support; ferguson; check out; police; sign; book; veterans; work; blog; children; war; 2; country; gop; living; thanks for the; report; freemarinea; auspol; u2019t; military; media; bbc; woman; house; men; u2026 http; truth; white; u2026 http t; u2026 http t co; http http; http http t; http http t co; posted; n nhttp; son; story; a great; photo http; n nhttp t; photo http t; photo http t co; law; n nhttp t co; healthy; america; dvfrpdjwn4z; state; tcot http; agree; mt; government; please check; god; kids; share; please check out; tcot http t; way; please check out my; case; bqtn0bi tcot

8 Discussion and Conclusions

This was our first effort at analyzing text from social media for mental health indicators. Our system here was informed by our experiences in other shared tasks for medical text, including the i2b2 Smoking Challenge (Pedersen, 2006; Uzuner et al., 2008), the i2b2 Obesity Challenge (Pedersen, 2008; Uzuner, 2009), and the i2b2 Sentiment Analysis of Suicide Notes Challenge (Pedersen, 2012; Pestian et al., 2012).

In those shared tasks we frequently observed that rule based systems fared reasonably well, and that machine learning methods were prone to over–fitting training data, and did not generalize terribly well. For this shared task we elected to take a very simple machine learning approach that did not attempt to optimize accuracy on the training data, in the hopes that it would generalize reasonably well.

However, this task is quite distinct in that the data is from Twitter. In the other shared tasks mentioned data came either from discharge notes, or suicide notes, all of which were generally written in standard English. We did not attempt to normalize abbreviations or misspellings, and we did not handle emoticons or URLs any differently than ordinary text. We also did not utilize any of the information available from Tweets beyond the text itself. These are all issues we plan to investigate in future work.

While it was clear that the Ngram 1–6 features performed better than bigrams, it would be interesting to know if the increased accuracy came from a particular length of Ngram, or if all the different Ngrams contributed equally to the success of Ngram 1–6. In particular we are curious as to whether or not the unigram features actually had a positive impact, since unigrams may tend to be both noisier and more semantically ambiguous.

Likewise, the binary weighting was clearly superior to the frequency based method. It seems important to know if there are a few very frequent features that are skewing these results, or if there are other reasons for the binary weighting to result in such better performance.

While is it difficult to generalize a great deal from these findings, there is some anecdotal evidence that these results have some validity. First, the user that was identified as most prone to Depression when compared to Control (in DvC) was different from the user identified as most prone to Depression when compared to PTSD (in DvP). This seems consistent with the idea that a person suffering from PTSD may also suffer from Depression, and so the DvC case is clearly distinct from the DvP since in the latter there may be confounding evidence of both conditions.

In reviewing the decision lists created by these systems, as well as the features that are actually found in user's Tweets, it seems clear that there were many somewhat spurious features that were included in the decision lists. This is not surprising given that features were included simply based on their frequency of occurrence - any Ngram that occurred 50 times more in one condition than the other would be included as a feature in the decision list. Moving forward having a more selective method for including features would surely help improve results, and provide greater insight into the larger problem of identifying mental illness in social media postings.

Acknowledgments

My thanks go to the CLPsych 2015 organizers for creating a very interesting and compelling task. This was not only a lot of fun to work on, but really presented some new and exciting challenges that will no doubt inspire a great deal of future work.

References

Satanjeev Banerjee and Ted Pedersen. 2003. The design, implementation, and use of the Ngram Statistics Package. In *Proceedings of the Fourth International Conference on Intelligent Text Processing and Computational Linguistics*, pages 370–381, Mexico City, February.

Glen Coppersmith, Mark Dredze, Craig Harman, Kristy Hollingshead, and Margaret Mitchell. 2015. CLPsych 2015 shared task: Depression and PTSD on Twitter. In *Proceedings of the Workshop on Computational Linguistics and Clinical Psychology: From Linguistic Signal to Clinical Reality*, Denver, Colorado, USA, June. North American Chapter of the Association for Computational Linguistics.

Ted Pedersen. 2006. Determining smoker status using supervised and unsupervised learning with lexical features. In *Working Notes of the i2b2 Workshop on Challenges in Natural Language Processing for Clinical Data*, Washington, DC, November.

Ted Pedersen. 2008. Learning high precision rules to make predictions of morbidies in discharge summaries. In *Proceedings of the Second i2b2 Workshop on Challenges in Natural Language Processing for Clinical Data*, Washington, DC, November.

Ted Pedersen. 2012. Rule-based and lightly supervised methods to predict emotions in suicide notes. *Biomedical Informatics Insights*, 2012:5 (Suppl. 1):185–193, January.

John Pestian, Pawel Matykiewicz, Michelle Linn-Gust, Brett South, Ozlem Uzuner, Jan Wiebe, Kevin Cohen, John Hurdle, and Chris Brew. 2012. Sentiment analysis of suicide notes: A shared task. *Biomedical Informatics Insights*, 2012:5 (Suppl. 1):3–16, January.

Ozlem Uzuner, Ira Goldstein, Yuan Luo, and Isaac Kohane. 2008. Identifying patient smoking status from medical discharge records. *Journal of the Medical Informatics Association*, 15(1):14–24.

Ozlem Uzuner. 2009. Recognizing obesity and co–morbidities in sparse data. *Journal of the Medical Informatics Association*, 16(4):561–570.

The University of Maryland CLPsych 2015 Shared Task System

Philip Resnik[2,4], **William Armstrong**[1,4], **Leonardo Claudino**[1,4], **Thang Nguyen**[3]
[1]Computer Science, [2]Linguistics, [3]iSchool, and [4]UMIACS, University of Maryland
{resnik,armstrow}@umd.edu
{claudino,daithang}@cs.umd.edu

1 Introduction

The 2015 ACL Workshop on Computational Linguistics and Clinical Psychology included a shared task focusing on classification of a sample of Twitter users according to three mental health categories: users who have self-reported a diagnosis of depression, users who have self-reported a diagnosis of post-traumatic stress disorder (PTSD), and control users who have done neither (Coppersmith et al., 2015; Coppersmith et al., 2014). Like other shared tasks, the goal here was to assess the state of the art with regard to a challenging problem, to advance that state of the art, and to bring together and hopefully expand the community of researchers interested in solving it.

The core problem under consideration here is the identification of individuals who suffer from mental health disorders on the basis of their online language use. As Resnik et al. (2014) noted in their introduction to the first ACL Workshop on Computational Linguistics and Clinical Psychology, few social problems are more costly than problems of mental health, in every possible sense of cost, and identifying people who need help is a huge challenge for a variety of reasons, including the fear of social or professional stigma, an inability of people to recognize symptoms and report them accurately, and the lack of access to clinicians. Language technology has the potential to make a real difference by offering low-cost, unintrusive methods for early screening, i.e. to identify people who should be more thoroughly evaluated by a professional, and for ongoing monitoring, i.e. to help providers serve their patients better over the long-term continuum of care (Young et al., 2014).

This paper summarizes the University of Maryland contribution to the CLPsych 2015 shared task. More details of our approach appear in Resnik et al. (2015), where we also report results on preliminary experimentation using the CLPsych Hackathon data (Coppersmith, 2015).

2 System Overview

In our system, we build on a fairly generic supervised classification approach, using SVM with a linear or RBF kernel and making use of baseline lexical features with TF-IDF weighting.

2.1 Variations explored

The innovations we explore center on using topic models to develop features that capture latent structure in the dataset, going beyond "vanilla" latent Dirichlet allocation (Blei et al., 2003) to include supervised LDA (Blei and McAuliffe, 2008, sLDA) as well as a supervised variant of the "anchor" algorithm (Arora et al., 2013; Nguyen et al., 2015, sAnchor). Putting together various combinations in our experimentation — linear vs. RBF kernel, big vs. small vocabulary, and four feature configurations (namely sLDA, sAnchor, lexical TF-IDF, and all combined), we evaluated a total of 16 systems for each of the three shared tasks (discriminating depression vs. controls, depression vs. PTSD, and PTSD vs. controls) for a total of 48 systems in all.

In general below, systems are named simply by concatenating the relevant elements of the description. For example, *combobigvocabSVMlinear_1* is the name of the system that uses (a) an SVM with linear kernel (*SVMlinear*), (b) models computed using the big vocabulary (*bigvocab*, details below), and (c) the "all combined" feature configuration

Proceedings of the 2nd Workshop on Computational Linguistics and Clinical Psychology: From Linguistic Signal to Clinical Reality, pages 54–60,
Denver, Colorado, June 5, 2015. ©2015 Association for Computational Linguistics

(*combo*). The numerical suffix is for internal reference and can be ignored. The names of all systems are shown in the legends of Figure 1 grouped by each pair of conditions.

As an exception to our general scheme, we also explored using sLDA to make predictions directly rather than providing topic posterior features for the SVM, i.e. by computing the value of the regression variable as a function of the posterior topic distribution given the input document (Blei and McAuliffe, 2008, sLDA). These systems are simply referred to as *SLDA Prediction*.

2.2 SLDA and SAnchor topic features

We briefly describe the features we used based on sLDA and sAnchor; see Resnik et al. (2015) for more details, as well as sample topics induced by these models on the closely related CLPsych Hackathon dataset. For both topic models, we used posterior topic distributions, i.e. the vector of $\Pr(\text{topic}_k|\text{document}), k = 1..K$ in a K-topic model, as features for supervised learning.

SLDA posteriors with informed priors. To take full advantage of the shared task's labeled training data in a topic modeling setting, we opted to use *supervised* topic models (sLDA, introduced by Blei and McAuliffe (2008)), as a method for gaining both clinical insight and predictive ability. However, initial exploration with the training dataset provided noisy topics of variable quality, many of which seemed intuitively unlikely to be useful as predictive features in the mental health domain. Therefore we incorporated an informed prior based on a model that we knew to capture relevant latent structure.

Specifically, we followed Resnik et al. (2013) in building a 50-topic model by running LDA on stream-of-consciousness essays collected by Pennebaker and King (1999) — a young population that seems likely to be similar to many authors in the Twitter dataset. These 50 topics were used as informed priors for sLDA.

Tables 3 to 5 show the top words in the sLDA topics with the 5 highest and 5 lowest Z-normalized regression scores, sLDA having been run with parameters: number of topics (k) $= 50$, document-topic Dirichlet hyper-parameter (α) $= 1$, topic-word Dirichlet hyper-parameter (β) $= 0.01$, Gaussian variance for document responses (ρ) $= 1$, Gaussian variance for topic's regression parameters (σ) $= 1$, Gaussian mean for topic's regression parameters (μ) $= 0.0$, using binary variables for the binary distinction in each experimental task.

Supervised anchor (SAnchor) posteriors. The anchor algorithm (Arora et al., 2013) provides a fast way to learn topic models and also enhances interpretability by automatially identifying a single "anchor" word associated with each topic. For example, one of the topics induced from the Hackathon tweets is associated with the anchor word *fat* and is characterized by the following most-probable words in the topic:

> *fat eat hate body sleep weight girl bed skinny cry fast beautiful die perfect cross hair ugh week sick care*

Nguyen et al. (2015) introduce SANCHOR, a supervised version of the anchor algorithm which, like sLDA, jointly models text content along with a per-document regression variable. We did not explore informed priors with SANCHOR in these experiments; this is left as a question for future work.

2.3 Classifier details

The majority of our experiments used SVM classifiers with either a linear or an RBF kernel. Specifically, we used the python *scikit-learn* module (*sklearn.svm.SVC*), which interfaces with the widely-used *libsvm*. Default parameters were used throughout except for the *class_weight* parameter, which was set to *None*.

In the *SLDA Prediction* experiments, we followed Blei and McAuliffe (2008) in computing the response value for each test document from $\eta^\top \bar{z}$ where $\bar{z}$ is the document's posterior topic distribution and the ηs are the per-topic regression parameters. SLDAPrediction_1 and SLDAPrediction_2 were conducted with small and big vocabularies, respectively.

2.4 Data Preparation

Data organization: weekly aggregation. To overcome potential problems for topic modeling with documents that are too small (individual tweets) or too large (all tweets for an author) we grouped tweets together by the week they were posted. Thus each author corresponded to several documents, one for each week they tweeted one or

Notes	Valence	Top 20 words
high emotional valence	e	life live dream change future grow family goal mind rest decision marry chance choice successful career set regret support true
high emotional valence	e	love life happy heart amaze hurt perfect crazy beautiful lose smile cry boy true fall real sad relationship reason completely
relationship problems	n	time boyfriend friend relationship talk person break doe happen understand hard trust care spend reason san situation antonio date leave
transition to college	n	school college student semester university experience hard grade parent graduate freshman campus learn texas attend teacher expect challenge adjust education
self-doubt	n	question realize understand completely idea sense level bring issue concern simply situation lack honestly admit mention fear step feeling act
poor ego control	n	yeah suck wow haha stupid funny hmm crap crazy blah freak type ugh weird lol min gosh hey bore hmmm
feeling ignored/annoyed *	n	call talk phone doe stop bad ring message loud head homework answer cell mad forget annoy sound hurt suppose mine
somatic complaints	n	cold hot feel sick smell rain walk start weather bad window foot freeze nice wait throat day heat hate warm
emotional distress *	n	feel happy day sad depress feeling cry scar afraid lonely head moment emotion realize confuse hurt inside guilty fear upset
family of origin issues	n	mom dad family sister parent brother kid child mother father grow doctor baby hard cousin die age cry proud husband
negative affect *	n	damn hell doe shit fuck smoke woman hate drink piss sex drug kid god bitch time real break screw cigarette
anxiety over failure	n	worry hard study test class lot grade focus mind start nervous stress concentrate trouble reason easier hop harder fail constantly
negative affect*	n	hate doe bad stupid care understand time suck happen anymore mad don mess scar horrible smart matter hat upset fair
sleep disturbance*	n	sleep tire night morning wake bed day time late stay hour asleep nap fall start tomorrow sleepy haven awake lay
somatic complaints	n	hurt eye hear itch hand air sound tire nose arm loud leg leave noise finger smell neck stop light water
social engagement	p	game football team win ticket excite school weekend week texas run lose night season saturday sport dallas longhorn coach fan
exercise, good self-care	p	run day feel walk class wear lose weight buy gym gain short fat dress shop exercise campus clothe body shirt

Table 1: LDA topics from Pennebaker stream-of-consciousness essays identified by a clinician as most relevant for assessing depression. Topics with negative valence (n) were judged likely to be indicators for depression, those with positive valence (p) were judged likely to indicate absence of depression, and those labeled (e) have strong emotional valence without clearly indicating likely assessment. Asterisked topics were viewed as the strongest indicators. Many more of the 50 topics from this model were intuitively coherent but not judged as particularly relevant for the depression-assessment task. This table is reproduced from Resnik et al. (2015).

more times; each document was treated as being labeled by the author's individual-level label. In preliminary experimentation, we found that this temporal grouping greatly improved the performance of our models, though it should be noted that organizing the data in this way fails to account for the fact that an author's mental health can vary greatly from week to week. For instance, a user identified as having depression at some point may not be experiencing symptoms in any given week, yet that week's document would still be labeled as positive for depression. This could potentially be mitigated in future work by attempting to identify the time of diagnosis and increasing the label weight on documents near that time.

Token pre-processing and vocabularies. All systems went through the same basic pre-processing: we first removed words with non-alphanumeric characters, emoticon character codes, and stop words.[1] The remaining tokens were further lemmatized.

For SVM classification we explored using systems with both *small* and *big* vocabularies. For the former, we first filtered out documents with less than 50 tokens and then selected tokens that appeared more than 100 documents; the latter was obtained in a similar fashion, except setting the word-per-document cutoff to 10 rather than 50, and the document-per-word cutoff to 30 instead of 100.[2]

For *sLDA* prediction, we used an external vocabulary produced from the set of 6,459 stream-of-consciousness essays collected between 1997 and 2008 by Pennebaker and King (1999), who asked students to think about their thoughts, sensations, and feelings in the moment and "write your thoughts as they come to you". As discussed in Section 2, running LDA on this dataset provided informative priors for sLDA's learning process on the Twitter training data. The student essays average approximately 780 words each, and for uniformity, we pre-processed them with the same tools as the Twitter set.[3] We created a shared vocabulary for our models by taking the union of the vocabularies from the two datasets, resulting in a roughly 10-20% increase in vocabulary size over the Twitter dataset alone.

Author-level features. In order to arrive at a single feature vector for each author based on documents aggregated at the weekly level, we weight-averaged features across weeks, where weights corresponded to the fraction of the author's tweets associated with each week alone. In other words, the more an author posted in a week, the more important that week's features would be, compared to the

[1]Unicode emoticons were left in, converted to the token EMOJI.

[2]When referring to vocabulary size, we use the terms *short* and *small* interchangeably.

[3]With the exception of the document count filters, due to the different number and sizes of documents, which were adjusted accordingly.

other weeks.

Data splits. We did an 80-20 partition into training and development sets, respectively. Since we did not do any hyper-parameter tuning, the dev set was used primarily for sanity checking and to get a preliminary sense of system performance. We report test set results based on models that were trained on the training set alone.[4]

3 Results

3.1 Overall results and ROCs

The ROC curves for all our submitted systems on the shared tasks (Section 2) are shown in Figure 1. The area under curve (AUC) scores for TF-IDF (baseline) and all configurations of combined features (best systems) are shown in Table 2, from which we see that the 8 best-performing feature configurations achieved an average AUC of about 0.84. We obtained the best overall results when we used a big vocabulary, combined all features, and trained a linear SVM. We saw that bigger vocabularies improved performance of linear SVMs but not RBF SVMs, and that, in general, linear SVMs did better.

The order of difficulty for these discrimination problems seems to be DvP > DvC > PvC, judging from the performance of our top 8 systems. This suggests that there may be greater overlap of linguistic signal between tweets from people who have self-reported PTSD and those who have self-reported depression, which is not entirely surprising since the two conditions often co-occur. According to Tull (2015), "Depression is one of the most commonly occurring disorders in PTSD... [A]mong people who have or have had a diagnosis of PTSD, approximately 48% also had current or past depression ...People who have had PTSD at some point in their life are almost 7 times as likely as people without PTSD to also have depression."

3.2 Qualitative discussion for sLDA

To get a sense of the role that supervised topic modeling may be playing, we take a brief qualitative look at the topics induced by sLDA on the training set. Tables 3,4, and 5 show the most polarized

[4]It is possible that modest improvements could be obtained by folding the dev set back into the training data, but we wished to avoid inspecting the dev set so that we can continue to use it for further development.

Feature configuration / Problem AUC	DvC	DvP	PvC
tfidfshortvocabSVMlinear	0.824	0.808	0.860
tfidfbigvocabSVMlineasr	0.845	0.827	0.884
tfidfshortvocabSVMrbf	0.831	0.812	0.872
tfidfbigvocabSVMrbf	0.815	0.798	0.855
comboshortvocabSVMlinear	0.841	0.832	0.879
combobigvocabSVMlinear	**0.860**	**0.841**	**0.893**
comboshortvocabSVMrbf	0.835	0.818	0.876
combobigvocabSVMrbf	0.830	0.811	0.869

Table 2: Area under curve (AUC) of selected feature configurations in Fig. 1 per each problem: depression vs. control (DvC), depression vs. PTSD (DvP) and PTSD vs. control (PvC). Boldface: big vocabulary, combined features, SVM linear. This setting was the best for all three tasks.

topics resulting from the sLDA models constructed on the DvC, DvP and PvC tasks respectively, where polarization is measured by the value of the sLDA regression variable for the topic. The topics we see are not as clean and coherent as the topics in Table 1, which is unsurprising since the latter topics came from LDA run on individually coherent documents (stream-of-consciousness essays) collected from a more uniform population (UT Austin college students) (Pennebaker and King, 1999), as contrasted with aggregations of tweets over time from a sample of Twitter users.

At the same time, there does seem to be interpretable signal distinguishing the high versus low polarity topics, at least in comparisons against controls. Comparing depression vs. control (Table 3), we see subdivisions of negative affect — for example, the most depression-oriented topic, as identified using positive regression values, is dominated by negatively oriented interjections (*fuck*, *shit*, *damn*, etc.), and the next most depression oriented topic appears to largely capture relationship discussion (*omg*, *cute*, *cry*, *guy*, *feel*, *hot*, *pretty*). Conversely, the least depression-oriented topics in the table, i.e. with the most negative regression values, contain not only many positive affect terms (*lol*, *haha*, etc.) but also activities related to family (*car*, *weekend*, *home*) and social activity (*food*, *tonight*, *party*, *dinner*, *weekend*).

In PTSD vs. control (Table 5), we see, among the topics more oriented toward PTSD users, topics that may be related to attention to veteran issues (*sign*, *support*, *homeless*, *petition*, *marine*), and possibly

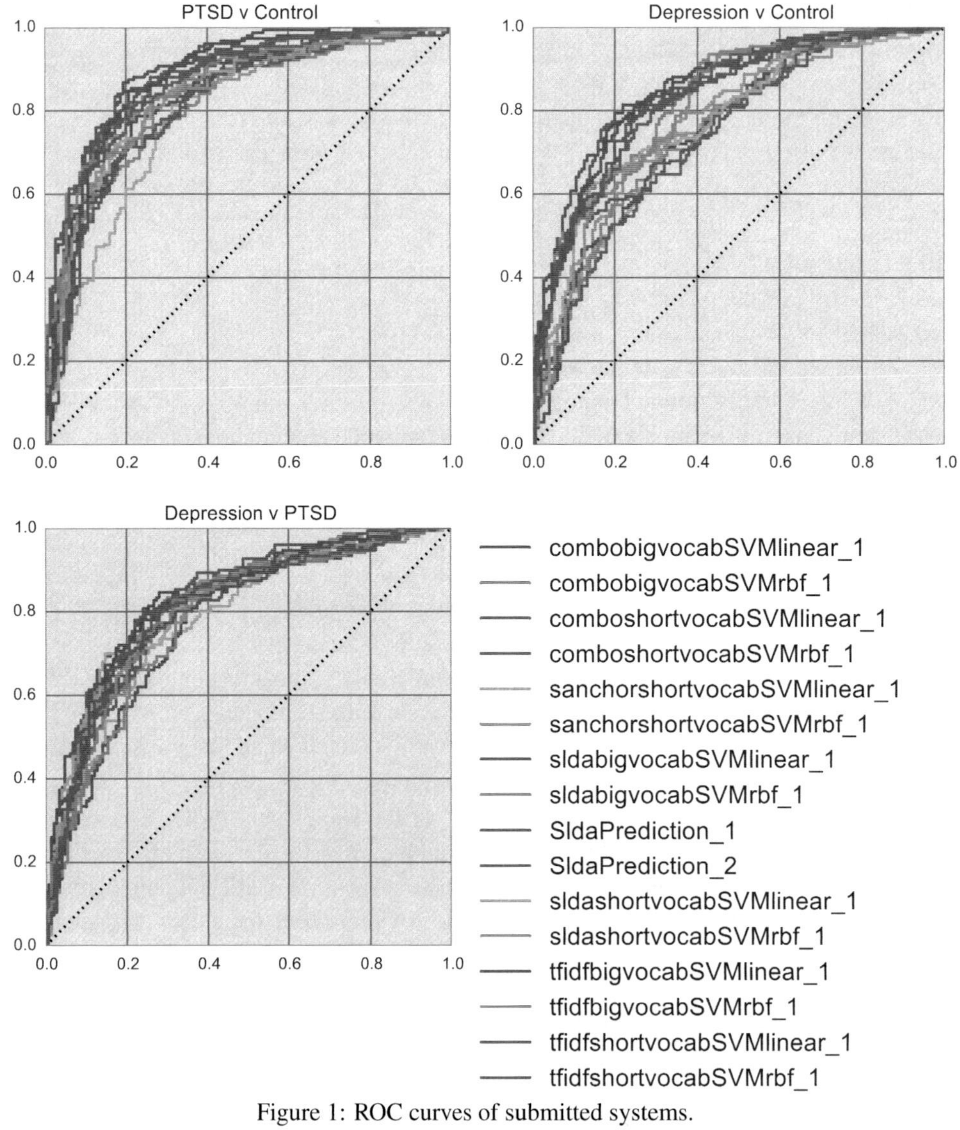

Figure 1: ROC curves of submitted systems.

Regression value	Top 20 words
5.362	fuck shit bitch sex smoke dick drink girl damn fuckin suck weed wanna life wtf hell gonna gay hate drug
4.702	omg cute cry gonna god guy demi idk literally feel wow hot pretty dont bye perfect pls ugh omfg laugh
4.204	line feel people cross friend comment doe start time link mental depression life live health submit deal talk lot issue
3.132	watch movie time episode read write season totally book favorite play character awesome scene star stuff cool horror start hug
2.877	week post baby inbox month day hey pain ago pregnant hun girl start doe bad boy feel time ive private
-1.689	food tonight truck night bring android party dinner tomorrow weekend awesome island game free wine lunch bar complete jack live
-1.87	nigga shit bitch hoe bout real tho gotta ima aint money lil wit bruh tryna mad yall damn ppl smh
-2.584	lol lmao damn smh yea gotta hell dude gon tho watch baby lmfao EMOJI wtf black bro idk boo funny
-2.966	car weekend home house drive summer miss week beach family rain weather run dog ready leave cancer race ride hour
-3.017	haha hahaha yeah hahahaha time night hahah wait watch ill love feel drink dad brother sleep phone sister eat miss

Table 3: Most extreme sLDA topics from Twitter training data (Depression (1) vs. Control (-1))

Regression value	Top 20 words
3.342	harry boy direction louis niall liam guy zayn demi fan tweet fandom laugh video tour day love concert people proud
2.984	EMOJI EMOJI night love EMOJI EMOJI EMOJI EMOJI EMOJI EMOJI EMOJI EMOJI tonight miss girl people EMOJI happy feel tomorrow
2.933	yeah pretty lot stuff play doe cool time send weird wait aww favourite kinda twitter awesome wow happen cat sound
2.708	bitch lmao nigga shit girl wanna hoe talk fuck dick bae damn baby lmfao pussy EMOJI text school boy lil
2.227	girl cute wanna boy guy friend love hate hair text life mom kiss hot feel fall relationship literally boyfriend date
-1.847	kid halloween call guy drink beer fun college throw sam hey dress pick scream play star remember walk porn doe
-2.11	child read change public agree abuse issue record system service kid pay refuse article response court lie business company doe
-2.357	obama tcot vote american ppl ebola america president gop gun country isi texas pay law lie idiot democrat military illegal
-2.568	food live beach town local fresh city coffee time life ago meet house chef fish street change nyc month san
-2.682	ptsd learn fear create canada meet experience speak positive step battle join voice awareness hear youth future world understand key

Table 4: Most extreme sLDA topics from Twitter training data (Depression (1) vs. PTSD (-1))

Regression value	Top 20 words
5.007	people woman doe call black white sex gay real kid word person twitter dude wrong lady marriage female marry tweet
3.581	sign support free share people day family time release send stand fight homeless petition marine pic hero home raise info
3.498	time doe cat lot tweet buy wife twitter feel haven move yep sit door house nice wear glad leave send
3.472	story child mother ptsd mom life son talk death surprise family mental parent woman care save daughter difference pls watch
3.238	feel day eat lose time fat body hard weight start run sleep gym workout fast cut stop food pain stay
-1.979	lol lmao ppl yea dat tho jus gotta wat smh kno dnt money yal dey damn cuz leo tht wen
-2.013	EMOJI love EMOJI EMOJI girl EMOJI day EMOJI EMOJI EMOJI EMOJI EMOJI EMOJI wanna miss people EMOJI EMOJI EMOJI night
-2.318	iphone apple player app phone bowl super youtube free update add ipad hand note box review pro game google play
-2.418	school class sleep tomorrow day feel hate bed tire home night hour homework study people teacher start wake boyfriend gonna
-2.743	haha hahaha yeah night love xxx sleep feel babe miss bed mum girl wait home ill bore boy phone tonight

Table 5: Most extreme sLDA topics from Twitter training data (PTSD (1) vs. Control (-1))

mental health issues including PTSD itself (*story*, *mother*, *ptsd*, *death*, *surprise*, *mental*).

Consistent with the lower performance on depression vs. PTSD (DvP), in Table 4 no topics jump out quite as forcefully as being polarized toward one condition or the other, except for the most PTSD-oriented topic, which appears as if it may concern efforts to draw attention to PTSD (*ptsd*, *learn*, *fear*, *speak*, *positive*, *step*, *battle*, *join*, *voice*, *awareness*). It may be, however, that in incorporating the depression vs. PTSD distinction, the model is actually capturing broader characteristics of relevant subpopulations: particularly in this dataset, people self-reporting a PTSD diagnosis may well be older on average than people self-reporting a depression diagnosis, if not chronologically than in terms of life experience. The topic with the most positive regression value in the table, i.e. leaning toward depression rather than PTSD, includes terms most likely related to youth/pop culture: *Niall* Horan, *Harry* Styles, *Liam* Payne, and *Louis* Tomlinson are the members of the pop boy band One Direction. Other positive- (i.e. depression-)leaning topics in the table also have a quality of disinhibition more characteristic of younger people. In contrast, the negative- (i.e. PTSD-)leaning topics in the table tend toward more mature topics, including, for example, politics and current affairs (*obama*, *tcot* (top conservatives on Twitter), *vote*, *ebola*).

Although our efforts are still in an early stage, our hope is that more sophisticated topic models can not only enhance predictive accuracy, as in Table 2, but also that observations like these about topics or themes might help create insight for clinicians. Examples like the ones in Tables 1 and 3-5 can help establish face validity with clinicians by showing that these models can capture things they already know about. Others can potentially lead to new questions worth asking, e.g. in Table 3, might the topic relating to entertainment (*watch*, *movie*, *episode*, *read*, *write*, *season*, *book*) suggest a closer look at social isolation (staying in watching movies, reading books) as a linguistically detectable online behavior that might correlate with increased likelihood of depression? If true, this would be consistent with, and complement, Choudhury et al. (2013), who look at non-linguistic measures of social engagement in Twitter among their potential depression-related attributes.[5]

4 Conclusions and Future Directions

In this paper we have briefly described the University of Maryland contribution to the CLPsych 2015 shared tasks. We found that TF-IDF features alone

[5] Although only an anecdotal observation involving two rather different datasets, the Depression v Control ROC curve in Figure 1 appears remarkably similar to the ROC curve in De Choudhury et al's Figure 4.

performed very well, perhaps surprisingly well, on all three tasks; TF-IDF combined with supervised topic model posteriors resulted in an even more predictive feature configuration.

In future work, we plan to conduct a thorough error analysis to see where the models go astray. We also plan to look at the extent to which our data organization may have influenced performance; in preliminary experimentation in Resnik et al. (2015), we found suggestive evidence that aggregating tweets by week, rather than as a single document per user, might make a significant difference, and that is the strategy we adopted here. This may not just be a question of document size — other time-based aggregations may be worth exploring, e.g. grouping tweets by time of day.

Acknowledgments

We are grateful to Rebecca Resnik for contributing her comments and clinical expertise, and we thank Glen Coppersmith, Mark Dredze, Jamie Pennebaker, and their colleagues for kindly sharing data and resources. This work was supported in part by NSF awards 1320538, 1018625, and 1211153. Any opinions, findings, conclusions, or recommendations expressed here are those of the authors and do not necessarily reflect the view of the sponsor.

References

Sanjeev Arora, Rong Ge, Yoni Halpern, David M. Mimno, Ankur Moitra, David Sontag, Yichen Wu, and Michael Zhu. 2013. A practical algorithm for topic modeling with provable guarantees.

David Blei and Jon McAuliffe. 2008. Supervised topic models. In J.C. Platt, D. Koller, Y. Singer, and S. Roweis, editors, *Advances in Neural Information Processing Systems 20*, pages 121–128. MIT Press, Cambridge, MA.

David M Blei, Andrew Y Ng, and Michael I Jordan. 2003. Latent Dirichlet allocation. *The Journal of Machine Learning Research*, 3:993–1022.

Munmun De Choudhury, Scott Counts, Eric Horvitz, and Michael Gamon. 2013. Predicting depression via social media. In *AAAI*. AAAI, July.

Glen Coppersmith, Mark Dredze, and Craig Harman. 2014. Quantifying mental health signals in Twitter. In *Proceedings of the Workshop on Computational Linguistics and Clinical Psychology: From Linguistic Signal to Clinical Reality*, pages 51–60, Baltimore, Maryland, USA, June. Association for Computational Linguistics.

Glen Coppersmith, Mark Dredze, Craig Harman, Kristy Hollingshead, and Margaret Mitchell. 2015. CLPsych 2015 shared task: Depression and PTSD on Twitter. In *Proceedings of the Workshop on Computational Linguistics and Clinical Psychology: From Linguistic Signal to Clinical Reality*, Denver, Colorado, USA, June. North American Chapter of the Association for Computational Linguistics.

Glen Coppersmith. 2015. [Un]Shared task: Computational linguistics and clinical psychology. `http://glencoppersmith.com/papers/CLPsych2015_hackathon_shared_task.pdf`.

Thang Nguyen, Jordan Boyd-Graber, Jeffrey Lund, Kevin Seppi, and Eric Ringger. 2015. Is your anchor going up or down? Fast and accurate supervised topic models. In *North American Chapter of the Association for Computational Linguistics*.

James W Pennebaker and Laura A King. 1999. Linguistic styles: language use as an individual difference. *Journal of personality and social psychology*, 77(6):1296.

Philip Resnik, Anderson Garron, and Rebecca Resnik. 2013. Using topic modeling to improve prediction of neuroticism and depression in college students. In *Proceedings of the 2013 Conference on Empirical Methods in Natural Language Processing*, pages 1348–1353, Seattle, Washington, USA, October. Association for Computational Linguistics.

Philip Resnik, Rebecca Resnik, and Margaret Mitchell, editors. 2014. *Proceedings of the Workshop on Computational Linguistics and Clinical Psychology: From Linguistic Signal to Clinical Reality*. Association for Computational Linguistics, Baltimore, Maryland, USA, June.

Philip Resnik, William Armstrong, Leonardo Claudino, Thang Nguyen, Viet-An Nguyen, and Jordan Boyd-Graber. 2015. Beyond LDA: exploring supervised topic modeling for depression-related language in Twitter. In *Proceedings of the 2nd Workshop on Computational Linguistics and Clinical Psychology (CLPsych)*.

Matthew Tull. 2015. PTSD and Depression. `http://ptsd.about.com/od/relatedconditions/a/depressionPTSD.htm`.

Bill Young, Chris Clark, John Kansky, and Erik Pupo. 2014. Definition: Continuum of care, May. `http://www.himss.org/ResourceLibrary/genResourceDetailPDF.aspx?ItemNumber=30272`.

Computational cognitive modeling of inflectional verb morphology in Spanish-speakers for the characterization and diagnosis of Alzheimer's Disease

del Castillo M.D.
Centro de Automática y Robótica, CAR, CSIC
Ctra. Campo Real, km. 0,200
28500 Madrid, Spain
md.delcastillo@csic.es

Serrano J.I.
Centro de Automática y Robótica, CAR, CSIC
Ctra. Campo Real, km. 0,200
28500 Madrid, Spain
jignacio.serrano@csic.es

Oliva J.
BBVA Data&Analytics
Avda. Burgos 16
28036 Madrid, Spain
jesus.oliva1984@gmail.com

Abstract

Alzheimer's Disease, as other mental and neurological disorders, is difficult to diagnose since it affects several cognitive abilities shared with other impairments. Current diagnostic mainly consists of neuropsychological tests and history obtained from the patient and relatives. In this paper we propose a methodology for the characterization of probable AD based on the computational cognitive modeling of a language function in order to capture the internal mechanisms of the impaired brain. Parameters extracted from the model allow a better characterization of this illness than using only behavioral data.

1 Introduction

Document "Dementia. A public health priority" by the World Health Organization[1] defines dementia as a syndrome, usually of a chronic or progressive nature, caused by a variety of brain illnesses that affect memory, thinking, orientation, comprehension, calculation, learning capacity, language, and judgment leading to an inability to perform everyday activities. Current data estimate over 35.6 million people worldwide affected by dementia and this number will double by 2030 and more than triple by 2050[2]. Dementia is among the seven priority mental and neurological impairments[1]. Although dementia is a collective concept including different possible causes or diseases (vascular, Lewy bodies, frontotemporal degeneration, Alzheimer), there are broad similarities between the symptoms of all them. Alzheimer's Disease (AD) is the most common cause of dementia. Its early diagnosis may help people to have information in the present for making decisions about their future and to receive treatment as soon as possible.

Clinical diagnosis of dementia happens after subjects realize memory loss or language difficulties affecting their everyday activities. Usually, the therapist takes note of these subjective impairments coupled with objective information given by some relative and then performs a battery of neuropsychological tests. Besides, neuroimaging techniques (MRI, PET) and biomarkers tests can strengthen the diagnosis process by discarding any other pathology. The drawback of these last techniques is their high cost. So, a key point in detecting this syndrome is to research about noninvasive and low cost diagnosis techniques whose application could be extended to everybody at a very early stage even before appearing any subjective or observable symptom.

One of the most common functions affected in dementia is language production (Hart and Semple, 1990). Many of the structures and processes involved in language processing are shared by different cognitive capacities. So, it would be possible to identify any cognitive impairment not directly

[1] www.who.int/mental_health/publications/
[2] www.who.int/mental_health/neurology/dementia/

Proceedings of the 2nd Workshop on Computational Linguistics and Clinical Psychology: From Linguistic Signal to Clinical Reality, pages 61–70,
Denver, Colorado, June 5, 2015.

related to language at an early stage by analyzing language processing.

The loss of communicative capability is detected in 80% of people at the first development stage of AD. Most research works relating AD and language have mainly focused their efforts on the lexical-semantics area (Cherktow and Bub, 1990) although there are also several studies showing linguistic problems in areas like phonology, syntax, pragmatics and inflectional morphology and how these problems evolve along the disease´s stages (Taller and Philips, 2008).

The majority of these works have been carried out in English but their results can be extended to other languages such as Spanish. An exhaustive analysis of linguistic processing in Spanish was performed by Cuetos el al. (2003) covering phonological, syntactical and semantic areas. However, there is no study dealing with verbal morphology in Spanish. The closest reference work examining the effects of AD in past-participle and present-tense production of real regular and irregular verbs as well as novel verbs of the two first morphological classes is in Italian (Walenski et al. 2009). The pattern found is the same as in English inflection: dementia patients are impaired at inflecting real irregular verbs but not real regular verbs for both tenses or novel verbs (Ullman, 2004).

Although there exist many neuropsychological tests used to diagnose dementia (Pasquier, 1999), like MMSE (Mini-Mental State Examination) (Folstein et al., 1975), they have a low sensibility at early stages and do not provide an individual and distinguishing measure of the disease. Language tests have proven to be very useful tools in identifying different types of mental disorders (Stevens et al., 1996).

In (Cuetos et al., 2003) the authors build a support model for the diagnosis of probable AD from the results of tasks belonging to phonological, syntactic and semantics areas by using a linear regression analysis. Other research work (Bucks et al., 2000) finds the predictive markers of probable AD by Principal Component Analysis (PCA) from measures of spontaneous narrative speech. The same kind of measures were processed by different machine learning methods resulting in classification models with a high predictive power (Thomas et al., 2005), which were able to detect the type of disorder even in pre-symptomatic subjects (Jarrold et al., 2010). These works demonstrate, on the one hand, the role of language use as a behavioral measure; on the other, the potential value of the computational analysis of language as a characterization and diagnostic means and, specifically, the capability of machine learning techniques to develop descriptive and predictive models of mental disorders from language use.

In other cognitive impairments related to language production (Oliva et al., 2014), the performance of classification models obtained with machine learning techniques have shown to be better than statistical methods like regression or lineal discriminant analyses. Nevertheless, to the best of our knowledge, there is no study about modeling by machine learning methods the behavior of native Spanish-speakers with dementia by using measures extracted from verbal morphology tests.

As stated before, there exist different types of dementia as a consequence of diverse diseases that share similar symptoms and behavioral patterns. A deeper knowledge about the specific structural or functional causes of this syndrome and so about the underlying disease can be gained by neuroimaging techniques. But these techniques are expensive and their use is not generally extended. The efficacy of a therapy or treatment depends on how the disease affects the patient individually. However, most studies present a profile of average behavior behind disorders. A novel way to overcome this lack of personalized information about the patient can be supplied by computational modeling of individual patients' behavior when patients perform a certain cognitive task.

A cognitive architecture is a general framework to develop behavior computational models about human cognition (Anderson and Lebiere, 1998). This type of architecture must take into account the abilities (i.e. memory, learning, perception, motor action) and the boundaries (i.e. forgetting) of the human being. As a general theory about the structure and function of a complete cognitive system, a cognitive architecture determines the way perceptual, cognitive and motor processes interact in producing behavior. The framework provided by a cognitive architecture allows the computational models supported by it to be neurologically and psychologically plausible. Computational modeling is an integral procedure for obtaining indirect measurements about structures and processes involved when people accomplish a cognitive task (Iglesias et al., 2012; Serrano et al., 2009). A good subject's model must fit the behavior of such a subject, that is, it must generate statistically equivalent data to the subject's data. A well-known cognitive architecture is ACT-R (Anderson, 2007). Its application to a language function as the task of acquiring verbal morphology in English (Taagten and Anderson, 2002) is based on the dual-mechanism theory (Pinker and Prince, 1988), which posits that irregular forms of verbs are stored in memory as entries in the mental lexicon while regular forms are computed by rules. This same paradigm has been used to model the acquisition of a highly inflected verbal system like Spanish (Oliva et al., 2010) and the behavior of children with Specific Language Impairment (SLI) (Oliva et al., 2013).

This paper presents a methodology for the characterization and diagnosis of probable AD (pAD) for native-Spanish speakers based on the computational cognitive modeling of the subjects' behavior when they perform verb inflection tasks. The set of variable values of each model are presented to supervised machine learning algorithms to learn a classification and predictive model of data. The results of the preliminary study that we have carried out show that the variables obtained from the computational cognitive models are very informative for the diagnosis process. Also it is important to note that this methodology can be easily extended to other languages and even to other cognitive impairments not necessarily related to language.

2 Method

As commented in the previous section, AD can present overlapping symptoms with other types of dementia and exhibit more deficits other than language use. So, any methodology for the diagnosis of cognitive or mental impairments should have two main goals: generality and individualization. The methodology should be adequate to diagnose different cognitive impairments and, at the same time, it should take into account the individual differences that are usually present on these impairments. Here we present a methodology that achieves these two objectives applied to the particular case of pAD consisting mainly in: i) finding the task that exhibits behavioral differences between healthy and impaired subjects, ii) preparing the computational cognitive architecture with the knowledge to deal with the selected task, iii) modeling the individual subject's behavior to obtain the parameters of the architecture specific to each participant, and iv) applying machine learning techniques on the information given by the cognitive models to learn the classification model that supports impairment diagnosis. Next, the different steps of the methodology are explained and applied to characterize and diagnose pAD.

2.1 Participants

Twenty-two native-Spanish speakers were initially selected to take part in this preliminary study by the Centro de Referencia Estatal de Discapacidad y Dependencia (CRE) de León, Spain, distributed into twelve patients of pAD (six men, six women) and ten healthy control subjects (five men, four women) age-matched. pAD participants were identified by the MEC (Lobo et al., 1979) and Barcelona tests (Peña-Casanova et al. 2005) for Spanish speakers.

Three participants with pAD were discarded due to two of them have a low educational level and the third one was not originally from Spanish. The final participants' demographic features can be seen in Table 1.

	pAD	control
Participants	9	10
Avg. Age (SD)	69.33 (6.42)	67.3 (2.58)
Sex	4F / 5M	5F / 5M

Table 1. Participants' demographic features. SD stands for Standard Deviation.

2.2 Define target task

The task to be carried out intends to reflect behavioral differences between pAD patients and control healthy individuals. Since patients with pAD have shown deficits with verbal morphology in English and Italian, we have selected a task of verb inflection consisting of two sets with 40 pairs of sentences. In selecting the sentences' verbs, we have avoided reflexive, recent and onomatopoeic verbs. In the first set, devoted to present tense, all the sentences were presented at first person, singular and together a frequency adverb to denote that the action is usually performed. An example of this set is: a) *A mí me gusta llevar pantalones vaqueros* (I like to wear jeans) and b) *Así que todos los días*

... *pantalones vaqueros* (So I ... jeans every day). In the second set, devoted to simple past, all sentences were presented at third person, singular and together the adverb "*ayer*" ("yesterday") to denote that the action was done in the past. An example of this set is: a) *A Lola le gusta comer temprano* (Lola likes to eat early) and b) *Así que ayer Lola ... temprano* (So Lola ... early yesterday).

In the two sets, 20 regular and 20 irregular verbs were used, respectively. These verbs were retrieved from the Reference Corpus of Current Spanish[3] and matched in frequency (regular = 44.79, irregular = 44.33, p = 0.98). All regular verbs, except one ("*comer*"-"to eat"), belonged to the first morphological class, or first conjugation, finishing the infinitival form of the verb with "–*ar*". Irregular verbs belonged to the second and third conjugation, finishing with "*–er*" and "*–ir*", respectively. Both regular and irregular matched in orthographical (Number of letters: Infinitive form: regular = 6.4, irregular = 5.85, p = 0.29; Inflected form: regular = 5.48, irregular = 5.58, p = 0.74) and phonological length (Number of syllables: Infinitive form: regular = 2.4, irregular = 2.25, p = 0.41; Inflected form: regular = 2.4, irregular = 2.35, p = 0.69), and consonant density (Infinitive form: regular = 1.62, irregular = 1.57, p = 0.62; Inflected form: regular = 1.18, irregular = 1.24, p = 0.43) in order to avoid phonological factors biasing results.

2.3 Behavioral profile

Next, the procedure performed to collect this kind of data and the results obtained are briefly described.

Procedure: 80 pairs of sentences were randomly sorted and presented to all the participants. Every participant had to read each sentence pair slowly and to fill the gap in the second sentence with the suited inflected form of the verb in the first sentence. The answers of each participant are categorized as follows: 1) Correct answers, 2) Overregularization or Irregularization errors, occurring when the expected form was irregular or regular, respectively, 3) Number or Person (NP) errors, when fails the number or person affix, 4) Mood, Tense or Aspect (MTA) errors, when fails the mood or tense or aspect affix, and 6) Other errors, not included in the previous categories.

Results: People with pAD made more mistakes when inflecting both past and present tenses. The results obtained show a clear deficit in producing irregular forms both in past and present tense in participants with pAD compared with controls, as seen in languages such as English (Ullman, 2004) and Italian (Walenski et al., 2009). Table 2 presents these results. Other types of errors made by participants with pAD holding statistical differences with the control group are overregularization ones in present tense and substitution errors of mood, tense or aspect. According to the dual-mechanism theory (Pinker and Prince, 1988), errors in irregular forms and MTA errors are focused on declarative memory fails since this memory stores irregular verb forms

			pAD	**control**
Present Tense	Regular Forms	Correct	0.983	0.995
		Irregularization	0	0
		NP Errors	0	0
		MTA Errors	0.006	0
		Other Errors	0.013	0.005
	Irregular Forms	Correct	0.911^{**}	0.985
		Irregularization	0.028^{*}	0.01
		NP Errors	0	0
		MTA Errors	0.039^{*}	0
		Other Errors	0.022	0.005
Past Tense	Regular Forms	Correct	0.978	0.99
		Irregularization	0	0
		NP Errors	0	0
		MTA Errors	0.011	0.005
		Other Errors	0.011	0.005
	Irregular Forms	Correct	0.9^{**}	0.98
		Irregularization	0.039	0.02
		NP Errors	0.006	0
		MTA Errors	0.033^{**}	0
		Other Errors	0.022^{*}	0

Table 2. Behavioral results.

and their abstract grammatical features. In the same way, overregularization errors are predicted by this mechanism due to the application by proce-

[3] RAE. 2012. Real Academia Española: Banco de datos (CREA). Corpus de Referencia del Español Actual. http://www.rae.es.

dural memory of a regular rule to produce an irregular form when this form is not found in the declarative memory.

2.4 Computational Cognitive Modeling

The next step is to build a personalized computational cognitive model for the target task. The psychological plausibility of the model is a key point. The cognitive architecture should be able to model the normal and the impaired behavior. It is also highly relevant how the architecture produces these behaviors because its parameters are to be used on the diagnosis process. The better the model mimics human behavior, the more useful would be the information obtained from it.

Each individual computational cognitive model is obtained from a dual-mechanism cognitive architecture for the acquisition of verbal morphology in highly inflected languages like Spanish along children' development. A more detailed description of this architecture can be found in (Oliva et al., 2010). We describe below the instantiation of this architecture to fit adults' features and behavior in the verb inflection task:

- Mechanisms: The architecture is based on two general strategies: memory retrieval and analogy. Using these two initial mechanisms, the architecture is able to use the regular rules and the irregular exceptions just using the examples from the input vocabulary.
- Parameters: The mechanisms of the architecture are controlled by a series of parameters that give shape to its behavior. These parameters form three main groups: declarative memory parameters that control the retrieval of learned facts from memory (RT-retrieval threshold, ANS-noise introduced into the memory retrieval process, BLL-forgetting factor, A_0-initial activation); procedural memory parameters that control the learning and execution of rules (α) and the noise in the process of selecting a rule to execute (EGS); and grammatical processing parameters that control how the architecture deals with the different grammatical features (γ_m, controls the noise introduced into the perception of morphological features, C-PM, NP-PM and MTA-PM, which control the sensitivity of the model to each grammatical feature as conjugation, number-person and mood-time-aspect, respectively) when retrieving a verb form from memory.
- Representation: The architecture uses semantic and morphological information. Each verb form is represented by its meaning and some grammatical features such as conjugation, number, person, mood, tense or aspect in the declarative memory.
- Input vocabulary: The architecture uses the same 20 regular verbs and 20 irregular verbs in present and past tense, retrieved from the Reference Corpus of Current Spanish (RAE, 2012) and engaged in the target task.

The procedure used to make the architecture mimic participants' behavior lies in presenting to it randomly each of the 40 verbs in infinitive form and to ask for the present tense of the first person of singular or the past tense of the third person of singular, depending on the sentence pair.

2.5 Subject modeling profile

Our proposal is to obtain for each participant the set of parameter values of the computational cognitive architecture that best fit the behavior of that participant.

Type	Attribute	Range
Declarative Memory	RT	-0.02 ± (5*0.62)
	ANS	0.43 ± (5*0.34)
	BLL	0.40 ± (5*0.31)
	A_0	-0.02 ± (5*0.62)
Procedural Memory	α	0.20 ± (5*0.03)
	EGS	0.13 ± (5*0.46)
Grammatical Processing	γ_m	0.1 ± 0.5
	Conj-PM	-2.8 ± 5
	NP-PM	-3.6 ± 5
	MTA-PM	-3.0 ± 5

Table 3. Attributes and their range of values in the search space.

Procedure: This stage of the methodology requires the use of an optimization algorithm for obtaining the architecture´s parameter values that adjust to the user´s behavior. We used an evolutionary strategy (Beyer and Schwefel, 2002), where the genotype consists of the 9 parameters of the cognitive architecture mentioned above. To constrain the search space to psychologically plausible values we used the database proposed by (Wong et al., 2010) shown in Table 3.

Subset	Type	Attribute	Index
Behavioral data	Present Regular	% Correct-PresReg	1
		% Irregul-PresReg	2
		% NP-PresReg	3
		% MTA-PresReg	4
		% Other-PresReg	5
	Present Irregular	% Correct-PresReg	6
		% Irregul-PresReg	7
		% NP-PresReg	8
		% MTA-PresReg	9
		% Other-PresReg	10
	Past Regular	% Correct-PresReg	11
		% Irregul-PresReg	12
		% NP-PresReg	13
		% MTA-PresReg	14
		% Other-PresReg	15
	Past Irregular	% Correct-PresReg	16
		% Irregul-PresReg	17
		% NP-PresReg	18
		% MTA-PresReg	19
		% Other-PresReg	20
Cognitive data	Declarative Memory	RT	21
		ANS	22
		BLL	23
		A_0	24
	Procedural Memory	α	25
		EGS	26
	Grammatical Processing	γ_m	27
		Conj-PM	28
		NP-PM	29
		MTA-PM	30

Table 4. Attributes used by machine learning methods.

In order to model individuals with impairment, the range allowed for each of the parameters is defined as the average value ± five standard deviations (Thomas et al., 2003). Since dementia is an impairment happening in adulthood, when most verbs have been yet acquired, verbs in declarative memory have associated a default activation value equal to the forgetting factor (RT). The fitness function used was the minimum mean square error between the participant's error rate vector and the model's error rate vector and the operators were Gaussian mutation, an intermediate crossover operator and 1:5 ratio for the parent population and the offspring sizes.

Results: The behavioral profile of every participant at inflecting verb forms was modeled by the architecture. The parameter values for each participant's model were computed as the average value for 10 runs of the evolutionary strategy, with a stop criterion of 200 generations. The global correlation between the participants' and models' error vectors was of 0.92, showing a very high fitting degree. The values of these personalized cognitive model data could aid to determine the status of specific cognitive structures and processes. The efficiency of the modeling process is not taken account since time is not an important constraint in this application.

2.6 Application of machine learning techniques

The final stage of the methodology has a two-fold goal: a) applying different machine learning techniques to both the behavioral and cognitive model data and analyzing their respective informative and discriminant power, and b) comparing both kind of data and the combination of them in the diagnosis process. Variables used by machine learning techniques are shown in Table 4.

Variable weighting: Cognitive model data provided further information than behavioral data for discriminating between pAD and control participants. First, variables of both behavioral profile and cognitive model sources were ordered by five attribute weighting methods, given by RapidMiner (Mierswa et al, 2006), which weight variables according to different criteria. Table 5 presents the ranking, computed by each method (Information Gain (I.G), Correlation (C.), Chi-square (Chi-sq.), Rule weighting (R-W), SVM weighting (SVM-W)), and the average ranking for every variable. From this, we also calculated the average ranking for each information source and the global average ranking, seeking for statistical differences between sources.

Figure 1 shows these average rankings with their standard deviations. In this figure, the variables related to cognitive model data have been indexed from 1 to 10 referring indexes from 20 to 30 in Table 4.

Index	I.G.	C.	Chi^2	R-W	SVM-W	Avg.
1	11	12	13	14	16	13.2
2	27	26	30	25	28	27.2
3	28	25	26	30	26	27.0
4	26	20	25	24	25	24.0
5	16	19	20	19	17	18.2
6	10	13	15	12	14	12.8
7	2	3	9	5	7	5.2
8	29	27	28	26	29	27.8
9	7	2	4	6	8	5.4
10	21	28	21	29	23	24.4
11	17	10	8	7	4	9.2
12	30	29	27	28	30	28.8
13	25	24	29	27	27	26.4
14	22	14	17	12	12	15.4
15	23	30	18	21	21	22.0
16	9	4	3	8	9	6.6
17	12	15	10	13	13	12.6
18	24	23	19	23	22	22.2
19	1	5	2	2	11	4.2
20	18	16	14	22	15	17.0
21	4	9	1	1	2	3.4
22	5	6	11	4	3	5.8
23	8	17	17	15	20	15.4
24	14	8	7	11	6	9.2
25	19	18	23	20	24	20.8
26	13	11	14	10	10	11.6
27	3	1	6	3	1	2.8
28	15	22	16	16	18	17.4
29	20	21	22	21	19	20.6
30	6	7	5	9	5	6.4

Table 5. Attributes sorted by 5 different attributes weighting methods and average rank (Avg.). The Index field refers to attributes' index in Table 4.

Behavioral data show that the most relevant variables are mood, tense and aspect substitutions both in present and past tense forms of irregular verbs, overregularization in present tense and the percentage of correct past tense forms of irregular verbs. The group of behavioral data achieves an average ranking significantly lower ($p<0.05$) than cognitive model data using a two-tailed t-test.

As can be seen in Figure 1, among the group of cognitive model data, the four variables with the lowest ranks present an average ranking of 4.6 that stand out on the six remaining variables, which have an average ranking of 15.83.

Two of these four variables are related to the declarative memory (RT and ANS, with indexes 1 and 2 in abscises of Fig. 1, respectively) and the other two to the grammatical processing (γ_m and MTA-PM, with indexes 7 and 10 in abscises of Fig. 1, respectively). These results indicate that the major differences between pAD and controls rely on internal structures and mechanisms involving declarative memory affecting the retrieval of irregular forms and of their grammatical features as predicted in (Ullman, 2001).

Predictive power: The full set of combined data had better performance metrics than individual data sets to correctly classify pAD. We evaluated the predictive power of data by four machine learning algorithms.

The algorithms are applied on the behavioral data, cognitive model data and the combined set of behavioral and cognitive model data to assess the informative and discriminant role of every information source in the classification performance. The cognitive model feature set is made only by the internal variables of the model (9 parameters). The behavioral feature set consists of the variables collected from participants (20 parameters corresponding to six error categories for four combinations tense-form). The third feature set is a combination of the two previous sets.

Subset	Metric	SVM	NB	DT	NN
Behavioral data	Sensitivity	0.61	0.65	0.50	0.54
	Specificity	0.64	0.73	0.54	0.63
	PR+	1.69	2.41	1.09	1.46
	PR-	0.61	0.48	0.93	0.73
	AUC	0.62	0.68	0.52	0.60
Cognitive data	Sensitivity	0.71	0.68	0.62	0.61
	Specificity	0.77	0.77	0.63	0.74
	PR+	3.09	2.96	1.68	2.35
	PR-	0.38	0.42	0.60	0.53
	AUC	0.73	0.72	0.62	0.68
Full set	Sensitivity	0.86	0.75	0.71	0.85
	Specificity	0.81	0.79	0.79	0.81
	PR+	4.53	3.57	3.38	4.47
	PR-	0.17	0.32	0.37	0.19
	AUC	0.58	0.76	0.76	0.82

Table 6. Sensitivity, Specificity, Positive Probability Rate (PR+), Negative Probability Rate (PR-) and AUC results obtained by the four classification algorithms and the three feature sets.

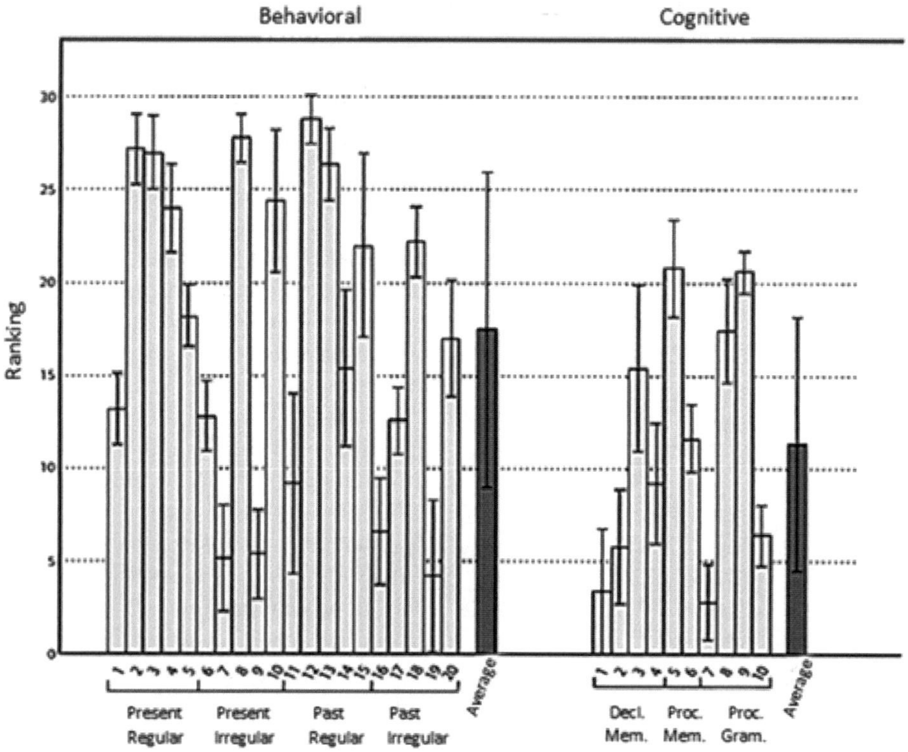

Figure 1. Average ranking and standard deviation for each attribute of the two attribute sets.

The classifiers used are a Support Vector Machine (SVM), a Naïve Bayes classifier (NB), a Neural Network (NN) and a Decision Tree (DT) (Mitchell, 1997). All the experiments were run under RapidMiner with its default parameter configuration (Mierswa et al, 2006). To evaluate each algorithm's performance, a leave-one-subject-out cross validation (LOOCV) was carried out and the sensitivity, specificity, positive and negative probability rates, and the Area Under Curve (AUC) metrics were computed.

Table 6 shows the results obtained for each one of the four classifiers and each feature set. A detailed analysis of all metrics confirms the importance of cognitive model data either alone or combined with behavioral features.

A one-way ANOVA test was carried out to check the differences among the performance of every classifier applied on each one of the three features set. Note that, given the preliminary nature of this study, the statistical power of them could be low. The SVM and DT classifiers improved statistically their sensitivity results ($p<0.05$) with the use of cognitive model variables regarding behavioral variables. Besides, DT and NN improved statistically their specificity results ($p<0.05$) with this feature set. The results are also better in sensitivity, specificity and AUC metrics for all classifiers with the use of complete feature set as compared to only behavioral feature set ($p<0.05$). The SVM and NN classifiers achieve sensitivity and specificity values higher than 80%, exceeding the threshold whereby a classification method can be considered a diagnosis support method (Plante and Vance, 1994). All these results confirm the relevant role of cognitive model variables supporting the diagnosis of pAD.

3 Discussion

In this paper we present a general methodology for the diagnosis of cognitive impairments when an inflectional verb task is carried out and we apply it to the particular case of pAD. The performed study corroborates the underlying hypothesis that computational cognitive modeling of a subject performing that inflection task provides a more charcharacteristic and discriminant information than only behavioral information extracted from neuropsychological tests. In spite of the low number of patients and types of verbs used, the results obtained in this preliminary study allow to identify significant differences useful for analyzing the relation between pAD and the verb morphology in Spanish. Beside, computational cognitive modeling could be a useful tool to have some kind of access to the processes that underlie normal and impaired behavior and this information could support the diagnosis process.

The average results of the five attribute weighting techniques rank informative ability of cognitive modeling variables above behavioral variables for discriminating pAD from control subjects when all of them perform an inflectional verb task. Besides, the full set of both cognitive modeling and behavioral variables lead to classifiers that improve sensitivity, specificity and AUC in comparison to only behavioral variables. All the results confirm the cross-linguistic generality of the pattern found in English an Italian: pAD patients are spared at processing regular inflected forms but impaired at irregular forms.

The methodology allows an individualized cognitive modeling for each subject and the parameter values obtained from the model can provide some clues about the underlying areas or mechanisms affected by the disease and their level of effects. The methodology has shown its successful application to cognitive impairments directly related to language like SLI (Oliva et al., 2013) as well as non-specific language impairment like pAD.

We conclude that the combination of machine-learning techniques with the information obtained through computational cognitive modeling could be a helpful methodology to support the diagnosis of pAD. Finally, it is important to note that this methodology is easily extensible to other languages, based on the language-independent nature of the mechanisms, parameters, representation and input vocabulary of the computational cognitive architecture used.

Acknowledgments

We are grateful to Mª Teresa Gutiérrez, Director of CRE-León for making available the behavioral data with Spanish-speaking adults, both with pAD and healthy ones. We also thank the financial support of FGCSIC, Obra Social La Caixa and CSIC, CP-Walker (DPI2012-39133-C03-01) and PIE-201350E070.

References

Anderson, JR. 2007. *How can the human mind occur in the physical universe?* Oxford University Press, New York.

Anderson, JR. and Lebiere, C. 1998. *The atomics components of thought.* Mahwah, NJ: Lawrence Erlbaum Associates.

Beyer, H. and Schwefel, H. 2002. Evolution strategies: A comprehensive introduction. *Natural Computing*, 1(1):3-52.

Bucks, R., Singh, S., Cuerden, J., and Wilcock, G. 2000. Analysis of spontaneous, conversational speech in dementia of Alzheimer type: Evaluation of an objective technique for analyzing lexical performance. *Aphasiology*, 14(1):71-91.

Cuetos, F., Martinez, T., Martinez, C., Izura, C., and Ellis, A. 2003. Lexical processing in Spanish patients with probable Alzheimer's Disease. *Cognitive Brain Research*, 17:549-561.

Cherktow, H. and Bub, D. 1990. Semantic memory loss in dementia of the Alzheimer's type. *Brain*, 113:397-417.

Folstein, M., Folstein, S., and McHugh, P. 1975. Mini-mental state. A practical method for grading the cognitive state of patients for the clinician. *Journal of Psychiatric Research*, 12(3):189-198.

Jarrold, W. L., Peintner, B., Yeh, E., Krasnow, R., Javitz, H., and Swan, G. 2010. Language analytics for assessing brain health: Cognitive impairment, depression and pre-symptomatic Alzheimer's disease. *Lecture Notes in Computer Science*, 6334: 299-307. Springer Berlin Heidelberg.

Iglesias, I., del Castillo, M.D., Serrano, J.I., and Oliva, J. 2012. A computational knowledge-based model for emulating human performance in the Iowa Gambling Task. *Neural Networks*, (33): 168-180.

Lobo, A., Esquerra,J., Gómez, F., Sala, J.M., Seva, A. (1979). El Mini-Exámen Cognoscitivo: un test sencillo y práctico para detectar alteraciones intelectuales en pacientes médicos. *Actas Luso Esp. Neurol. Psiquiatr.*, 3: 189-202.

Mierswa, I., Wurst, M., Klinkenberg, R., Scholz, M., and Euler, T. 2006. Yale: Rapid prototyping for complex data mining tasks. *Proceedings of the 12th ACM SIGKDD International Conference on Knowledge Discovery and Data Mining*, 935-940, NY, USA. ACM.

Mitchell, T. 1997. *Machine Learning*. McGraw-Hill.

Oliva, J., Serrano, J. I., Del Castillo, M. D., and Iglesias, A. 2010. Cognitive modeling of the acquisition of a highly inflected verbal system. *Proceedings of the*

10th International Conference on Cognitive Modeling, 181-186, Philadelphia, PA. Drexel University.

Oliva, J., Serrano, J., del Castillo, M., and Iglesias, A. 2013. Computational cognitive modeling for the diagnosis of Specific Language Impairment. *Proceedings of the EFMI-STC Data and Knowledge for Medical Support Systems Conference*, Praga.

Oliva, J., Ignacio Serrano, J.I., del Castillo, M.D., and Iglesias, A. 2014. A methodology for the characterization and diagnosis of cognitive impairments. Application to specific language impairment. *Artificial Intelligence in Medicine*, 61(2):89-96.

Pasquier, F. 1999. Early diagnosis of dementia: neupsychology. *Journal of Neurology*, 246:6-15.

Peña-Casanova, J., Monllau, A., Böhm, P., Blesa R., Aguilar, M., Sol, JM., Hernández, G. (2005). *Correlación cognitivo-funcional en la de demencia tipo Alzheimer: A propósito del Test Barcelona Abreviado*. Neurología 20: 4-8.

Pinker, S. and Prince, A. 1988. On language and connectionism: analysis of a distributed processing model of language acquisition. *Cognition*, 28:73-193.

Plante, E. and Vance, R. 1994. Selection of preschool language tests: A data-base approach. *Language, Speech and Hearing Services in School*, 25:15-24.

Serrano, JI., del Castillo, MD., and Iglesias, A. 2009. Dealing with written language semantics by a connectionist model of cognitive reading. *Neurocomputing*, 72(4-6):713-725.

Hart, S., and Semple, J.M. 1990. *Neuropsychology and the dementias*. Psychology Press

Stevens, S., Harvey, R., and Kelly, C. 1996. Characteristics of language performance in four groups of patients attending a memory clinic. *International Journal of Geriatric Psychiatry*, 11:973-982.

Taatgen, N. and Anderson, J. 2002. Why do children learn to say "broke", a model of learning the past tense without feedback? Cognition, 86:123-155.

Taler, V. and Phillips, N. 2008. Language performance in Alzheimer's disease and mild cognitive impairment: a comparative review. *Journal of Clinical Experimental Neuropsychology*, 30(5):501-556

Thomas, C., Keselj, V., Cercone, N., Rockwood, K., and Asp, E. 2005. Automatic detection and rating of dementia of Alzheimer type through lexical analysis of spontaneous speech. *Proceedings of IEEE ICMA*, 1569-1574.

Ullman, M. 2001. A neurocognitive perspective on language: the declarative/procedural model, *Nature Reviews Neuroscience*, 2 (10):717–726.

Ullman, M. 2004. Contributions of memory circuits to language: the declarative/procedural model. *Cognition*, 92:231-270.

Walenski, M., Sosta, K., Cappa, S., and Ullman, M. 2009. Deficits on irregular verbal morphology in Italian-speaking Alzheimer's disease patients. *Neuropsychologia*, 47:1245-1255.

Wong, T., Cokely, E., and Schooler, L. 2010. An online database of ACT-R parameters: Towards a transparent community-based approach to model development. *Proceedings fo ICCM - 2010 Tenth International Conference on Cognitive Modeling*, 282-286, Philadelphia, USA.

Recursive Neural Networks for Coding Therapist and Patient Behavior in Motivational Interviewing

Michael Tanana[1], Kevin Hallgren[2], Zac Imel[1], David Atkins[2], Padhraic Smyth[3], and Vivek Srikumar[4]
[1] Department of Educational Psychology, University of Utah, Salt Lake City, UT
[2] Department of Psychiatry and Behavioral Sciences, University of Washington, Seattle, Washington
[3] Department of Computer Science, University of California, Irvine, CA
[4] School of Computing, University of Utah, Salt Lake City, UT
michael.tanana@utah.edu khallgre@uw.edu zac.imel@utah.edu
datkins@u.washington.edu smyth@ics.uci.edu svivek@cs.utah.edu

Abstract

Motivational Interviewing (MI) is an efficacious treatment for substance use disorders and other problem behaviors (Lundahl and Burke, 2009). However, little is known about the specific mechanisms that drive therapeutic change. A growing body of research has focused on coding within-session language to better understand how therapist and patient language mutually influence each other and predict successful (or unsuccessful) treatment outcomes. These studies typically use human raters, requiring considerable financial, time, and training costs for conducting such research. This paper describes the development and testing of a recursive neural network (RNN) model for rating 78,977 therapist and patient talk turns across 356 MI sessions. We assessed the accuracy of RNNs in predicting human ratings for client speech and compared them to standard n-gram models. The RNN model showed improvement over ngram models for some codes, but overall, all of the models performed well below human reliability, demonstrating the difficulty of the task.

1 Introduction

1.1 Motivational Interviewing

Motivational Interviewing (MI) (Miller and Rollnick, 2012) is a counseling style that attempts to highlight and resolve patient ambivalence about behavioral change. To achieve these aims, MI theory emphasizes that therapists should use specific MI-consistent strategies, such as fostering collaboration rather than confrontation, emphasizing patient autonomy rather than therapist authority, and eliciting discussion of the factors that motivate patients to change or not change their behavior. During MI sessions, therapists are instructed to attend to patient *change talk* (i.e., language that indicates a desire, reason, or commitment to make a behavioral change), and *sustain talk* (i.e., language that indicates a desire, reason, or commitment against making a behavioral change). Therapists are further instructed to respond to such change and sustain talk in specific, MI-consistent manners. For example, therapists are instructed to frequently use open questions and to reflect patient language with the goal of eliciting change talk from patients. Likewise, therapists are instructed to minimize their use of behaviors such as confrontation, warning, and giving advice without permission.

MI researchers have developed several coding systems for identifying these types of patient and therapist language. The information provided by these MISC ratings often provides critical data for a variety of research and training purposes. For example, such coding data can be used to assess therapists' fidelity to using MI (e.g., based on the amount of MI-consistent and MI-inconsistent therapist behaviors), to understand the temporal relationships between therapist and patient behaviors (e.g., through sequential analysis of therapist and patient codes), or to understand how in-session behaviors predict out-of-session behavioral change (e.g., therapist and patient language predicting reductions in substance use). These coding systems typically require human coders to listen to psychotherapy sessions and manually label each therapist and patient utterance using codes derived from MI theory. For example, one of the most versatile but time consuming coding systems, the Motivation Interview-

Proceedings of the 2nd Workshop on Computational Linguistics and Clinical Psychology: From Linguistic Signal to Clinical Reality, pages 71–79,
Denver, Colorado, June 5, 2015.

ing Skill Code (Houck et al., 2012) assigns codes to every therapist and patient utterance (defined as a single idea within a section of speech) using over 30 different predefined codes (See examples below in Figure 1).

> **Counselor**: "How do you feel about your progress so far?" **(Open Question)**
> **Patient**: "Everyone's getting on me about my drinking." **(Follow-Neutral)**
> **Counselor**: "Kind of like a bunch of crows pecking at you." **(Complex Reflection)**
> **Patient**: "I'm not sure I can finish treatment." **(Sustain Talk)**
> **Counselor**: "You're not sure if you can finish treatment." **(Simple Reflection)**
> **Patient**: "I drank a couple of times this week when I was with my brother **(Sustain Talk)**. I want to quit so badly **(Change Talk)**, but I don't think I can do it." **(Sustain Talk)**

Figure 1: Example of MISC codes from (Houck et al., 2012)

1.2 Machine Learning and Psychotherapy Coding

There are few studies that have used machine learning to assess therapist and patient behavior in psychotherapy sessions. Most of these methods have relied heavily on n-grams (i.e., specific words or phrases) and have used a bag of words approach where the temporal ordering of n-grams within an utterance is mostly ignored, thereby losing information about the functional relationships between words.

For example (Atkins et al., 2014) used topic modeling to predict utterance-level MISC codes in 148 MI sessions obtained from studies of primary care providers in public safety net hospitals and brief interventions for college student drinking. The topic models were able to predict human ratings of utterances with high accuracy for many codes, such as open and closed questions or simple and complex reflections (Cohen's kappa all >0.50). However, the topic models struggled to accurately predict other codes, such as patient *change talk* and *sustain talk* (Cohen's kappa all <0.25). The limitations in the prediction model were attributed to multiple sources, including low inter-rater agreement among the human raters, the limited information provided within the relatively small number of n-grams contained in single utterances, the inability to incorporate the local context of the conversation in the predictive model, and the lack of a uniform linguistic style associated with some codes (e.g., questions typically contain keywords such as "what" or "how", but *change talk* does not).

Using a subset of the same data, (Can et al., 2012) used multiple linguistic features to predict utterance-level therapist reflections with reasonably high accuracy, F1 = 0.80. Specifically, Can et al. used N-grams (i.e., specific words and phrases), similarity features (i.e., overlapping N-grams between therapist utterances and patient utterances that preceded), and contextual meta-features (i.e., words in the surrounding text) with a maximum-entropy Markov model and found improved performance relative to models that did not include similarity or meta-features. However, this study did not test the prediction of language categories that were difficult to predict in Atkins et al., such as *change talk* and *sustain talk*.

1.3 Aims

An important problem with the word and n-gram based models is that they do not account for syntactic and semantic properties of the text. In this work, we study the question of using dense vector features and their compositions to address this issue

To our awareness, no research to date has tested the use of recursive neural networks (RNNs) for predicting MISC codes. It is possible that a model capturing semantic and syntactic similarity in text can perform better than n-gram models in identifying reflections in MI sessions. The present study aimed to test (1) whether recursive neural networks (RNNs) (Socher, 2014) can be used to predict utterance-level patient MISC codes and (2) whether RNNs can improve the prediction accuracy of these codes over n-gram models.

Following the basic procedure described in (Socher, 2014), we developed a Recursive Neural

Network model to achieve these aims. We used the Stanford parser (Klein and Manning, 2003) to create parse trees that modeled the language structure of patient and therapist utterances. These sentence-level models were then used as input into a Maximum Entropy Markov Model (MEMM), a type of sequence model that uses the sentence and surrounding context to predict MISC codes. The recursive neural networks were designed using the 'standard' model (Socher et al., 2011) with a single weight matrix to combine each node in the tree.

We tested both a standard RNN model and an RNN that utilized a dependency parsing of the sentence. Once a final model was tuned, the performance of each model predicting *change talk* and *sustain talk* codes was examined by comparing RNNs with an n-gram based model using cross-validation.

The main goals of this paper are to

1. Define the challenging and interesting problem of identifying client *change* and *sustain talk* in psychotherapy transcripts.
2. Explore and evaluate methods of using continuous word representations to identify these types of utterances and
3. Propose future directions for improving the performance of these models

2 Data

We used the dataset constructed as part of a collaborative project between psychologists at the University of Utah and the University of Washington and computer scientists and engineers at the University of California, Irvine and University of Southern California. The dataset consists of 356 psychotherapy sessions from 6 different studies of MI, including the 5 studies (148 sessions) reported in (Atkins et al., 2014). The original studies were designed to assess the effectiveness of MI at a public safetynet hospital (Roy-Byrne et al., 2014), the efficacy of training clinicians in using MI (Baer et al., 2009), and the efficacy of using MI to reduce college student drinking (Tollison et al., 2008; Neighbors et al., 2012; Lee et al., 2013; Lee et al., 2014). All sessions have utterance level MISC ratings totaling near 268,000 utterances in 78,977 talk turns. A subset of sessions was coded by multiple raters to estimate inter-rater reliability, which serves as a theoretical lower-bound for the predictive performance.

3 Modeling MISC Codes

3.1 Sequence Labeling

All of the models attempted to correctly label utterances as a single sequence. For example, a patient may speak two or three times in a row, then the therapist may speak once. Each utterance code is predicted by the preceding utterance label, regardless of the speaker. Both patient and therapist utterances were combined into this sequence model.

All sequence models were Maximum Entropy Markov Models (MEMM)(McCallum and Freitag, 2000). At test time, the sequences for the codes were inferred using the Viterbi algorithm. The models all differed in their feature inputs into the MEMM. The N-gram model used sparse input vectors representing the presence of the various unigrams, bigrams and trigrams in each utterance. The RNN models used the final sentence vector as the input into the MEMM model. The RNN models were allowed to learn from the mistakes in the MEMM models through backpropogation.

Even though the purpose of this model was to predict patient change and sustain talk, we attempted to predict all codes in the sequence to assist in the task due to the relationship between change talk, sustain talk, and other MISC codes. Other codes identified by the models included reflect, affirm, giving information, facilitate, open questions, closed questions, advise, confront, and follow-neutral (See (Houck et al., 2012)).

It should be noted that the MEMM models only used the previous utterance codes (or predicted codes) and the current utterance for feature inputs. We were attempting in this study to identify the best sentence model. At a later point in time, similar work will be done testing various iterations of sequence models to find the optimal version, after the best sentence level model has been chosen. One of the reasons for choosing a MEMM over a conditional random field was to allow for joint training of the RNN models and the sequence model (with a MEMM, it is easy to backpropogate errors from the sequence model to the sentence model).

3.2 Word Based Features

Our first feature set for utterances is defined using indicators for n-grams. In all cases, the speaker of the utterance (patient or therapist) was considered to be known. That is, the models only had to distinguish between codes applicable for each speaker role and did not have to distinguish the roles of the speakers as patient or therapist. We trained two different models – one that uses indicators for only unigrams in the utterance and the second that uses indicators for unigrams, bigrams and trigrams in the utterance.

3.3 Recursive Neural Network

Our second feature set uses recursive neural network (RNN) models, which are variants of the ideas presented in (Socher, 2014). The models were initialized with word vectors (i.e., numeric representations of word tokens) that were pre-trained using word vectors generated by the Glove model (Pennington et al., 2014). The RNNs in this paper relied mostly on the standard model for combining nodes of a recursive tree. For example, for combining word vector 1 a_1 (e.g., numeric representation of "hate") and word vector 2 a_2 (e.g., numeric representation of "hangovers"), the two vectors are multiplied through a weight matrix W_m that is shared across the tree in order to combine the individual words (e.g., "hate" and "hangovers") into a new vector that combines the meaning of both inputs, $a_{1,2}$ (e.g., "hate hangovers"). This is performed through the function:

$$p_{1,2} = tanh\left(W_m \begin{bmatrix} a_1 \\ a_2 \end{bmatrix} + b\right)$$

where a_1,a_2 and $p_{1,2}$ are all $\mathbb{R}^{dx1}$ where d is dimensionality value for the word vectors that is chosen by the researcher. Typically, several sizes of word vectors are tried to discover the optimal length for different types of problems. Based on cross-validated comparisons of different vector lengths, 50 dimensional word vectors were found to have the best overall performance and were used in the present study. Importantly, the non-linearity of hypertangent is used, which constrains the outputs to be between -1 and +1.

The top level vector of the RNN, which represents the whole linguistic utterance, was used as input into a MEMM to combine individual utterances with information from the surrounding linguistic context.

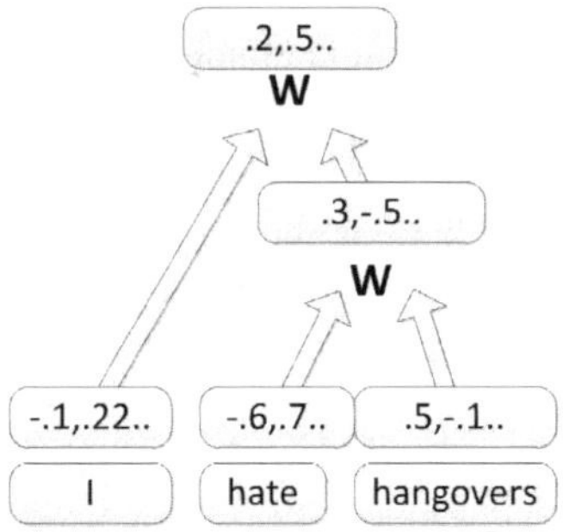

Figure 2: RNN Model. Each level of the parse tree is represented by a vector of 50 numeric values. Higher-level phrases and subphrases are modeled by multiplying the child node vectors through a weight matrix W_m.

The learning utilized backpropagation through structure (Goller and Kuchler, 1996). In other words, errors made at the top of the tree structure gave information that allowed the parameters lower in the model to learn, improving prediction accuracy. Weight updates were performed using adagrad with the diagonal variant (see Technical Appendix)(Duchi et al., 2011). The advantage of this weight update method is that it allows the model to learn faster for more rare words and to learn more slowly for frequently seen words.

3.4 Dependency RNN

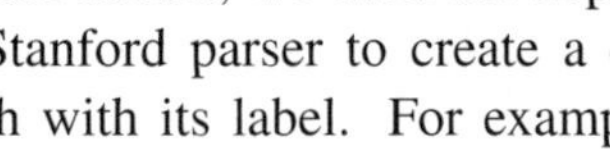

Figure 3: Example Dependency Parse

The final feature vector we tested was based on (Socher et al., 2014), with some important differences. In our model, we used the dependency tree from the Stanford parser to create a collection of edges, each with its label. For example, in figure 3 the dependency parse can be thought of as having three node with two labeled edges. The edge between "I" and "hate" has the label *nsubj* for nominal subject. In our dependency RNN we multiply the word vectors for "I" (the child node) and "Hate" (the parent node) through a weight matrix that is specific to the label *nominal subject*.

The model cycles through all of the edges in the dependency tree, then sums the output vectors. After summing, a hypertangent nonlinearity is applied to get the final feature vector for the sentence. Formally, this can be written as follows:

$$p_s = tanh\left(\sum\nolimits_{(p,c,\ell)\in D(s)} W_\ell \begin{bmatrix} a_p \\ a_c \end{bmatrix} + b\right)$$

a_p is the parent word vector and a_c is the child word vector. In this case, W_ℓ is the weight matrix specific to the dependency relationship for that specific label. The model sums over all parent p, child c and label ℓ triads in the dependency parse of the sentence ($D(s)$) and then adds an intercept vector b. The weight matrix is initialized to the shared weight matrix from the pre-trained standard RNN, but then is allowed to learn through backpropagation. The final model combines the output of the standard RNN and the dependency RNN as adjacent vectors. Both models share their word vectors and learn these vectors jointly.

4 Evaluation

To evaluate the performance of the RNN and n-gram models we compared precision (i.e., proportion of model-derived codes that matched human raters), recall (i.e., proportion of human-rated codes that were correctly identified by the model), and F1 scores (i.e., the harmonic mean of precision and recall) for each model. The current results are an early stage in the process toward developing a final model. As such, all models were evaluated using 5 fold cross validation on the section of the dataset that is designated as training data (which is two thirds of the total dataset). The cross validation subsets were divided by session (so each session could only occur in one or the other subsets). The testing section of the data will be used at a later date when the modeling process is complete.

5 Results

5.1 Prediction Accuracy

When predicting change talk (see table 1), the models varied in their performance. Unigram-only and unigram, bigram, and trigram models had F1 scores of 0.17 and 0.21, respectively. The standard RNN had a much lower F1 score of 0.06. The dependency RNN outperformed both the n-gram models and the standard RNN on F1 score (0.22). While the dependency RNN performed best on F1 score and precision, the Uni,Bi and tri-gram model tied for recall of change talk. These values were all relatively low compared to the theoretical upper bound of predictive performance based on the estimated human agreement, F1 = 0.61.

Table 1: Cross Validation Results: Change Talk

Model	Precision	Recall	F1
Uni-gram	.24	.13	.17
Uni,Bi,Tri-Gram	.28	**.18**	.21
Standard RNN	.15	.03	.06
Dependency RNN	**.29**	**.18**	**.22**
Human Agreement	.73	.42	.61

Table 2: Cross Validation Results: Sustain Talk

Model	Precision	Recall	F1
Uni-gram	.26	.20	.22
Uni,Bi,Tri-Gram	**.33**	.20	**.24**
Standard RNN	.19	**.23**	.21
Dependency RNN	.26	.19	.22
Human Agreement	.66	.53	.59

When predicting sustain talk (table 2), the unigram model, unigram, bigram, and trigram model, and the standard RNN all performed similarly in terms of F1 scores (F1 = 0.21 to 0.24), with the Uni, Bi and trigram model performing the best (.24). The Standard RNN had the highest recall (.23), but had the lowest precision (.19) As with change talk, all models had relatively low F1 scores compared to the F1 scores between human raters, F1 = 0.59.

5.2 Examples

Figure 4 shows two example sentences from the test sample of the dataset, one which was predicted correctly from the dependency RNN and one that was predicted incorrectly. Below each sentence is a chart with the predicted probability that it was change talk, sustain talk or follow-neutral (i.e., neither change talk or sustain talk). In the first example, the dependency RNN did well at identifying a simple change statement. Similarly simple utterances, such as "I don't want to drink anymore" or "I enjoy drinking alcohol" were typically coded correctly as change talk or sustain talk. But more complicated utterances, like the second example in figure 4 were less likely to be coded correctly. (Note that the second utterance depends more than the context of previous statements in the conversation, which involved the patient discussing reasons for smoking marijuana.)

"Because I don't really want to have to smoke more" (Change Talk)

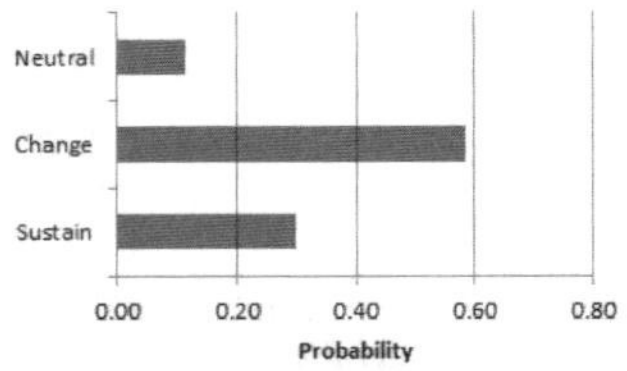

"I don't have to lay there in bed for three hours staring at the ceiling being like why am I still awake" (Sustain Talk)

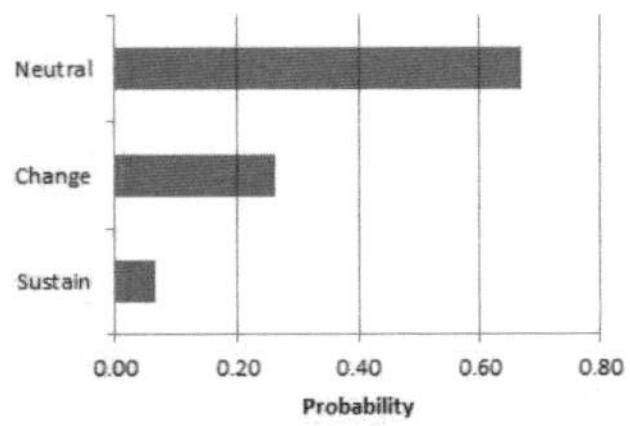

Figure 4: Example Codings

6 Conclusions

In general, predicting change and sustain talk is a non-trivial task for machine learning. It involves a subtle understanding of the context of a phrase and involves more than just the words in a single sentence. These early models are able to correctly identifying many statements as change talk or sustain talk, particularly for sentences with simple structures such as "I want to stop drinking". However, these models appear have a harder time with sentences that are longer and have greater complexity and sentences that require more contextual information based on previous statements. These initial results show that our dependency RNN has the ability to outperform n-gram models on identifying client change talk, but this performance gain did not apply to sustain talk.

As shown in (Can et al., 2012) and (Atkins et al., 2014), machine learning techniques are able to reliably identify important linguistic features in MI. This study represents an initial attempt at predicting the more difficult-to-identify patient behaviors, which are central to much of the research on MI. More work is needed to improve these models, and it is likely that performance could be improved by going beyond word counting models, for example, by using the syntactic structure of sentences as well as the context of surrounding utterances.

NLP applications have been successful in areas in which human annotators can clearly label the construct of interest (e.g., sentiment in movie reviews(Socher et al., 2013b), classifying news articles(Rubin et al., 2012)). Psychotherapy generally and 'change talk' within MI specifically are often concerned with latent psychological states of human experience. Verbalizations of reducing drug use are hypothesized to be observed indicators of a patient's inclination to change their behavior and is mutually dependent on both their own previous linguistic behavior as well as the therapist's. This is a challenging, new arena for NLP application and development, and one that will only be successful through the tight collaboration of NLP researchers and domain experts.

6.1 Limitations

There were some important limitations to this initial study. First, we have not yet systematically explored all of the possible options for discrete word models. For example, one could use the dependency tree to create non-sequential n-grams that capture longer range dependencies than traditional n-grams. We acknowledge that part of the advantage given to the RNN is the information the dependency tree provides and that it is possible for discrete word models to use this type of information as well. Second, not all of the possible combinations of word dimensions and word models were tried. Because of limitations in available compute capacity, only promising combinations were tested. Third, there was a moderate degree of disagreement between human raters. These human ratings were required for training each method and were used as the criterion for classifying correct or incorrect ratings, and error in these ratings limits the performance of the models.

References

David C Atkins, Mark Steyvers, Zac E Imel, and Padhraic Smyth. 2014. Scaling up the evaluation of psychotherapy: evaluating motivational interviewing fidelity via statistical text classification. *Implementation science : IS*, 9(1):49, January.

John S. Baer, Elizabeth a. Wells, David B. Rosengren, Bryan Hartzler, Blair Beadnell, and Chris Dunn. 2009. Agency context and tailored training in technology transfer: A pilot evaluation of motivational interviewing training for community counselors. *Journal of Substance Abuse Treatment*, 37(2):191–202.

Leon Bottou. 2014. From Machine Learning to Machine Reasoning. *Machine Learning*, 94(2):133–149.

Dogan Can, Panayiotis G. Georgiou, David C Atkins, and Shrikanth Narayanan. 2012. A Case Study: Detecting Counselor Reflections in Psychotherapy for Addictions using Linguistic Features. In *Proceedings of InterSpeech*.

John Duchi, E Hazan, and Y Singer. 2011. Adaptive subgradient methods for online learning and stochastic optimization. *The Journal of Machine Learning ...*, pages 1–40.

Christoph Goller and Andreas Kuchler. 1996. Learning task-dependent distributed representations by backpropagation through structure. *Proceedings of International Conference on Neural Networks (ICNN'96)*, 1.

Jon. M. Houck, TheresaB. Moyers, William R. Miller, Lisa. H. Glynn, and Kevin. A. Hallgren. 2012. ELICIT Motivational Interviewing Skill Code (MISC) 2.5 coding manual. Technical report, Unpublished coding manual, University of New Mexico.

Dan Klein and CD Manning. 2003. Accurate unlexicalized parsing. In *ACL '03 Proceedings of the 41st Annual Meeting on Association for Computational Linguistics - Volume 1*, pages 423–430.

Christine M Lee, Jason R Kilmer, Clayton Neighbors, David C Atkins, Cheng Zheng, Denise D Walker, and Mary E Larimer. 2013. Indicated Prevention for College Student Marijuana Use: A Randomized Controlled Trial. *Journal of consulting and clinical psychology*, 81(4):702–709.

Christine M Lee, Clayton Neighbors, Melissa a Lewis, Debra Kaysen, Angela Mittmann, Irene M Geisner, David C Atkins, Cheng Zheng, Lisa a Garberson, Jason R Kilmer, and Mary E Larimer. 2014. Randomized controlled trial of a Spring Break intervention to reduce high-risk drinking. *Journal of consulting and clinical psychology*, 82(2):189–201.

Brad W. Lundahl and Brian L. Burke. 2009. The effectiveness and applicability of motivational interviewing: A practice-friendly review of four meta-analyses.

Andrew McCallum and Dayne Freitag. 2000. Maximum entropy markov models for information extraction and segmentation. *Proceedings of the 17th International Conference on Machine Learning*, pages 591–598.

William R. Miller and Stephen Rollnick. 2012. *Motivational Interviewing, Third Edition: Helping People Change*. The Guilford Press, New York, NY, third edit edition.

Clayton Neighbors, Christine M. Lee, David C. Atkins, Melissa a. Lewis, Debra Kaysen, Angela Mittmann, Nicole Fossos, Irene M. Geisner, Cheng Zheng, and Mary E. Larimer. 2012. A randomized controlled trial of event-specific prevention strategies for reducing problematic drinking associated with 21st birthday celebrations. *Journal of Consulting and Clinical Psychology*, 80(5):850–862.

Jeffrey Pennington, Richard Socher, and Christopher D Manning. 2014. GloVe: Global Vectors for Word Representation. In *Proceedings of the 2014 Conference on Empirical Methods in Natural Language Processing*.

Peter Roy-Byrne, Kristin Bumgardner, Antoinette Krupski, Chris Dunn, Richard Ries, Dennis Donovan, Imara I. West, Charles Maynard, David C. Atkins, Meredith C. Graves, Jutta M. Joesch, and Gary a. Zarkin. 2014. Brief Intervention for Problem Drug Use in Safety-Net Primary Care Settings. *Jama*, 312(5):492.

Timothy N. Rubin, America Chambers, Padhraic Smyth, and Mark Steyvers. 2012. Statistical topic models for multi-label document classification. *Machine Learning*, 88:157–208.

Richard Socher, Jeffrey Pennington, and EH Huang. 2011. Semi-supervised recursive autoencoders for predicting sentiment distributions. *Proceedings of the EMNLP*, (ii):151–161.

Richard Socher, John Bauer, CD Manning, and AY Ng. 2013a. Parsing with compositional vector grammars. In *Proceedings of the ACL conference*.

Richard Socher, Alex Perelygin, Jean Y Wu, Jason Chuang, Christopher D. Manning, Andrew Y. Ng, and C. Potts. 2013b. Recursive deep models for semantic compositionality over a sentiment treebank. *Proceedings of the Conference on Empirical Methods*.

Richard Socher, Andrej Karpathy, Quoc V Le, Christopher D Manning, and Andrew Y Ng. 2014. Grounded

Compositional Semantics for Finding and Describing Images with Sentences. *Transactions of the Association for Computational Linguistics (TACL)*, 2:207–218.

Richard Socher. 2014. *Richard Socher August 2014*. Dissertation, Stanford.

Sean J. Tollison, Christine M. Lee, Clayton Neighbors, Teryl a. Neil, Nichole D. Olson, and Mary E. Larimer. 2008. Questions and Reflections: The Use of Motivational Interviewing Microskills in a Peer-Led Brief Alcohol Intervention for College Students. *Behavior Therapy*, 39:183–194.

7 Technical Appendix

7.1 General Details on Learning

The loss function for all outputs o was: $E = \frac{1}{2}\sum_{o}(t_o - y_o)^2$. All of the weights were given random initialization between -.001 and .001. The selection of all hyper-parameters including ada-grad learning rate, weight decay and word vector size were chosen using 5 fold cross validation in the training set of data. As mentioned in the paper, these results will be tested on a third of the data reserved for testing at a later stage in this process when we have selected a final set of models. The optimal learning rate for the RNN models was .1, and the optimal weight decay was 1×10^{-7}. It should be noted that selection of hyperparameters had a major impact on the success of the RNN models. Different learning rates would often result in RNN models that performed half as well as the optimal models.

All models were pre-trained on the general psych corpus (The corpus is maintained and updated by the Alexander Street Press (http://alexanderstreet.com/) and made available via library subscription) using an idea from (Bottou, 2014) called a corrupted frame classifier. The idea is to try to get the model to predict which parts of its parse tree are 'real' sentences and which ones are 'corrupted', that is, one word has been replaced with a random word. Early testing found this unsupervised pre-training significantly improves the performance of the final models.

7.2 Ada-Grad

The training for both the Recursive Neural Nets and the Maximum Entropy Markov Models in this paper utilize stochastic gradient descent, based on common conventions in the machine learning literature, with one important exception. We used the adaptive gradient descent algorithm to adjust our learning rate (Duchi et al., 2011). We opted to use the diagonal variant for simplicity and conservation of memory. The Ada-grad variant to stochastic gradient descent, basically adapts the change in the gradient so that parameters that have many updates will update more slowly over time. Whereas, the parameters that have very few updates will make larger changes. It is obvious that this is advantageous given the fact that in RNN's, the main weight parameters might update on every case, whereas certain word vectors may only have a couple of presentation of an entire corpus. The classic weight update for stochastic gradient descent is $\theta_{t+1} = \theta_t - \alpha G_t$ Where θ are the weights that are being estimated and α is the learning rate. G_t is the gradient at time t. For Ada-grad, we just need to save a running total of the squared gradient, elementwise (we call it γ here):

$$\gamma_t = \gamma_{t-1} + G_t^2$$

And then we add an adjustment to the update step (again, elementwise). Divide the gradient by the square root of the running total sum of squared gradients:

$$\theta_{t+1} = \theta_t - \alpha_t \frac{G_t}{\sqrt{\gamma_t} + \beta}$$

Where β is a constant.

7.3 Notes on Code

Most of the code for this project was written specifically for this problem, but some additional libraries were used. All matrix operations used the Universal Java Matrix Package: http://sourceforge.net/projects/ujmp/files/. Some spell checking was required of some of the data and the open source Suggester was used: http://www.softcorporation.com/products/suggester/ . Version 3.2 of the Stanford parser was used to create the parse trees for the RNN's. (Klein and Manning, 2003; Socher et al., 2013a)

Putting Feelings into Words: Cross-Linguistic Markers of the Referential Process

Sean M. Murphy
New York Psychoanalytic Society and Institute
247 East 82nd Street
New York, NY 10028, USA
smurphy1@gmail.com

Bernard Maskit
Mathematics Department
Stony Brook University
Stony Brook, NY 11794, USA
daap@optoline.net

Wilma Bucci
Derner Institute
Adelphi University
Garden City, NY 11530, USA
wbucci@optonline.net

Abstract

The use of language to convey emotional experience is of significant importance to the process of psychotherapy, the diagnosis of problems with emotion and memory, and more generally to any communication that aims to evoke a feeling in the recipient. Bucci's theory of *the referential process* (1997) concerns three phases whereby a person activates emotional, or bodily experience (*Arousal Phase*), conveys the images and events associated with it (*Symbolizing Phase*), and reconsiders them (*Reorganizing Phase*). The Symbolizing Phase is the major focus of this study and is operationalized by a measure called *referential activity* (RA) based on judges' ratings of the concreteness, specificity, clarity and imagery of language style. Computational models of RA have previously been created in several languages, however, due to the complexity of modeling RA, different modeling strategies have been employed for each language and common features that predict RA across languages are not well understood. Working from previous computational models developed in English and Italian, this study specifies a new model of predictors common to both languages that correlates between r = .36 and.45 with RA. The components identified support the construct validity of the referential process and may facilitate the development of measures in other languages.

1 Introduction

Emotional states are generally accompanied by the retrieval of specific images and events. Similar methods are used to activate emotional states in both research and clinical contexts. For example, appraisal researchers may ask a participant to describe an experience of being angry at oneself in as much vivid detail as possible (Ellsworth and Tong, 2006). Prompting retrieval of images and events also underlies imaginal exposure in treatments for Post Traumatic Stress Disorder (PTSD) and other anxiety disorders (Powers et al., 2010).

Bucci (1997) theorized that the process of putting sensory, visceral and emotional experiences into words requires connection of symbols (words) to non-verbal and non-discrete, analogic (or subsymbolic) information through what she terms the *referential process.*

1.1 The referential process.

Arousal Phase: According to the theory, in the Arousal Phase, material that cannot yet be described or thought of in verbal terms is activated. This may include bodily sensations, or plans for motor action. The speaker is often unsure of what to talk about and may shift loosely from association to association. Language may have greater disfluency (e.g. 'um', 'uh'), more false starts, or non-sequiturs. The proportion of disfluency in a text is used as a major indicator of the Arousal Phase.

Symbolizing Phase: As the activated material is processed it coalesces into a prototypic im-

Proceedings of the 2nd Workshop on Computational Linguistics and Clinical Psychology: From Linguistic Signal to Clinical Reality, pages 80–88,
Denver, Colorado, June 5, 2015. ©2015 Association for Computational Linguistics

age or plan for action. This is the preliminary part of the Symbolizing Phase, when the material is brought into symbolic form but is not yet expressed in language. The latter part of this phase is the expression of this material in words by telling about an image, or event. The language of this phase will tend to be more specific, will focus on describing a single idea or frame, will refer more to the concrete or sensate properties of things, and will tend to evoke imagery in the listener, or reader. This style of language has been operationalized by *referential activity* (RA), which is understood as the connection of words to nonverbal experience, including bodily and emotional experiences that are *subsymbolic*. This measure is the focus of the current study and will be discussed in greater detail below along with computational models of referential activity.

Reorganizing Phase: Once symbolically expressed, such ideas are open for reflection and reorganization which takes place during the Reorganizing Phase. The restructuring that occurs during this phase encourages psychological development, and can begin the referential process anew by raising new questions, thoughts or feelings in response to the revelations that have occurred. The language of this phase is marked by references to cognitive processes, logical operations and reasoning. Such references are operationalized by a dictionary of 'Reflection' words (REF) which is used as a measure of the reorganizing phase and is discussed in greater detail below and in Maskit et al. (2015, this conference).

1.2 Referential activity (RA).

Referential activity was first operationalized by Bucci through a scoring system whereby judges rate language segments on dimensions of concreteness, specificity, clarity and imagery. Each scale is scored from zero to ten. The four dimensions are significantly inter-correlated for most speakers and most texts and are understood as reflecting different aspects of the same general dimension. For this reason, the average of the four scales is taken as the overall referential activity (RA) score of the segment (Bucci et al., 2004). Using these four scales, raters are able to achieve excellent inter-rater reliability with standardized item alphas exceeding .90 (Bucci et al., 2004, p. 24). The RA scales (as defined above) have been used in many studies (e.g. Appelman, (2000); Bucci, (1984); Dodd & Bucci, (1987); Fretter, Bucci, Broitman, Silberschatz, & Curtis, J., (1994); Horowitz, et al. (1993); Jepson & Bucci (1999); Langs, Bucci, Udoff, Cramer, & Thomson, (1993); Watson, J., (1996); also see Samstag, (1997) for a review of dissertations utilizing these scales).

1.3 The referential process and psychotherapy process.

In order to function well in life we need to be able to connect our sensory and emotional experiences to the people and events of our life so that we can make the best possible judgments regarding how to respond. We need to take in new information and modify our understanding of the world and our relationships as we and our life situations change.

In talk therapies, Bucci argues that psychological change occurs through the referential process. In the Arousal Phase, activation of a problematic experience can be gradually tolerated as the relationship develops between therapist and patient. In the Symbolizing Phase, the person talks about an episode of life, a dream or fantasy that is connected to this problematic experience. The representation of the experience in share-able symbolic form allows for new information to be brought in and connected with it. Once shared, there is an opportunity for a Reorganizing Phase where the meaning of the events may be reconsidered and further explored.

1.4 Clinical studies of the referential process.

Clinical studies have demonstrated that measures of the referential process are meaningful predictors of good psychotherapy process and outcome. Bucci and Maskit (2007) showed that the referential activity of a series of sessions in a single case design of a psychoanalytic treatment had strong correlations with the process ratings of expert clinicians who read and scored these sessions. Higher RA in therapist process notes, understood as indicating greater emotional engagement of the therapist, was associated with better treatment outcome as assessed by independent raters (Bucci et al., 2012). Mariani et al. (2013) found that RA (measured by the Italian Weighted Referential Activity Dictionary IWRAD) increased over the course of three psychotherapy treatments that showed improvement in personality functioning.

1.5 RA as an indicator of episodic memory capability and impairment.

In their 2008 paper, Nelson, Moskowitz and Steiner found a robust correlation ($r_s(53) = .69, p < .001$) between a measure of narrativity and the WRAD in a sample of high school students talking about their most stressful time. In their paper, Nelson et al. (2008) noted the similarity between the "story-now grammar" of narratives (Clark, 1996; Fleischman, 1990) and Tulving's concept of episodic memory as "time travel" (1972). Maskit et al. (2014) directly compared WRAD with measures of episodic memory strength using data provided by Schacter and scored by Addis, Wong and Schacter (2008), and also found strong correlations between the two measures. In line with these findings WRAD has been shown to differentiate populations with impairments in episodic memory such as participants with Schizophrenia (Lewis et al., 2009) and with Alzheimer's dementia (Nelson and Polignano, 2009) from nonclinical controls.

1.6 Previous computational models of referential activity.

The first computerized model of RA was the Computerized Referential Activity (CRA) of Mergenthaler and Bucci (1999), based on modeling very high and very low RA scale scores. The technique used to develop this measure was refined to develop the second generation computer model, the Weighted Referential Activity Dictionary (WRAD) (Bucci and Maskit, 2006). The WRAD was developed through a process of modeling the frequency with which words appeared in texts at several levels of RA as scored by judges, producing a weighted dictionary. In comparison to the CRA the WRAD represents an improvement in the correlation between computerized and judge based RA scoring in six of the seven samples utilized to model and test the dictionary. Correlations between WRAD and judges scoring of RA ranged between $r = .38$ and $r = .60$ in these samples. A detailed explanation of the modeling procedure for the WRAD dictionary may be found in Bucci and Maskit (2006).

The WRAD is a weighted dictionary with weights lying between -1, for words used more frequently in low RA speech, and $+1$ for words used more frequently in high RA speech. The WRAD comprises 697 frequently used items, primarily function words, including personal pronouns such as 'she', conjunctions such as 'and', and articles such as 'the'. Because of the dominance of such extremely frequent function words, the dictionary covers approximately 85% of the tokens used in the sample from which the dictionary was derived.

The structure of the Italian language is different from that of English; thus modeling strategies based on a restricted number of core types was less successful when modeling referential activity in Italian. (See Mariani, Maskit, Bucci and De Coro, 2013). This led to a model that includes a much larger number of types (9596). The IWRAD covers approximately 97% of the tokens used in the sample from which the dictionary was derived and correlates between $r = .24$ and $r = .91$ with samples used to develop and test the model.

1.7 The need for understanding common predictors of RA across languages.

Successful computational models have been built for referential activity (RA) in several languages including: English (Bucci and Maskit, 2006); Italian (Mariani et al., 2013); Spanish (Roussos and O'Connel, 2005) and German (Ehrman, 1997); however, each model was built separately and without a common basis. The current study seeks to identify a model that may be applied across languages based on a common definition of the features associated with referential activity.

We address this question by identifying those predictors in English and Italian that are most strongly associated with RA scores and have shared meaning. We hope that this model will be validated in other languages and develop into a generalized model that may be applied across languages. The value of such a model is twofold. First, there is pragmatic value as we receive requests from psychotherapy researchers who are working in various languages for which no computational model exists.[1] Second, the development of a generalized model provides a unique opportunity to study the construct validity of the referential process. To the degree that we can describe how the process of putting feelings into words plays out across languages we will have a more accurate description of this basic psychological process.

2 Methods and Results

2.1 Spoken corpora.

This study utilized segments from the same corpora that were used to build the English (N=763 segments) and Italian (N=936 segments) Weighted Referential Activity Dictionaries. The segments in the English sample had an average length of 163 words (SD 115) and in the Italian sample had an average length of 83 words (SD 60). Both corpora included psychotherapy and other spoken narrative material such as interviews, monologues, early memories and stories told to pictures. These materials were reliably segmented and scored for referential activity by judges following instructions from Bucci et al. (2004) and in Italian following a translation of this manual by De Coro and Caviglia (2000). All of the texts were scored for the four RA scales by at least two trained raters who had achieved high inter-rater reliability. The average of the scales was taken as the RA score. Detailed descriptions of the composition of these samples and scoring procedures may be found in Bucci & Maskit (2006), for the English sample and Mariani et al. (2013), for the Italian sample.

For the current study both the English and Italian corpora were subdivided into training, testing and validation subsets. The training subset (English N=362, Italian N=472) was used to develop the model in this study and the test subset (English N=209, Italian N=272) was used to test interim models. The validation subset (English N=192, Italian N=192) was reserved for final validation of the model.

2.2 The Discourse Attributes Analysis Programs (DAAP) and (IDAAP).

The Discourse Attributes Analysis Program (DAAP) is a computer-based text analysis system designed by Bernard Maskit, whose features include the use of both weighted and unweighted dictionaries. The Italian version of the software differs mainly in its ability to handle accented letters from a variety of text formats. The English version of the software is publicly available at: https://github.com/DAAP/DAAP09.6

2.3 Existing referential process dictionaries.

The phases of the referential process are operationalized by three main measures: disfluency (Arousal Phase), referential activity (Symbolizing Phase), and reflection (Reorganizing Phase). In addition there are several other dictionary based measures that are routinely used in studies of the referential process. These dictionaries were created using standard procedures for computerized text analysis that involve compiling word lists for a large source of texts and selecting items based on agreement among judges following the conceptual definitions of the dictionaries which follow below. The dictionaries listed below were created independently in English and Italian except where otherwise indicated.

Disfluency (DF): A limited set of six items that people use when struggling to communicate such as 'um', 'uh', 'hmmm', etc. Disfluent language is also associated with cognitive load and effort in speech planning (Bortfeld et al., 2001). In addition to matching types in the disfluency dictionary DAAP also counts incomplete

[1] We have received requests for measures of referential activity in: Bulgarian, French, German, Hebrew, Mandarin, Norwegian, Polish and Portuguese.

words (indicated by transcribers using a dash), repeated words and repeated two word phrases as disfluencies.

Reflection (REF): A dictionary of 1436 words that concern how people think and communicate thoughts. This dictionary includes words referring to cognitive or logical functions, e.g., 'assume', 'think', 'plan'.

Affect (AFF): Words that concern how people feel and communicate feelings directly such as, 'angry', 'sad', and 'happy'. The global measure of these words is the 'Affect Sum' dictionary (AFFS 2452 words). These are further classified as 'Positive' (AFFP; 620 words), 'Negative' (AFFN; 1470 words) and 'Mixed' affect (AFFZ; 362 words) words. The definitions of positive and negative affect are self explanatory; mixed affect words are words that seem to have an affective or emotional loading, but are neither positive, nor negative, e.g., 'anticipate', 'overwhelmed', 'serious'.

Sensory Somatic (SENS): A set of 1936 words pertaining to bodily and or sensory experience, e.g., 'dizzy', 'eye', 'face', 'listen'.

Negation (NEG): A limited set of 26 items that people use when negating in communication. e.g., 'no', 'not', 'never'; this may be seen as a function of the logic mode. This dictionary was not created independently in Italian.

2.4 Test of automated translation of existing dictionaries.

In order to test how well dictionaries might work in direct translation by automated means, all of the dictionaries described above in English and Italian were translated using Google Translate (through Google Sheets). The translated dictionaries were then run on the corpora described above using the English and Italian versions of the DAAP. Tables 1 and 2 show the correlations of the native language to the translated dictionaries.

The translation of the dictionaries used here, based largely on content words including nouns, verbs and adjectives, showed moderate to strong correlations both from and to Italian. Though manual translation would likely show stronger results, these results indicate that even automated translation of these dictionaries shows good correspondence with the dictionaries created by native speakers. The two computational models of RA, which are more dominated by function words, though strongly correlated with Judges' RA in both languages (English $r(761) = .53, p < .001$; Italian $r(934) = .73, p < .001$) were only weakly correlated and in the opposite of the expected direction in Italian (as shown in Tables 1 and 2). The translated dictionaries were also weakly related to judge scored RA (English $r(761) = -.03, p = .363$; Italian $r(934) = .04, p = .130$). The difficulty of trans-

Dictionary	Correlation
Negative Affect	.75***
Positive Affect	.33***
Mixed Affect	.69***
Affect Sum	.66***
Reflection	.44***
Sensory Somatic	.62***
Disfluency[2]	.66***
WRAD & IWRAD-T	-.10**
Note: N=763; *p<.05; **p<.01; ***p<.001	

Table 1: Pearson's correlations of English DAAP dictionaries with translated Italian DAAP dictionaries (translated using Google Translate).

Dictionary	Correlation
Negative Affect	.27***
Positive Affect	.57***
Mixed Affect	.34***
Affect Sum	.40***
Reflection	.33***
Sensory Somatic	.40***
Disfluency	.23**
IWRAD & WRAD-T	.16***
Note: N=936; *p<.05; **p<.01; ***p<.001	

Table 2: Pearson's correlations of Italian DAAP dictionaries with translated English DAAP dictionaries (translated using Google Translate).

[2]Since there are core differences in typical words used as disfluencies in English, such as, 'like', and Italian, such as 'boh' the full dictionary in each language was compared to a common subset of lexical items, e.g., 'uh' and 'um'.

lating these dictionaries based on style rather than content underscore the need for the current study.

2.5 New model development.

In order to develop a more universal model of referential activity, impact scores were created for the current English and Italian WRAD dictionaries by multiplying the WRAD weight for each dictionary term by the frequency with which it occurred in the corpus from which the dictionary was derived. These lists were then sorted by this impact score and compared. Words in the top 50 of both lists that had shared translated meaning were selected. Finally, the word 'uno' (ranked 97) was added as the masculine of 'una' (ranked 13), the word 'mia' (ranked 86) was added as the feminine of 'mio' (ranked 44) and the word 'ed' (ranked 99) was added as an additional translation of the English 'and'. Table 3 below shows the selected words along with the proportion of the corpus each represents.[3]

2.6 New 'Universal Weighted Referential Activity Dictionary' (UWRAD) regression model.

All types[4] in Table 3 were entered into a regression model predicting the RA score for the Italian training set along with the following dictionaries translated to Italian from English using Google Translate: SENS, DF, REF, NEG, and AFFS. All entries that were significant at the .10 level or better were retained, all others were dropped. This left 'and', 'to', 'he / she', 'the', 'was', SENS and NEG in the final model shown in Table 4.

2.7 New model performance.

Table 5 shows the correlations of the UWRAD model with judge scored referential activity in each of the sub-samples of the two corpora.

[3]The number 50 was an arbitrary choice intended to include a high proportion of the positive predictors of RA in both languages.

[4]She / He was added as a single type all others were kept separate.

English	Proportion	Italian	Proportion
and	4.3%	e	2.7%
		ed	0.1%
		poi	0.6%
the	3.2%	il	1.1%
		le	0.6%
		gli	0.4%
		lo	0.5%
		i	0.5%
		la	1.6%
a	1.9%	un	1.8%
		una	1.2%
		uno	0.2%
my	0.8%	mio	0.5%
		mia	0.6%
all	0.3%	tutti	0.2%
from	0.2%	da	0.6%
to	2.9%	a	1.8%
		al	0.3%
		per	1%
in	1.3%	in	1.2%
she	2.1%	lei	0.4%
he	1.2%	lui	0.5%
they	0.7%	sono	1%
me	0.6%	mi	1.6%
		me	0.5%
there	0.5%	là	1.6%
		lì	0.2%
was	1.6%	era	0.6%
		ero	0.2%
had	0.6%	aveva	0.2%
		avevo	0.2%
	22%		**24%**

Table 3: Predictors of RA with shared translated meaning. These types were selected by comparing the top 50 positive predictors of referential activity in English and Italian from previous computational models.

As for the UWRAD's relation to other indices of the referential process, the model correlated $r(761) = -.38, p < .001$ with Reflection in English and $r(934) = -.28, p < .001$ in Italian. UWRAD also correlated $r(761) = -.16, p < .001$ with Disfluency[5] in English and

[5]Disfluency was modified for this comparison as discussed above by removing all language specific indicators.

	Dependent variable:
	RA Score
and	8.370***
	(2.240)
to	6.780**
	(2.580)
he / she	6.880†
	(3.910)
the	8.470***
	(2.060)
was	16.300**
	(6.120)
Sensory Somatic	6.120*
	(2.430)
Negation	−12.900***
	(2.140)
Constant	4.140***
	(0.180)
Observations	472
R^2	0.197
Adjusted R^2	0.185
Residual Std. Error	1.320 (df = 464)
F Statistic	16.200*** (df = 7; 464)
Note:	† p<.10; *p<.05; **p<.01; ***p<.001

Table 4: 'Universal Weighted Referential Activity' (UWRAD) model.

$r(934) = -.23, p < .001$ in Italian. This pattern of correlations, which is typically observed in studies of the referential process, indicate that the Arousal, Symbolizing and Reorganizing phases are distinct from one another[6] and thus provide support for the construct validity of the UWRAD as developed here.

[6]Correlations of Reflection and Disfluency were $r(761) = -.02, p = .567$ and $r(934) = .02, p = .571$, suggesting that these dimensions are orthogonal.

Sample	Correlation
English (N=736)	.43***
Training (n=362)	.41***
Testing (n=209)	.44***
Validation (n=192)	.45***
Italian (N=936)	.41***
Training (n=472)	.44***
Testing (n=272)	.38***
Validation (n=192)	.36***
Note: *p<.05; **p<.01; ***p<.001	

Table 5: Pearson's correlations of the 'Universal Weighted Referential Activity Dictionary' (UWRAD) with judge scored RA for all subsets in English and Italian

3 Discussion

This study identified a single model comprised of seven common components that accounted for 13% to 20% of the variance in judges' scores of referential activity in two languages. As this model was able to function in translation between English and Italian, which have quite different lexical structures, it holds promise to translate into other languages as well. Future research will explore this modeling strategy in additional languages by comparing the model identified here to the scoring of referential activity by native speakers in similar corpora to those utilized here. Future research will also test this model for stability in additional samples of English and Italian.

While this study shows promise to facilitate the development of computational models of referential activity in other languages it also represents an opportunity to better understand the construct of referential activity. We believe that the components identified by this model support the idea that referential activity represents the language of scene construction. As evidence, the model makes use of definite object references ('the') sensate and experience near content (Sensory Somatic), the movement of actors and objects ('to') and orientation in time ('was'), all of which are consistent with the detailed description of images and events. A higher density of 'and' suggests that such texts may be similarly dense in details and events which require connection to one another in the context of a scene.

The inclusion of the third person singular animate pronouns 'he' and 'she' is consistent with an emphasis on concrete immediate experience with other people as opposed to internal reflection and consideration which may be more likely to involve a more reflective or abstract point of view. Similarly, negations as strong negative predictors of RA suggest that when speakers are using high RA language they are not engaged in reconsideration and qualification involving logical operations.

Scene construction is consistent with the idea of the Symbolizing Phase of the referential process which suggests that our felt experience is most effectively conveyed by telling about the events and images that give rise to a feeling so that others may become engaged in the event in their own bodily, sensory and emotional experience. This basic function is central to communicating emotional experience to others, and to making sense of our own experience. Such a dimension is necessarily important for understanding emotion in interpersonal communication in clinical contexts such as psychotherapy and the diagnosis of problems with memory and emotion, and in non-clinical contexts such as inspiration in political speech, clarity in effective teaching, or connection in interpersonal relationships.

References

Donna Rose Addis, Alana T Wong, and Daniel L Schacter. 2008. Age-related changes in the episodic simulation of future events. *Psychological science*, 19(1):33–41, January.

Eva Appelman. 2000. Attachment experiences transformed into language. *American Journal of Orthopsychiatry*, 70(2):192–202.

H Bortfeld, S. D. Leon, J. E. Bloom, M. F. Schober, and S. E. Brennan. 2001. Disfluency rates in conversation: Effects of age, relationship, topic, role, and gender. *Language and Speech*, 44(2):123–147, June.

Wilma Bucci and Bernard Maskit. 2006. A weighted dictionary for referential activity. In James G. Shanahan, Yan Qu, and Janyce Wiebe, editors, *Computing attitude and affect in text: Theory and applications*, volume 20 of *The Information Retrieval Series*. Springer-Verlag, Berlin/Heidelberg.

Wilma Bucci and Bernard Maskit. 2007. Beneath the surface of the therapeutic interaction: the psychoanalytic method in modern dress. *Journal of the American Psychoanalytic Association*, 55(4):1355–1397, December.

Wilma Bucci, R. Kabasakalian-McKay, and The RA Research Groups. 2004. Scoring Referential Activity instructions for use with transcripts of spoken texts.

Wilma Bucci, Bernard Maskit, and Leon Hoffman. 2012. Objective measures of subjective experience: the use of therapist notes in process-outcome research. *Psychodynamic psychiatry*, 40(2):303–40, June.

Wilma Bucci. 1984. Linking words and things: Basic processes and individual variation. *Cognition*, 17(2):137–153, July.

Wilma Bucci. 1997. *Psychoanalysis and cognitive science: A multiple code theory.* Guilford Press, New York, NY, US.

Herbert H. Clark. 1996. *Using language.* Cambridge University Press, Cambridge.

A. De Coro and G. Caviglia. 2000. La valutazione dell'Attivita' Referenziale.

Michael Dodd and Wilma Bucci. 1987. The relationship of cognition and affect in the orientation process. *Cognition*, 27(1):53–71, October.

Susanne Ehrman. 1997. *Computer measures of the cycles model: The german version.* Ph.D. thesis, Adelphi University.

Phoebe C Ellsworth and Eddie M W Tong. 2006. What does it mean to be angry at yourself? Categories, appraisals, and the problem of language. *Emotion (Washington, D.C.)*, 6(4):572–86, November.

Suzanne Fleischman. 1990. *Tense and narrativity: From medieval performance to modern fiction.* Austin: University of Texas Press.

Polly Fretter, Wilma Bucci, Jessica Broitman, George Silberschatz, and John Curtis. 1994. How the Patient's Plan Relates to the Concept of Transference. *Psychotherapy Research*, 4(1):58–72, January.

Mardi J. Horowitz, Charles Stinson, Deborah Curtis, and Mary Ewert. 1993. Topics and signs: Defensive control of emotional expression. *Journal of Consulting and Clinical Psychology*, 61(3):421–430.

Lisa Jepson and Wilma Bucci. 1999. Object relations and referential activity in physically abused adolescents. *Adolescence*, 34:780–792.

Robert J. Langs, Wilma Bucci, Andrea L. Udoff, Gail Cramer, and Lenore Thomson. 1993. Two methods of assessing unconscious communication in psychotherapy. *Psychoanalytic Psychology*, 10(1):1–16.

Katie Lewis, Sean Murphy, and Yuko Hanakawa. 2009. Uncovering episodic memory through linguistic measures in schizophrenia. In *Poster session at the Association for Psychological Science Annual Convention*, San Francisco.

Rachele Mariani, Bernard Maskit, Wilma Bucci, and Alessandra De Coro. 2013. Linguistic measures of the referential process in psychodynamic treatment: the English and Italian versions. *Psychotherapy research: Journal of the Society for Psychotherapy Research*, 23(4):430–47, January.

Bernard Maskit, Wilma Bucci, and Sean Murphy. 2014. Computer based measures of referential activity and their use as measures of episodic memory.

Bernard Maskit, Wilma Bucci, and Sean Murphy. 2015. A computer program for tracking the evolution of a psychotherapy treatment. In *Computational Linguistics and Clinical Psychology Workshop at NAACL HLT 2015*.

Erhard Mergenthaler and Wilma Bucci. 1999. Linking verbal and non-verbal representations: Computer analysis of referential activity. *British Journal of Medical Psychology*, 72(3):339–354, September.

Kristin Nelson and Michael Polignano. 2009. Referential activity in negative episodic 'flashbulb' memories from patients. In *Poster session at the Association for Psychological Science Annual Convention*, San Francisco, CA.

Kristin L. Nelson, Damian J. Moskovitz, and Hans Steiner. 2008. Narration and Vividness as Measures of Event-Specificity in Autobiographical Memory. *Discourse Processes*, 45(2):195–209, March.

Mark B Powers, Jacqueline M Halpern, Michael P Ferenschak, Seth J Gillihan, and Edna B Foa. 2010. A meta-analytic review of prolonged exposure for posttraumatic stress disorder. *Clinical psychology review*, 30(6):635–41, August.

Andres Roussos and Manuela O'Connel. 2005. Construcción de un diccionario ponderado en español para medir la Actividad Referencial. *Revista del Instituto de Investgaciones de la Facultad de Psicología / UBA*, 10.(2):99–119.

Nicolas Samstag. 1997. A meta-analysis of referential activity. *Dissertation Abstracts International: Section B: The Sciences and Engineering*, 57(9-B), 5.

Endel Tulving. 1972. Episodic and semantic memory. In *Organization of memory*, volume 1, pages 381–403.

J C Watson. 1996. The relationship between vivid description, emotional arousal, and in-session resolution of problematic reactions. *Journal of consulting and clinical psychology*, 64:459–464.

Towards Developing an Annotation Scheme for Depressive Disorder Symptoms: A Preliminary Study using Twitter Data

Danielle L Mowery
Department of Biomedical Informatics
University of Utah
421 Wakara Way
Salt Lake City, UT 84115
danielle.mowery@utah.edu

Craig Bryan
Department of Psychology
University of Utah
260 S. Central Campus Dr
Salt Lake City, UT 84112
craig.bryan@utah.edu

Mike Conway
Department of Biomedical Informatics
University of Utah
421 Wakara Way
Salt Lake City, UT 84115
mike.conway@utah.edu

Abstract

Major depressive disorder is one of the most burdensome and debilitating diseases in the United States. In this pilot study, we present a new annotation scheme representing depressive symptoms and psycho-social stressors associated with major depressive disorder and report annotator agreement when applying the scheme to Twitter data.

1 Introduction

Major depressive disorder — one of the most debilitating forms of mental illness — has a lifetime prevalence of 16.2% (Kessler et al., 2003), and a 12-month prevalence of 6.6% (Kessler and Wang, 2009) in the United States. In 2010, depression was the fifth biggest contributor to the United State's disease burden, with only lung cancer, lower back pain, chronic obstructive pulmonary disease, and heart disease responsible for more poor health and disability (US Burden of Disease Collaborators, 2013).

Social media, particularly Twitter, is increasingly recognised as a valuable resource for advancing public health (Ayers et al., 2014; Dredze, 2012), in areas such as understanding population-level health behaviour (Myslín et al., 2013; Hanson et al., 2013), pharmacovigilance (Freifeld et al., 2014; Chary et al., 2013), and infectious disease surveillance (Chew and Eysenbach, 2010; Paul et al., 2014). Twitter's value in the mental health arena — the focus of this paper — is particularly marked, given that it provides access to first person accounts of user behaviour, activities, thoughts, feelings, and relationships, that may be indicative of emotional wellbeing.

The main contribution of this work is the development and testing of an annotation scheme, based on DSM-5 depression criteria (American Psychiatric Association, 2013) and depression screening instruments[1] designed to capture depressive symptoms in social media data, particularly Twitter. In future work, the annotation scheme described here will be applied to a large corpus of Twitter data and used to train and test Natural Language Processing (NLP) algorithms.

The paper is structured as follows. Section 2 describes related work. Section 3 sets out the methodology used, including a list of semantic categories related to depression and psycho-social stressors derived from the psychology literature, and a description of our annotation process and environment. Section 4 presents the results of our annotation efforts and Section 5 provides commentary on those results.

[1]For example, the 10-item HANDS scale (Harvard Department of Psychiatry/NDSD) (Baer et al., 2000).

Proceedings of the 2nd Workshop on Computational Linguistics and Clinical Psychology: From Linguistic Signal to Clinical Reality, pages 89–98,
Denver, Colorado, June 5, 2015.

2 Background

2.1 Mental Health, NLP, and Social Media

Significant research effort has been focused on developing NLP methods for identifying mental health risk factors. For example, Huang et al., in a large-scale study of electronic health records, used structured data to identify cohorts of *depressed* and *non-depressed* patients, and — based on the narrative text component of the patient record — built a regression model capable of predicting depression diagnosis one year in advance (Huang et al., 2014). Pestian et al. showed that an NLP approach based on machine learning performed better than clinicians in distinguishing between suicide notes written by suicide completers, and notes elicited from healthy volunteers (Pestian et al., 2010; Pestian et al., 2012). Using machine learning methods, Xuan et al. identified linguistic characteristics — e.g. impoverished syntax and lexical diversity — associated with dementia through an analysis of the work of three British novelists, P.D. James (no evidence of dementia), Agatha Christie (some evidence of dementia), and Iris Murdoch (diagnosed dementia) (Xuan et al., 2011).

More specifically focused on Twitter and depression, De Choudhury et al. describes the creation of a corpus crowdsourced from Twitter users with depression-indicative CES-D scores[2], then used this corpus to train a classifier, which, when used to classify geocoded Twitter data derived from 50 US states, was shown to correlate with US Centers for Disease Control (CDC) depression data (De Choudhury et al., 2013). Jashinsky et al. used a set of Twitter keywords organised around several themes (e.g. depression symptoms, drug use, suicidal ideation) and identified strong correlations between the frequency of suicide-related tweets (as identified by keywords) and state-level CDC suicide statistics (Jashinsky et al., 2014). Coppersmith et al. identified Twitter users with self-disclosed depression diagnoses ("I was diagnosed with depression") using regular expressions, and discovered that when depressed Twitter users' tweets where compared with a cohort of non-depressed Twitter users' tweets there were significant differences between the two groups in their expression of anger, use of pronouns, and frequency of negative emotions (Coppersmith et al., 2014).

[2]Center for Epidemiologic Studies Depression Scale (Radloff, 1977)

2.2 Annotation Studies

Annotation scheme development and evaluation is an important subtask for some health and biomedical-related NLP applications (Conway et al., 2010; Mowery et al., 2013; Roberts et al., 2007; Vincze et al., 2008; Kim et al., 2003). Work on building annotation schemes (and corpora) for mental health signals in social media is less well developed, but pioneering work exists. For example, Homan et al. created a 4-value distress scale for rating tweets, with annotations performed by novice and expert annotators (Homan et al., 2014). To our knowledge, there exists no clinical depression annotation scheme that explicitly captures elements from common diagnostic protocols for the identification of depression symptoms in Twitter data.

3 Methods

Our first step was the iterative development of a Depressive Disorder Annotation Scheme based on widely-used diagnostic criteria (Section 3.1). We then went on to evaluate how well annotators were able to apply the schema to a small corpus of Twitter data, and assessed pairwise inter-annotator agreement across the corpus (Section 3.2).

3.1 Depressive Disorder Annotation Scheme

3.1.1 Classes

Our Depressive Disorder Annotation Scheme is hierarchally-structured and is comprised of two mutually-exclusive nodes - **No evidence of clinical depression** and **Evidence of clinical depression**. The **Evidence of clinical depression** node has two non-mutually-exclusive types, **Depression Symptom** and **Psycho-Social Stressor**, derived from our literature review (top-down modeling) and dataset (bottom-up modeling). A summary of the scheme is shown in Figure 1.

For **Depression Symptom** classes, we identified 9 of the 10 parent-level depression symptoms from five resources for evaluating depression:

Figure 1: Radial representation of Depressive Disorder Annotation Scheme

1. Diagnostic and Statistical Manual of Mental Disorders, Edition 5 (DSM-5) (American Psychiatric Association, 2013)
2. Behavioral Risk Factors Surveillance System BRFSS depression inventory (BRFSS)(Centers for Disease Control, 2014)[3]
3. The Harvard Department of Psychiatry National Depression Screening Day Scale (HANDS) (Baer et al., 2000)

[3]www.webcitation.org/6Ws1k4tki

4. Patient Health Questionnaire (PHQ-9) (Kroenke et al., 2001)
5. The Quick Inventory of Depressive Symptomatology (QIDS-SR) (Rush et al., 2003)

Additionally, we included a suicide related class, **Recurrent thoughts of death, suicidal ideation**, which consisted of child level classes derived from the Columbia Suicide Severity Scale (Posner et al., 2011).

For **Psycho-Social Stressor** classes, we synthesised 12 parent-level classes based on the Diagnostic and Statistical Manual of Mental Disorders, Edition 4 (DSM IV) Axis IV "psychosocial and environmental problems" (American Psychiatric Association, 2000) and work by Gilman et al. (Gilman et al., 2013). We identified other potential parent classes based on annotation of 129 randomly-selected tweets from our corpus. The hierarchical structure of the scheme, emphasising parent and child classes assessed in this study, is depicted in Figure 2.

In the following subsections, **3.1.1.1 Depression Symptom Classes** and **3.1.1.2 Psycho-Social Stressor Classes**, we list some example tweets for each Depression Symptom and Psycho-Social Stressor class.

3.1.1.1 Depression Symptom Classes

- **No evidence of clinical depression**: political stance or personal opinion, inspirational statement or advice, unsubstantiated claim/fact, NOS
  E.g."People who eat dark chocolate are less likely to be depressed"
- **Low mood**: feels sad, feels hopeless, "the blues", feels down, NOS
  E.g. "Life will never get any better #depression"
- **Anhedonia**: loss of interest in previous interests, NOS
  E.g. "Cant seem to jam on this guitar like the old days #depressionIsReal"
- **Weight change or change in appetite**: increase in weight, decrease in weight, increase in appetite, decrease in appetite, NOS
  E.g. "At least I can now fit into my old fav jeans again #depressionWeightLossProgram"
- **Disturbed sleep**: difficulty in falling asleep, difficulty staying awake, waking up too early, sleeping too much, NOS
  E.g. "I could sleep my life away; I'm a depressed sleeping beauty"
- **Psychomotor agitation or retardation**: feeling slowed down, feeling restless or fidgety, NOS
  E.g. "I just feel like I'm talking and moving in slow motion"
- **Fatigue or loss of energy**: feeling tired, insufficient energy for tasks, NOS
  E.g. "I just cannot muster the strength to do laundry #day20 #outOfUnderwear"
- **Feelings of worthlessness or excessive inappropriate guilt**: perceived burdensome, self-esteem, feeling worthless, inappropriate guilt, NOS
  E.g. "I just can't seem to do anything right for anybody"
- **Diminished ability to think or concentrate, indecisiveness**: finding concentration difficult, indecisiveness, NOS
  E.g. "Should I do my homework or the laundry first? What does it matter anyway?"
- **Recurrent thoughts of death, suicidal ideation**: thoughts of death, wish to be dead, suicidal thoughts, non-specific active suicidal thoughts, active suicidal ideation with any method without intent to act, active suicidal ideation with some intent to act, without specific plan, active suicidal ideation with specific plan and intent, completed suicide, NOS
  E.g. "Sometimes I wish i would fall asleep and then not wake up"

3.1.1.2 Psycho-Social Stressor Classes

- **Problems with expected life course with respect to self**: serious medical condition, failure to achieve important goal, NOS
  E.g. "If it wasn't for my chronic pain, I could have made the Olympics. Now what?!"
- **Problems with primary support group**: death of a family member, health problem in a family member, serious disability of a family member, separation/divorce/end of serious relationship, serious disagreement with or estrangement from friend, NOS
  E.g. "I've been so depressed since my brother passed this year"
- **Problems related to the social environment**: death of friend, death of celebrity or person of interest, social isolation, inadequate social support personal or romantic, living alone, experience of discrimination, adjustment to lifestyle transition, NOS
  E.g. "Since Robin Williams's death, I've only known dark days"

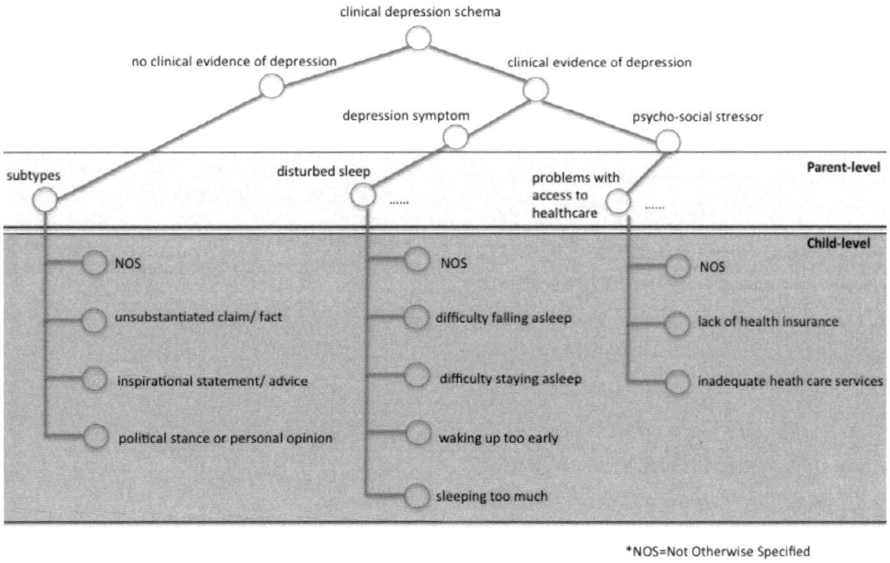

Figure 2: Annotation scheme hierarchy. light gray=parent classes; dark gray=child classes. **NOS** (**N**ot **O**therwise **S**pecified indicates the parent class by default)

- **Educational problems**: academic problems, discord with teachers or classmates, inadequate or dangerous school environment, NOS
  E.g. "This MBA program is the worst! I feel like I'm leaving Uni with no skill sets"
- **Occupational problems**: firing event, unemployment, threat of job loss, stressful work situation, job dissatisfaction, job change, difficult relationship with boss or co-worker, NOS
  E.g. "What kind of life is this working 12 hour days in a lab??"
- **Housing problems**: homelessness, inadequate housing, unsafe neighbourhood, discord with neighbours or landlord, NOS
  E.g. "My dad threw me out of the house again. I didn't want to live under his roof anyway"
- **Economic problems**: major financial crisis, regular difficulty in meeting financial commitments, poverty, welfare recipient, NOS
  E.g."My clothes have more patches than original cloth. #whateverItTakes"
- **Problems with access to healthcare**: inadequate health care services, lack of health insurance, NOS
  E.g. "These generic pills do nothing to subside my depressed thoughts"
- **Problems related to the legal system/crime**: problems with police or arrest, incarceration, litigation, victim of crime, NOS
  E.g. "3 years in the joint and life hasn't changed at all on the outside #depressingLife"
- **Other psychosocial and environmental problems**: natural disaster, war, discord with caregivers, NOS
  E.g. "I lost everything and my mind to Hurricane Katrina"
- **Weather**: NOS
  E.g. "Rainy day - even the weather agrees with my mood" [NOT A DSM IV PSYCHO-SOCIAL STRESSOR]
- **Media**: music, movie or tv, book, other, NOS
  E.g. "After reading Atonement I became really bummed out" [NOT A DSM IV PSYCHO-SOCIAL STRESSOR]

3.2 Pilot Annotation Study

The goal of this preliminary study was to assess how reliably our annotation scheme could be applied to Twitter data. To create our initial corpus, we queried the Twitter API using lexical variants of "depression" e.g., "depressed" and "depressing", and randomly sampled 150 tweets from the data set[4]. Of these 150 tweets, we filtered out 21 retweets (RT). The remaining tweets (n=129 tweets) were annotated with the annotation scheme and adjudicated with consensus review by the authors (A1, A2), both biomedical informaticists by training. Two clinical psychology student annotators (A3, A4) were trained to apply the guidelines using the extensible Human Oracle Suite of Tools (eHOST) annotation tool (South et al., 2012) (Figure 3). Following this initial training, A3 and A4 annotated the same 129 tweets as A1 and A2.

In this study, we calculated the frequency distribution of annotated classes for each annotator. In order to assess inter-annotator agreement, we compared annotator performance *between* annotators (IAA_{ba} — *b*etween *a*nnotators) and *against* the adjudicated reference standard (IAA_{ar} — *a*gainst the *r*eference standard) using F1-measure. Note that F1-measure, the harmonic mean of sensitivity and positive predictive value, is equivalent to positive specific agreement which can act as a surrogate for kappa in situations where the number of true negatives becomes large (Hripcsak and Rothschild, 2005). We also assessed IAA_{ar} performance compared to the reference standard at both parent and child levels of the annotation scheme hierarchy (see Figure 2 for example parent/child classes). In addition to presenting IAA_{ar} by annotator for each parent class, we also characterise the following distribution of disagreement types:

1. Presence/absence of clinical evidence (CE)
   e.g., **No evidence of clinical depression** *vs.* **Fatigue or loss of energy**
2. Spurious class (SC)
   e.g., false class annotation
3. Missing class (MC)
   e.g., missing class annotation
4. Other (OT)
   e.g., errors not mentioned above

[4]The Twitter data analysed were harvested from the Twitter API during February 2014. Only English language tweets were retained.

4 Results

In Table 1, we report the distribution of annotated classes per tweet. The prevalence of tweets annotated with one class label ranged from 83-97%, while the prevalence of tweets annotated with two class labels ranged from 3-16%. A3 and A4 annotated all 129 tweets. Annotators annotated between 133-149 classes on the full dataset.

	A1	A2	A3	A4
1	106 (83)	116 (91)	121 (94)	125 (97)
2	20 (16)	12 (9)	8 (6)	4 (3)
3+	1 (1)	0 (0)	0 (0)	0 (0)
tws	127	128	129	129
cls	149	140	137	133

Table 1: Count (%) distribution for annotated classes per tweet; total annotated tweets (tws); total annotated classes (cls)

Table 2 shows assessed pair-wise IAA_{ba} agreement between annotators. We observed moderate (A1/A2: 68; A2/A4: 43) to low (A2/A3: 30; A1/A4:38) IAA_{ba} between annotators.

In Table 3, we report IAA_{ar} for each annotator compared to the reference standard for both parent and child classes. IAA_{ar} ranged from 60-90 for the parent classes (e.g. **Media**) and 41-87 for child classes (e.g. **Media: book**). The IAA_{ar} difference between parent and child class performance ranged from 3-36 points.

Table 4 enumerates IAA_{ar} for the observed parent classes. Note that only 12 (55%) of the parent classes were observed in the reference standard. A1 had variable agreement levels including 4 subtypes between 80-100, 6 subtypes between 60-79, and 3 subtypes between 40-59. A2 had consistently high agreement with 10 subtypes between 80-100 followed by 1 subtype IAA_{ar} between 20-39 IAA_{ar}. A3 achieved 3 subtypes between 60-79 and 1 subtype between 40-59. A3 performed with 2 subtypes between 80-100, 3 subtypes between 60-79, 1 subtype between 40-59, and 2 subtypes between 20-39.

	A1	A2	A3	A4
A1		68	24	38
A2			30	43
A3				28
A4				

Table 2: Pairwise IAA_{ba} between annotators

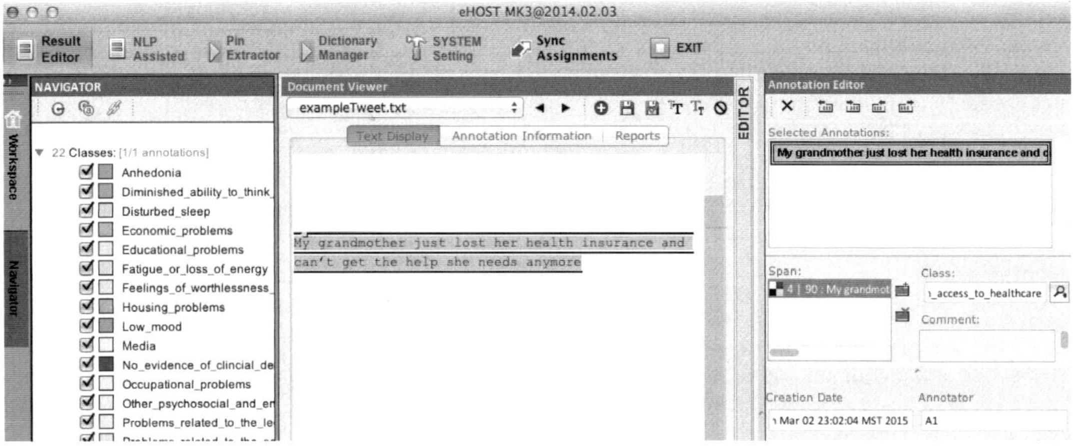

Figure 3: eHOST annotation tool

	A1	A2	A3	A4
parent	75	90	66	60
child	63	87	30	41

Table 3: Overall IAA_{ar} for each annotator at parent and child levels compared against the reference standard

We observed between 15-57 disagreements across annotators when compared to the reference standard (see Table 5), with **No evidence of clinical depression** accounting for 60-77% of disagreements. Missing classes accounted for 16-33% of disagreements.

5 Discussion

We developed an annotation scheme to represent depressive symptoms and psychosocial stressors associated with depressive disorder, and conducted a pilot study to assess how well the scheme could be applied to Twitter tweets. We observed that content from most tweets can be represented with one class annotation (see Table 1), an unsurprising result given the constraints on expressivity imposed by Twitter's 140 character limit. In several cases, two symptoms or social stressors are expressed within a single tweet, most often with **Low mood** and a second class (e.g. **Economic problems**).

We observed low to moderate IAA_{ba} between annotators (Table 2). Annotators A1 and A2 achieved highest agreement suggesting they have a more similar understanding of the schema than all other pair combinations. Comparing our kappa scores to related work is challenging. However, Homan et al. reports a comparable, moderate kappa (50) between two novice annotators when annotating whether a tweet represents distress.

When comparing IAA_{ar}, annotators achieved moderate to high agreement at the parent level against the reference standard (Table 3). Annotators A1 and A2 had higher parent and child level agreement than annotators A3 and A4. This may be explained by the fact that the schema was initially developed by A1 and A2. Additionally, the reference standard was adjudicated using consensus between A1 and A2. Around half of the depressive symptoms and psycho-stressors were not observed during the pilot study (e.g. **Anhedonia**, **Fatigue or loss of energy**, **Recurrent thoughts of death or suicidal ideation** — see Table 4) although may well appear in a larger annotation effort. The reference standard consists mainly of **No evidence of clinical depression** and **Low mood** classes suggesting that other depressive symptoms and psycho-stressors (e.g. **Psychomotor agitation or retardation**) are less often expressed or more difficult to detect without more context than is available in a single tweet. For these most prevalent subtypes, good to excellent agreement was achieved by all 4 annotators. Considerably lower agreement was observed for annotators A3 and A4 for less prevalent classes. In contrast, A1 and A2 maintained similar moderate and high agreement, respectively. In future experiments, we will leverage all annotators' annotations when generating the reference standard (i.e. the reference standard will be created using majority vote).

The most prevalent disagreement involved iden-

Parent Classes	Ct	A1	A2	A3	A4
All	148	75	90	66	60
No evidence of clinical depression	73	77	94	74	66
Low mood	52	75	91	70	63
Problems related to social environment	6	80	80	40	22
Media	4	67	33	0	31
Problems with expected life course wrt. self	3	86	0	0	0
Weather	3	86	100	0	50
Education problems	2	67	80	0	0
Disturbed sleep	1	100	100	0	100
Economic problems	1	50	100	0	0
Occupational problems	1	67	100	0	100
Problems with primary support group	1	50	100	0	0
Weight or appetite change	1	50	100	0	0
Fatigue or loss of energy	0	0	0	0	0
Housing problems	0	0	0	0	0
Psychomotor agitation or retardation	0	0	0	0	0

Table 4: Agreement for parent classes between annotator & reference standard; darker gray=higher IAA_{ar}, lighter gray=lower IAA_{ar}. Note that not all classes are listed.

	A1	A2	A3	A4
CE	25 (65)	9 (60)	36 (74)	44 (77)
MC	8 (21)	5 (33)	8 (16)	9 (16)
SC	3 (8)	1 (7)	2(4)	0 (0)
OT	2 (5)	0 (0)	3 (6)	4 (7)
Total	38	15	49	57

Table 5: Count (%) of disagreements by type for each annotator compared against the reference standard

tifying a tweet as containing **No evidence of clinical depression** (see Table 5). The line between the presence and absence of evidence for clinical depression is difficult to draw in these cases due to the use of humour ("So depressed :) #lol"), misuse or exaggerated use of the term ("I have a bad case of post concert depression"), and lack of context ("This is depressing"). In very few cases, disagreements were the result of other differences such as specificity (**Media vs Media: book**) or one-to-one mismatch (**Weather: NOS** vs **Media: book**). This result is unsurprising given that agreement tends to reduce as the number of categories become large, especially for less prevalent categories (Poesio and Vieira, 1998). We acknowledge several limitations in our pilot study, notably the small sample size and initial queried term. We will address these limitations in future work by annotating a significantly larger corpus (over 5,000 tweets) and querying the Twitter API with a more diverse list of clinician-validated keywords than was used in this pilot annotation study.

6 Conclusions

We conclude that there are considerable challenges in attempting to reliably annotate Twitter data for mental health symptoms. However, several depressive symptoms and psycho-social stressors derived from DSM-5 depression criteria and depression screening instruments can be identified in Twitter data.

Acknowledgements

We would like to thank Dr Murray Stein (University of California San Diego, Department of Psychiatry) and Dr Gary Tedeschi (California Smokers Helpline) for their comments on an early draft of the annotation scheme described in this paper. We would also like to thank Mr Soumya Smruti Mishra (University of Utah, Department of Computer Science) for help with diagram creation, and both Mr Tyler Cheney and Ms Hilary Smith (University of Utah, Department of Psychology) for their annotation efforts. This work was funded by a grant from the National Library of Medicine (R00LM011393).

Ethics Statement

This study was granted an exemption from review by the University of Utah Institutional Review Board (IRB_00076188). Note that in order to protect tweeter anonymity, we have not reproduced tweets verbatim. Example tweets shown were generated by the researchers as exemplars only.

References

American Psychiatric Association. 2000. *Diagnostic and Statistical Manual of Mental Disorders, 4th Edition, Text Revision (DSM-IV-TR)*. American Psychiatric Association.

American Psychiatric Association. 2013. *Diagnostic and Statistical Manual of Mental Disorders, Fifth Edition (DSM-5)*. American Psychiatric Publishing.

J Ayers, B Althouse, and M Dredze. 2014. Could behavioral medicine lead the web data revolution? *JAMA*, 311(14):1399–400, Apr.

L Baer, D G Jacobs, J Meszler-Reizes, M Blais, M Fava, R Kessler, K Magruder, J Murphy, B Kopans, P Cukor, L Leahy, and J O'Laughlen. 2000. Development of a brief screening instrument: the HANDS. *Psychother Psychosom*, 69(1):35–41.

Centers for Disease Control. 2014. *BRFSS - Anxiety and Depression Optional Module*.

M Chary, N Genes, A McKenzie, and A Manini. 2013. Leveraging social networks for toxicovigilance. *J Med Toxicol*, 9(2):184–91, Jun.

C Chew and G Eysenbach. 2010. Pandemics in the age of Twitter: content analysis of tweets during the 2009 H1N1 outbreak. *PLoS One*, 5(11):e14118.

M Conway, A Kawazoe, H Chanlekha, and N Collier. 2010. Developing a disease outbreak event corpus. *J Med Internet Res*, 12(3):e43.

G Coppersmith, M Dredze, and C Harman. 2014. Quantifying mental health signals in Twitter. In *Proceedings of the Workshop on Computational Linguistics and Clinical Psychology: From Linguistic Signal to Clinical Reality*, pages 51–60, Baltimore, Maryland, USA, June. Association for Computational Linguistics.

M De Choudhury, S Counts, and E Horvitz. 2013. Social media as a measurement tool of depression in populations. In *Proceedings of the 5th Annual ACM Web Science Conference*, pages 47–56. ACM.

M Dredze. 2012. How social media will change public health. *Intelligent Systems, IEEE*, 27(4):81–84.

C Freifeld, J Brownstein, C Menone, W Bao, R Filice, T Kass-Hout, and N Dasgupta. 2014. Digital drug safety surveillance: monitoring pharmaceutical products in Twitter. *Drug Saf*, 37(5):343–50, May.

S Gilman, N Trinh, J Smoller, M Fava, J Murphy, and J Breslau. 2013. Psychosocial stressors and the prognosis of major depression: a test of Axis IV. *Psychol Med*, 43(2):303–16, Feb.

C Hanson, B Cannon, S Burton, and C Giraud-Carrier. 2013. An exploration of social circles and prescription drug abuse through Twitter. *J Med Internet Res*, 15(9):e189.

C Homan, R Johar, T Liu, M Lytle, V Silenzio, and C Ovesdotter Alm. 2014. Toward macro-insights for suicide prevention: analyzing fine-grained distress at scale. In *Proceedings of the Workshop on Computational Linguistics and Clinical Psychology: From Linguistic Signal to Clinical Reality*, pages 107–117, Baltimore, Maryland, USA, June. Association for Computational Linguistics.

G Hripcsak and A Rothschild. 2005. Agreement, the f-measure, and reliability in information retrieval. *JAMIA*, 12(3):296–298.

S Huang, P LePendu, S Iyer, M Tai-Seale, D Carrell, and N Shah. 2014. Toward personalizing treatment for depression: predicting diagnosis and severity. *J Am Med Inform Assoc*, 21(6):1069–75, Nov.

J Jashinsky, S Burton, C Hanson, J West, C Giraud-Carrier, M Barnes, and T Argyle. 2014. Tracking suicide risk factors through Twitter in the US. *Crisis*, 35(1):51–9.

R Kessler and P Wang. 2009. Handbook of Depression. chapter Epidemiology of Depression, pages 5–22. Guilford Press, 2nd edition.

R Kessler, P Berglund, O Demler, R Jin, D Koretz, K Merikangas, A Rush, E Walters, P Wang, and National Comorbidity Survey Replication. 2003. The epidemiology of major depressive disorder: results from the national comorbidity survey replication (NCS-R). *Journal of the American Medical Association*, 289(23):3095–105.

J-D Kim, T Ohta, Y Tateisi, and J Tsujii. 2003. Genia corpus–semantically annotated corpus for bio-textmining. *Bioinformatics*, 19 Suppl 1:i180–2.

K Kroenke, R Spitzer, and J Williams. 2001. The PHQ-9: validity of a brief depression severity measure. *J Gen Intern Med*, 16(9):606–13, Sep.

D Mowery, P Jordan, J Wiebe, H Harkema, J Dowling, and W Chapman. 2013. Semantic annotation of clinical events for generating a problem list. *AMIA Annu Symp Proc*, 2013:1032–41.

M Myslín, S-H Zhu, W Chapman, and M Conway. 2013. Using Twitter to examine smoking behavior and perceptions of emerging tobacco products. *J Med Internet Res*, 15(8):e174.

M Paul, M Dredze, and D Broniatowski. 2014. Twitter improves influenza forecasting. *PLoS Curr*, 6.

J Pestian, H Nasrallah, P Matykiewicz, A Bennett, and A Leenaars. 2010. Suicide note classification using natural language processing: a content analysis. *Biomed Inform Insights*, 2010(3):19–28, Aug.

J Pestian, P Matykiewicz, and M Linn-Gust. 2012. What's in a note: construction of a suicide note corpus. *Biomed Inform Insights*, 5:1–6.

M Poesio and R Vieira. 1998. A corpus-based investigation of definite description use. *Comput. Linguist.*, 24(2):183–216, June.

K Posner, G Brown, B Stanley, D Brent, K Yershova, M Oquendo, G Currier, G Melvin, L Greenhill, S Shen, and J Mann. 2011. The Columbia-Suicide Severity Rating Scale: initial validity and internal consistency findings from three multisite studies with adolescents and adults. *Am J Psychiatry*, 168(12):1266–77, Dec.

L Sawyer Radloff. 1977. The CES-D scale: a self-report depression scale for research in the general population. *Applied Psychological Measurement*, 1(3):385–401.

A Roberts, R Gaizauskas, M Hepple, N Davis, G Demetriou, Y Guo, J Kola, I Roberts, A Setzer, A Tapuria, and B Wheeldin. 2007. The CLEF corpus: semantic annotation of clinical text. *AMIA Annu Symp Proc*, pages 625–9.

A Rush, M Trivedi, H Ibrahim, T Carmody, B Arnow, D Klein, J Markowitz, P Ninan, S Kornstein, R Manber, M Thase, J Kocsis, and M Keller. 2003. The 16-item Quick Inventory of Depressive Symptomatology (QIDS), clinician rating (QIDS-C), and self-report (QIDS-SR): a psychometric evaluation in patients with chronic major depression. *Biol Psychiatry*, 54(5):573–83, Sep.

B South, S Shen, J Leng, T Forbush, S DuVall, and W Chapman. 2012. A prototype tool set to support machine-assisted annotation. In *Proceedings of the 2012 Workshop on Biomedical Natural Language Processing*, BioNLP '12, pages 130–139, Stroudsburg, PA, USA. Association for Computational Linguistics.

US Burden of Disease Collaborators. 2013. The state of US health, 1990-2010: burden of diseases, injuries, and risk factors. *JAMA*, 310(6):591–608, Aug.

V Vincze, G Szarvas, R Farkas, G Móra, and J Csirik. 2008. The Bioscope corpus: biomedical texts annotated for uncertainty, negation and their scopes. *BMC Bioinformatics*, 9 Suppl 11:S9.

L Xuan, I Lancashire, G Hirst, and R Jokel. 2011. Longitudinal detection of dementia through lexical and syntactic changes in writing: a case study of three British novelists. *Literary and Linguistic Computing*, 26(435-461).

Beyond LDA: Exploring Supervised Topic Modeling for Depression-Related Language in Twitter

Philip Resnik[2,4], **William Armstrong**[1,4], **Leonardo Claudino**[1,4],
Thang Nguyen[3], **Viet-An Nguyen**[1,4], **and Jordan Boyd-Graber**[3,5]
[1]Computer Science, [2]Linguistics, [3]iSchool, and [4]UMIACS, University of Maryland
[5]Computer Science, University of Colorado Boulder
{resnik,armstrow}@umd.edu
{claudino,daithang,vietan}@cs.umd.edu
{daithang,jbg}@umiacs.umd.edu

Abstract

Topic models can yield insight into how depressed and non-depressed individuals use language differently. In this paper, we explore the use of supervised topic models in the analysis of linguistic signal for detecting depression, providing promising results using several models.

1 Introduction

Depression is one of the most prevalent forms of mental illness: in the U.S. alone, 25 million adults per year suffer a major depressive episode (NAMI, 2013), and Katzman et al. (2014) observe that "[by] 2020, depression is projected to be among the most important contributors to the global burden of disease". Unfortunately, there are significant barriers to obtaining help for depression and mental disorders in general, including potential stigma associated with actively seeking treatment (Rodrigues et al., 2014) and lack of access to qualified diagnosticians (Sibelius, 2013; APA, 2013). When patients suffering from depression see a primary care physician, the rates of misdiagnosis are staggering (Vermani et al., 2011).

These considerations have helped to motivate a recent surge of interest in finding accessible, cost effective, non-intrusive methods to detect depression and other mental disorders. Continuing a line of thought pioneered by Pennebaker and colleagues (Pennebaker and King, 1999; Rude et al., 2004, and others), researchers have been developing methods for identifying relevant signal in people's language use, which could potentially provide inexpensive early detection of individuals who might require a specialist's evaluation, on the basis of their naturally occurring linguistic behavior, e.g. (Neuman et al., 2012; De Choudhury et al., 2013; Coppersmith et al., 2014). Critical mass for a community of interest on these topics has been building within the computational linguistics research community (Resnik et al., 2014).

To date, however, the language analysis methods used in this domain have tended to be fairly simple, typically including words or n-grams, manually defined word categories (e.g., Pennebaker's LIWC lexicon, Pennebaker and King (1999)), and "vanilla" topic models (Blei et al., 2003, latent Dirichlet allocation (LDA)). This stands in contrast to other domains of computational social science in which more sophisticated models have been developed for some time, including opinion analysis (Titov and McDonald, 2008), analysis of the scientific literature (Blei and Lafferty, 2007), and computational political science (Grimmer, 2010).

In this paper, we take steps toward employing more sophisticated models in the analysis of linguistic signal for detecting depression, providing promising results using supervised LDA (Blei and McAuliffe, 2007) and supervised anchor topic models (Nguyen et al., 2015), and beginning some initial exploration of a new supervised nested LDA model (SNLDA).

2 Data

Our primary experimental dataset is the Twitter collection created by Coppersmith et al. (2014)

Proceedings of the 2nd Workshop on Computational Linguistics and Clinical Psychology: From Linguistic Signal to Clinical Reality, pages 99–107,
Denver, Colorado, June 5, 2015.

and used in the CLPsych Hackathon (Coppersmith, 2015). The raw set contains roughly 3 million tweets from about 2,000 twitter users, of which roughly 600 self-identify as having been clinically diagnosed with depression (by virtue of having publicly tweeted "I was diagnosed with depression today" or similar, with manual validation by the individuals preparing the data). We grouped all tweets by an individual user into a single document, and a base vocabulary was created by pre-processing documents using standard NLP tools, specifically: (1) keeping alphanumeric words and word-encoded emoticons, (2) removing stopwords using the MALLET stopword list, and (3) lemmatizing using NLTK's WordNetLemmatizer. We then filtered out words that appeared in fewer than 20 documents, words only appearing in documents of fewer than 50 words (fewer than 10 users), and URLs. The resulting set of 1,809 documents was randomly divided into train/dev/test subsets to create a 60-20-20% split. We model documents from the Twitter datasets depression subset as having a regression value of 1 and those from the control subset as having a regression value of -1.

In building some of our models, we also use a collection of 6,459 stream-of-consciousness essays collected between 1997 and 2008 by Pennebaker and King (1999), who asked students to think about their thoughts, sensations, and feelings in the moment and "write your thoughts as they come to you". As discussed in Section 3.1, running LDA on this dataset provides informative priors for sLDA's learning process on the Twitter training data. The student essays average approximately 780 words each, and Resnik et al. (2013) showed that unsupervised topic models based on this dataset can produce very clean, interpretable topical categories, a number of which were viewed by a clinician as relevant in the assessment of depression, including, for example, "vegetative" symptoms (particularly related to sleep and energy level), somatic symptoms (physical discomfort, e.g. headache, itching, digestive problems), and situational factors such as homesickness.

For uniformity, we preprocessed the stream-of-consciousness dataset with the same tools as the Twitter set.[1] We created a shared vocabulary for our models by taking the union of the vocabularies from the two datasets, leading to a roughly 6% increase in vocabulary size over the Twitter dataset alone.

3 Models

3.1 LDA

LDA (Blei et al., 2003) uncovers underlying structure in collections of documents by treating each document as if it was generated as a "mixture" of different topics. As a useful illustration, replicating Resnik et al. (2013), we find that using LDA with 50 topics on the Pennebaker stream-of-consciousness essays produces many topics that are coherent and meaningful. We had a licensed clinical psychologist review these to identify the topics most likely to be relevant in assessing depression, shown in Table 1.[2] This step exploiting domain expertise can be viewed as a poor-man's version of interactive topic modeling (Hu et al., 2014), which we intend to explore in future work.

3.2 Supervised LDA

Basic (sometimes referred to as "vanilla") LDA is just the entry point when it comes to characterizing latent topical structure in collections of documents, and extensions to LDA have proven valuable in other areas of computational social science. *Supervised* topic models (sLDA, introduced by Blei and McAuliffe (2007)), extend LDA in settings where the documents are accompanied by labels or values of interest, e.g. opinion analysis (reviews accompanied by k-star ratings) or political analysis (political speeches accompanied by the author's political party). The advantage of supervised topic modeling is that the language in the documents and the accompanying values are modeled jointly — this means that the unsupervised topic discovery process seeks to optimize not just the coherence of the topics underlying the discourse, but the model's ability to predict the associated values. So, for example, in modeling Amazon reviews, vanilla LDA might discover a topic containing opinion words (*great*, *enjoy*, *dislike*, etc.) but sLDA would be more likely to separate these out into a positive opinion-word topic

[1] With the exception of the document count filters, due to the different number and sizse of documents; instead, we allowed all non stopwords that appear in more than one document.

[2] Many other topics were coherent and meaningful, but were judged as falling below the clinician's intuitive threshold of relevance for assessing depression.

Notes	Valence	Top 20 words
high emotional valence	e	life live dream change future grow family goal mind rest decision marry chance choice successful career set regret support true
high emotional valence	e	love life happy heart amaze hurt perfect crazy beautiful lose smile cry boy true fall real sad relationship reason completely
relationship problems	n	time boyfriend friend relationship talk person break doe happen understand hard trust care spend reason san situation antonio date leave
transition to college	n	school college student semester university experience hard grade parent graduate freshman campus learn texas attend teacher expect challenge adjust education
self-doubt	n	question realize understand completely idea sense level bring issue concern simply situation lack honestly admit mention fear step feeling act
poor ego control	n	yeah suck wow haha stupid funny hmm crap crazy blah freak type ugh weird lol min gosh hey bore hmmm
feeling ignored/annoyed *	n	call talk phone doe stop bad ring message loud head homework answer cell mad forget annoy sound hurt suppose mine
somatic complaints	n	cold hot feel sick smell rain walk start weather bad window foot freeze nice wait throat day heat hate warm
emotional distress *	n	feel happy day sad depress feeling cry scar afraid lonely head moment emotion realize confuse hurt inside guilty fear upset
family of origin issues	n	mom dad family sister parent brother kid child mother father grow doctor baby hard cousin die age cry proud husband
negative affect *	n	damn hell doe shit fuck smoke woman hate drink piss sex drug kid god bitch time real break screw cigarette
anxiety over failure	n	worry hard study test class lot grade focus mind start nervous stress concentrate trouble reason easier hop harder fail constantly
negative affect*	n	hate doe bad stupid care understand time suck happen anymore mad don mess scar horrible smart matter hat upset fair
sleep disturbance*	n	sleep tire night morning wake bed day time late stay hour asleep nap fall start tomorrow sleepy haven awake lay
somatic complaints	n	hurt eye hear itch hand air sound tire nose arm loud leg leave noise finger smell neck stop light water
social engagement	p	game football team win ticket excite school weekend week texas run lose night season saturday sport dallas longhorn coach fan
exercise, good self-care	p	run day feel walk class wear lose weight buy gym gain short fat dress shop exercise campus clothe body shirt

Table 1: LDA topics from Pennebaker stream-of-consciousness essays identified by a clinician as most relevant for assessing depression. Topics with negative valence (n) were judged likely to be indicators for depression, those with positive valence (p) were judged likely to indicate absence of depression, and those labeled (e) have strong emotional valence without clearly indicating likely assessment. Asterisked topics were viewed as the strongest indicators.

(*great*, *enjoy*, etc.) predicting higher star ratings and a negative opinion-word topic (*dislike*, *sucks*, etc.) predicting lower ratings.

Table 2 illustrates topics we obtained by running 50-topic SLDA on the Pennebaker stream-of-consciousness dataset, using, as each essay's regression variable, the student's degree of neuroticism — a personality trait that can be a risk factor for internalizing disorders such as depression and anxiety — as assessed using the Big-5 personality inventory (John and Srivastava, 1999). The neuroticism scores are Z-score normalized, so the more positive (negative) a topic's regression value, the more (less) the supervised model associates the topic with neuroticism. As was done for Table 1, we had a clinician identify the most relevant topics; these were presented in random order without the neuroticism regression values in order to avoid biasing the judgments. The SLDA neuroticism values for topics in Table 2 pattern nicely with the clinician judgments: negative neuroticism scores are associated with clinician-judged positive valence topics, and positive neuroticism scores with negative valence. Scores for the p and n valence items differ significantly according to a Mann-Whitney U test ($p < .005$).

Table 3 shows topics derived using SLDA on the Twitter training data; owing to space limitations, we show the topics with the 5 highest and 5 lowest Z-normalized regression scores.

We also derive topics on Twitter training data using a "seeded" version of SLDA in which the 50 topics in Section 3.1 provide informative priors; recall that these came from the Pennebaker stream-of-consciousness data. We were motivated by the hypothesis that many of the topics emerging cleanly in Pennebaker's population of college students would be relevant for the Twitter dataset, which also skews toward a younger population but is significantly messier. Although the SLDA runs with and without informative priors produce many similar topics, Table 4 shows a number of topics identified by SLDA with informative priors, that were not among the topics found without them.

3.3 Supervised Anchor Model

As another extension to LDA-based modeling, we explore the use of the the anchor algorithm (Arora et al., 2013, hence ANCHOR), which provides a fast way to learn topic models and also enhances interpretability by identifying a single "anchor" word associated with each topic. Unlike SLDA, which examines every document in a dataset, ANCHOR requires only a V by V matrix Q of word cooccurrences, where V is the size of the vocabulary, to discover topics. Nguyen et al. (2015) introduces a *supervised* anchor algorithm (hence SANCHOR), which, like SLDA, takes advantage of joint modeling with document-level metadata to learn better topics and enable prediction of regression variables.

Briefly, the anchor algorithm assumes that each

Notes	Valence	Regression value	Top 20 words
social engagement	p	-1.593	game play football team watch win sport ticket texas season practice run basketball lose soccer player beat start tennis ball
social engagement	p	-1.122	music song listen play band sing hear sound guitar change remind cool rock concert voice radio favorite awesome lyric ipod
social engagement	p	-0.89	party night girl time fun sorority meet school house tonight lot rush drink excite fraternity pledge class frat hard decide
social engagement	p	-0.694	god die church happen day death lose doe bring care pray live plan close christian control free hold lord amaze
high emotional valence	e	-0.507	hope doe time bad wait glad nice happy worry guess lot fun forget bet easy finally suck fine cat busy
somatic complaints	n	-0.205	cold hot hair itch air light foot nose walk sit hear eye rain nice sound smell freeze weather sore leg
poor ego control; immature	n	0.177	yeah wow minute haha type funny suck hmm guess blah bore gosh ugh stupid bad lol hey stop hmmm stuff
relationship issues	n	0.234	call talk miss phone hope mom mad love stop tonight glad dad weird stupid matt email anymore bad john hate
homesick; emotional distress	n	0.34	home miss friend school family leave weekend mom college feel parent austin stay visit lot close hard boyfriend homesick excite
social engagement	p	0.51	friend people meet lot hang roommate join college nice fun club organization stay social totally enjoy fit dorm conversation time
negative affect*	n	0.663	suck damn stupid hate hell drink shit fuck doe crap smoke piss bad kid drug freak screw crazy break bitch
high emotional valence	e	0.683	life change live person future dream realize mind situation learn goal grow time past enjoy happen control chance decision fear
sleep disturbance*	n	0.719	sleep night tire wake morning bed day hour late class asleep fall stay nap tomorrow leave mate study sleepy awake
high emotional valence	e	0.726	love life happy person heart cry sad day feel world hard scar perfect feeling smile care strong wonderful beautiful true
memories	n	0.782	weird talk doe dog crazy time sad stuff funny haven happen bad remember day hate lot scar guess mad night
somatic complaints*	n	0.805	hurt type head stop eye hand start tire feel time finger arm neck move chair stomach bother run shoulder pain
anxiety*	n	1.111	feel worry stress study time hard lot relax nervous test focus school anxious concentrate pressure harder extremely constantly difficult overwhelm
emotional discomfort	n	1.591	feel time reason depress moment bad change comfortable wrong lonely feeling idea lose guilty emotion confuse realize top comfort happen
homesick; emotional distress*	n	2.307	hate doe sick feel bad hurt wrong care happen mess horrible stupid mad leave worse anymore hard deal cry suppose

Table 2: SLDA topics from Pennebaker stream-of-consciousness essays identified by a clinician as most relevant for assessing depression. Supervision (regression) is based on Z-scored Big-5 neuroticism scores.

Regression value	Top 20 words
2.923	eat fat cut hate fuck weight cross line body sleep scar die food cry fast ugh gym skinny boyfriend week
1.956	omg cry school god cute literally hair gonna hate mom ugh idk wow sleep omfg laugh wear picture tbh sad
1.703	book write read episode twitter story tweet fan cover movie awesome win doctor alex season character yeah film happen week
1.676	fuck shit bitch gonna wanna hate damn man dick wtf suck dude smoke god drink gay sex girl hell piss
1.602	pls depression donate kindly film support mental word ocd health package producer hour anxiety mind tomorrow hun teamfollowback disorder visit
-1.067	game win team play coach season run player state tonight fan football baseball lead brown dodger ohio score red week
-1.078	game man win play team damn fan lebron tonight dude gonna football heat ball bro nba hell boy basketball bull
-1.354	man goal fan win unite game arsenal play team player league score season madrid football match manchester cup sign chelsea
-1.584	EMOJI EMOJI EMOJI EMOJI EMOJI EMOJI EMOJI EMOJI EMOJI EMOJI EMOJI EMOJI EMOJI EMOJI birthday EMOJI bae EMOJI lmao EMOJI
-2.197	birthday class tonight week literally hour tomorrow weekend summer college home break party favorite excite game die beach drive study

Table 3: Most extreme SLDA topics from Twitter training data

Regression value	Top 20 words
4.119	happiness cut line depression post cross anxiety mental read view eat suicide scar die ago family connect month account hospital
1.68	brain episode doctor fan season week movie link tumblr comment finally read story ago scene buy gaga write order hey
0.054	eat sleep morning hour home food bed drink week run dinner tomorrow wake dog fat coffee tire buy tonight lunch
0.039	girl baby boy hot beautiful kiss date heart sexy dance babe week sweet hair marry birthday lady retweet nice miley
-0.641	tonight dress beautiful fashion style cute party beauty hair nail black shop lady free beach vip bottle outfit buy ticket
-1.199	wanna baby sleep phone hate home mad bore tire bitch text morning hurt play man ready tomorrow leo stay ima

Table 4: Selected SLDA topics from Twitter training data with informative priors

Anchor	Top 20 words
business	business market plan lead build birmingham car city support social pay company system legal financial deal service design creative control
college	college school class girl week student study hour test learn summer parent high hate sit tomorrow senior mom wear teacher
dance	dance girl school amaze tonight wear song funny movie picture beautiful pretty fun sing omg hot high drink hair boy
fat	fat eat hate body sleep weight girl bed skinny cry fast beautiful die perfect cross hair ugh week sick care
friday	friday tonight weekend week tomorrow party monday saturday morning thursday tuesday sunday club meet drink hour wednesday queen card movie
fuck	fuck shit hate bitch girl wanna gonna sleep care school drink damn die suck yeah break kill text stupid phone
god	god heart man jesus lord bless pray person men mind church trust woman care truth girl walk hear matter true
haha	haha yeah tomorrow gonna bed pretty omg xx nice sleep excite tweet fun week hour yay mum amaze hate tonight
music	music song album awesome single grey rock hear justin meet band gonna light sound tour grab concert artist tonight amaze
play	play game tonight man fan team radio hey season sound hour yeah episode nice buy hear football ball beat player
win	win game team fan tonight vote season player goal football man chance final card coach score week luck usa top

Table 5: Examples of topics identified by SANCHOR on Twitter training data.

topic has at least one anchor word that unambiguously identifies that topic — when you see an anchor in a document, you know for sure that that topic is relevant somewhere in it.[3] For instance, *fifa* might be an anchor word for the soccer topic. Words such as *ball*, *net*, or *player* are related to the soccer topic, but they cannot be anchor words because they are also mentioned in topics such as baseball or networking. The supervised anchor algorithm (SANCHOR) extends ANCHOR by expanding the word co-occurrence data to include word-level conditional probabilities for the regression variable of interest (Nguyen et al., 2015). Table 5 illustrates a number of the topics discovered by SANCHOR in the Twitter training data.[4] See the Appendix for more details.

3.4 Supervised Nested Latent Dirichlet Allocation

Like all topic models, SNLDA is based on a generative model in which each document is created by selecting a probability distribution over topics it will contain, and then selecting words based on that topic distribution; that is, every document can be viewed as coming from a mixture of topics. Like SLDA (Section 3.2), SNLDA allows us to connect each topic with a regression variable of interest; however, in SNLDA we additionally assume that the underlying topics are organized into a tree. The additional hierarchy is intended to improve our ability to represent more complicated text and account for the fact that a single topic can contribute to either side of the regression parameter depending on its subcontext.

The input of SNLDA is identical to that of SLDA, namely a collection of D documents, each associated with a response variable. The output is a tree $\mathcal{T}$, with fixed height L and a pre-defined number of children K_l for each level l of the tree. At each node, we have a process similar to SLDA: we draw (a) a topic ϕ_k specifying what this node k is about and (b) a regression parameter η_k specifying the weight of k in capturing the response variable. A child node is connected with its parent node, topically, by drawing its topic distribution from a Dirichlet prior $\mathrm{Dir}(\beta_{l_k}\phi_{p_k})$ whose mean vector ϕ_{p_k} is the topic of the parent node p_k. See the Apendix for more details.

Features	P, R=0.5	P, R=0.75	P, R=1
(A) Unigrams	0.607	0.483	0.342
(B) LIWC	0.571	0.479	0.344
(C) LDA-50 (Mallet)	0.447	0.402	0.349
(D) SLDA features, uninformative priors	0.308	0.352	0.341
(E) SLDA **features, informative priors**	**0.648**	**0.584**	**0.353**
(F) **SANCHOR**	**0.638**	**0.529**	**0.348**
(G) SLDA prediction, uninformative priors	0.568	0.479	0.271
(H) SLDA prediction, informative priors	0.643	0.436	0.303
(I) Combining A+B+C+E+F	0.632	0.526	0.342

Table 7: Evaluation on Twitter test set, showing precision at three levels of recall.

The structure of this model is similar in spirit to SHLDA (Nguyen et al., 2013), and it is intended to serve a similar purpose, namely inducing structure in such a way that sub-topics meaningfully specialize their parent nodes. Nguyen et al. illustrate how this can be useful in the political domain — for example, in an analysis of Congressional floor debates, the model identifies taxation as a first-level topic, with one child node that captures Democrats' framing of the subject (with terms like *child support*, *education*, *students*, and *health care*, i.e. the social services that taxes pay for) and another child node capturing Republican framing (with terms like *death tax*, *jobs*, *family businesses*, and *equipment*, related to the implications of taxation for businesses). Here our goal is to use a similarly structured model, but jointly modeling authors' language with their depression status as the regression variable rather than their political affiliation.

Tables 6 provide some illustrative examples of SNLDA topics induced from the Twitter training data. The hierarchical organization is apparent in, for example, Topic 8, where a sports topic is subdivided into subtopics related to, among others, soccer and professional wrestling; Topic 9 on politics/news, subdividing into, among others, education, India, Britain, and controversies involving race and law enforcement (Ferguson, the Travyon Martin shooting); and Topic 6, which our clinician characterizes as issues that tend to be discussed on social media by women, e.g. relationships, body issues, parenting, and physical maladies.

[3]This assumption can be violated, but the truer it is, the better the model.

[4]Note that SANCHOR does not produce regression values for each topic in the way that SLDA does.

Topic:Subtopic	Regression value	Top 20 words
8	-3.279	game win team play player fan season football coach basketball score lebron nfl baseball nba ball beat lead ohio brown
8:3	-0.15	goal dodger cup madrid match brazil usa chris soccer germany worldcup ronaldo messi spain ucla ger fifa orlando oscar att
8:5	-0.021	spur wrestle match wwe raw danny podcast wrestler fantastic batman title fan cont cena nxt wrestlemania corbin debut manu kick
9	-1.874	obama vote news report support government police bob president tax plan obamacare labour campaign business law leader election birmingham city
9:1	-0.244	student art education teach college teacher visa africa university scholarship mandela literacy typhoon science digital haiyan nelson child phot
9:2	-0.23	india medium hindu saint allegation conspiracy indian follower delhi fake diwali expose police sai rape truth false support jail fir
9:3	-0.056	manchester tory bbc ukip lib britain cut british event dems council library thatcher clegg guardian dem england farage unite mail
9:7	0	ferguson black williams prison crochet police topic false morning zimmerman trayvon chicago woman angeles family community ebay guest sxsw discus
6	0.093	lol sleep haha hate wanna omg ugh eat mom tire gonna baby idk bed yeah tomorrow wake hurt bore hair
6:0	0.102	anxiety vlog stress weightloss anxious panda migraine tire guinea therapy shift interview EMOJI remedy mind relief irritable chil
6:1	0.171	skype husband lols hubby dream reply week meet edit youi nowplaying owner instagram steam beautiful yup birthday notice amaze admin
6:4	0.972	fat eat cut weight cross calorie skinny fast line body burn workout account food water weigh gain exercise leg healthy

Table 6: Selected SNLDA topics

4 Quantitative results

An established use of topic models in predictive modeling is to create a K-topic model using some relevant document collection (which might or might not include the training set), and then, for training and test documents, to use the posterior topic distribution $\Pr(z_k|d), k = 1..K$ as a set of K features (Resnik et al., 2013; Schwartz et al., 2014). These features can be useful because the automatically discovered topics sometimes capture higher-level properties or "themes" in authors' language that have predictive value beyond individual words or phrases. Our experimentation used these features from LDA, sLDA, and sANCHOR; using topic posteriors from SNLDA is left for future work.

To assess the ability of the models/features and how they compare to baseline methods, we trained a linear support vector regression (SVR) model on the union of the Twitter train and dev sets, evaluated on the test set. We chose regression over classification despite having binary labels in our data in order to more easily evaluate precision at various levels of recall, which can be done simply by thresholding the predicted value at different points in order to obtain different recall levels. In addition, SVR has been shown to be an adequate choice to other similar text regression problems (Kogan et al., 2009), and in future analyses the use of the linear kernel will allow us to further see the contributions of each feature from the weights assigned by the regression model. We follow standard practice in using unigram features and LIWC categories as baseline feature sets, and we also use topic posteriors from a 50-topic LDA model built on the Twitter training data.[5]

As shown in Table 7, we evaluated alternative models/feature sets by fixing the percentage of recalled (correctly classified) depression subjects at levels R=1, 0.75, and 0.5 and looking at precision, or, equivalently, the rate of misdiagnosed control subjects.[6] When R=1, it means the classification threshold was set to the smallest value such that all depressed subjects were correctly classified. The results show that all methods perform similarly badly at 100% recall: when required to identify all depressed individuals, two thirds or so of the flagged individuals are false positives. When allowed to trade off recall for improved precision, sLDA performs well *if* provided with informative priors, and the supervised anchor method (without informative priors) is not far behind.

For completeness, we also used the sLDA models directly for prediction, i.e. computing the expected response value for a test document from $\eta^\top \bar{z}$ where $\bar{z}$ is the document's posterior topic distribution and the ηs are the per-topic regression parameters. These results are shown as "sLDA prediction" (lines G and H) in the table. The utility of this technique is illustrated on the model without informative priors (G), where it yielded a substantial improvement over the use of the posterior topics as features for both LDA (line C) and sLDA with uninformative priors (line D). This suggests that sLDA-based features (D) may have performed so poorly because they failed to sufficiently leverage the added value of the regression parameter, making them no better than vanilla LDA (C). SNLDA models can similarly be used to predict a test document's expected

[5]Not to be confused with the LDA model built using the stream-of-consciousness dataset in Section 3.1, which was used to provide informative priors for sLDA.

[6]Owing to an error discovered late in the writing process, 4 out of 396 test items were excluded from the SANCHOR evaluation. If accepted, this will be corrected in the final version.

response value; we will explore this in future work.

To the extent that this test set is representative of the real world, the results here seem promising: with R=0.75, 3 of 4 depressed individuals are detected at the cost of roughly 1 false positive per 3 individuals predicted. The representativeness of the experiment, however, depends heavily on the true prevalence of depression. On the one hand, the prevalence in the Coppersmith (2015) dataset — in the vicinity of 30% — is consistent with Vermani et al. (2011), who cite four prior studies when stating that "major depressive disorder has been shown to be one of the most common mental disorders seen in primary care patients, with prevalence rates ranging from 23% to 35%". In their own study of 840 primary care patients in Canada, they found that 27.2% met criteria for major depressive disorder. On the other hand, those numbers seem quite high: Vermani et al. also cite a WHO study finding that 10.4% of screened patients met criteria for current depression, and that number is more in line with NIMH's 12-month prevalence figures.[7]

Although it introduces a mismatch between training and test data prevalence, therefore, we experimented with randomly down-sampling the number of positive examples in the test data (but not the training set) to get a test-set prevalence of 10%. Table 8 shows the mean ± standard deviation results.[8] The absolute numbers are significantly lower, but the same trend persists in the comparison across models/features.

Elsewhere in this volume, a companion paper describes our participation in the CLPsych 2015 Shared Task (Coppersmith et al., 2015), providing experimentation on shared task datasets and further discussion and analysis (Resnik et al., 2015).

5 Conclusions

Our goal in this paper has been to go beyond simple, "vanilla" topic models to explore the potential utility of more sophisticated topic modeling in the automatic identification of depression. Qualitative examples have confirmed that LDA, and now additional LDA-like models, can uncover meaningful and potentially useful latent structure, and our quantitative experimentation using the CLPsych Hackathon dataset has shown more sophisticated topic models exploiting supervision, such as SLDA and SANCHOR, can improve on LDA alone.

One of the additional take-aways here is that informative priors can make a meaningful difference in performance; we plan to pursue this further using interactive topic modeling (Hu et al., 2014) with our domain expert, and also by providing informative priors for anchor methods.

Another important observation is that prevalence matters, and therefore further work is needed exploring the sensivity of early screening approaches to changes in the proportion of the target signal represented in the data.

Finally, a third interesting observation coming out of our experimentation was that aggregation might matter a great deal. Rather than aggregating by author, we defined a *set* of documents for each author as their tweets aggregated on a weekly basis, i.e. one document per author per week. Although just a preliminary experiment with one model, we found with SANCHOR that the weekly grouping improved precision at R=0.5 to 74% and precision at R=0.75 to 62%. The improvement makes intuitive sense, since topics and emotional state vary over time and language samples grouped on a weekly basis are likely to have more internal coherence than samples aggregated over long periods. This led us to adopt weekly aggregation in the CLPsych 2015 shared task, with good results (Resnik et al., 2015), and other forms of aggregation therefore seem like a fruitful area for further exploration.

Features	P, R=0.5	P, R=0.75	P, R=1
Uni	0.239 ± 0.047	0.165 ± 0.042	0.108 ± 0.010
SANCHOR	0.271 ± 0.045	0.189 ± 0.033	0.126 ± 0.015
SLDA-inf	0.267 ± 0.042	0.216 ± 0.035	0.119 ± 0.022

Table 8: Mean ± stdev precision (P) and recall (R) scores of linear SVR for the3 best-performing models/features in Table 7 (SLDA with informative priors, SANCHOR and unigrams) on test sets where the prevalence of depression was randomly downsampled to 10%.

[7] http://www.nimh.nih.gov/health/statistics/prevalence/major-depression-among-adults.shtml

[8] To obtain means and standard deviations we down-sampled 100 times.

Acknowledgments

We appreciate the helpful comments of the anonymous reviewers, we are grateful to Rebecca Resnik for contributing her comments and clinical expertise, and we thank Glen Coppersmith, Mark Dredze, Jamie Pennebaker, and their colleagues for kindly sharing data and resources. This work was supported in part by NSF awards 1320538, 1018625, and 1211153. Any opinions, findings, conclusions, or recommendations expressed here are those of the authors and do not necessarily reflect the view of the sponsor.

Appendix

The Appendix is available online at `http://www.umiacs.umd.edu/~resnik/pubs/clpsych2_appendix.pdf`.

References

APA. 2013. The critical need for psychologists in rural America. http://www.apa.org/about/gr/education/rural-need.aspx, Downloaded September 16, 2013.

Sanjeev Arora, Rong Ge, Yoni Halpern, David M. Mimno, Ankur Moitra, David Sontag, Yichen Wu, and Michael Zhu. 2013. A practical algorithm for topic modeling with provable guarantees.

David M Blei and John D Lafferty. 2007. A correlated topic model of science. *The Annals of Applied Statistics*, pages 17–35.

David M Blei and Jon D McAuliffe. 2007. Supervised topic models. In *Advances in Neural Information Processing Systems*, pages 121–128.

David M Blei, Andrew Y Ng, and Michael I Jordan. 2003. Latent Dirichlet allocation. *The Journal of Machine Learning Research*, 3:993–1022.

Glen Coppersmith, Mark Dredze, and Craig Harman. 2014. Quantifying mental health signals in Twitter. In *Proceedings of the Workshop on Computational Linguistics and Clinical Psychology: From Linguistic Signal to Clinical Reality*, pages 51–60, Baltimore, Maryland, USA, June. Association for Computational Linguistics.

Glen Coppersmith, Mark Dredze, Craig Harman, Kristy Hollingshead, and Margaret Mitchell. 2015. CLPsych 2015 shared task: Depression and PTSD on Twitter. In *Proceedings of the Workshop on Computational Linguistics and Clinical Psychology: From Linguistic Signal to Clinical Reality*, Denver, Colorado, USA, June. North American Chapter of the Association for Computational Linguistics.

Glen Coppersmith. 2015. [Un]Shared task: Computational linguistics and clinical psychology. `http://glencoppersmith.com/papers/CLPsych2015_hackathon_shared_task.pdf`.

Munmun De Choudhury, Scott Counts, and Eric Horvitz. 2013. Predicting postpartum changes in emotion and behavior via social media. In *Proceedings of the 2013 ACM annual conference on Human factors in computing systems*, pages 3267–3276. ACM.

Justin Grimmer. 2010. A Bayesian hierarchical topic model for political texts: Measuring expressed agendas in Senate press releases. *Political Analysis*, 18(1):1–35.

Yuening Hu, Jordan Boyd-Graber, Brianna Satinoff, and Alison Smith. 2014. Interactive topic modeling. *Machine Learning*, 95(3):423–469.

Oliver P John and Sanjay Srivastava. 1999. The big five trait taxonomy: History, measurement, and theoretical perspectives. *Handbook of personality: Theory and research*, 2:102–138.

Martin A Katzman, Leena Anand, Melissa Furtado, and Pratap Chokka. 2014. Food for thought: understanding the value, variety and usage of management algorithms for major depressive disorder. *Psychiatry research*, 220:S3–S14.

Shimon Kogan, Dimitry Levin, R. Bryan Routledge, S. Jacob Sagi, and A. Noah Smith. 2009. Predicting risk from financial reports with regression. In *Proceedings of Human Language Technologies: The 2009 Annual Conference of the North American Chapter of the Association for Computational Linguistics*, pages 272–280. Association for Computational Linguistics.

NAMI. 2013. Major depression fact sheet, April. http://www.nami.org/Template.cfm?Section=depression.

Yair Neuman, Yohai Cohen, Dan Assaf, and Gabbi Kedma. 2012. Proactive screening for depression through metaphorical and automatic text analysis. *Artif. Intell. Med.*, 56(1):19–25, September.

Viet-An Nguyen, Jordan Boyd-Graber, and Philip Resnik. 2013. Lexical and hierarchical topic regression. In *Proceedings of Advances in Neural Information Processing Systems*, pages 1106–1114.

Thang Nguyen, Jordan Boyd-Graber, Jeffrey Lund, Kevin Seppi, and Eric Ringger. 2015. Is your anchor going up or down? Fast and accurate supervised topic models. In *North American Chapter of the Association for Computational Linguistics*.

James W Pennebaker and Laura A King. 1999. Linguistic styles: language use as an individual difference. *Journal of personality and social psychology*, 77(6):1296.

Philip Resnik, Anderson Garron, and Rebecca Resnik. 2013. Using topic modeling to improve prediction of neuroticism and depression in college students. In *Proceedings of the 2013 Conference on Empirical Methods in Natural Language Processing*, pages 1348–1353, Seattle, Washington, USA, October. Association for Computational Linguistics.

Philip Resnik, Rebecca Resnik, and Margaret Mitchell, editors. 2014. *Proceedings of the Workshop on Computational Linguistics and Clinical Psychology: From Linguistic Signal to Clinical Reality*. Association for Computational Linguistics, Baltimore, Maryland, USA, June.

Philip Resnik, William Armstrong, Leonardo Claudino, and Thang Nguyen. 2015. The University of Maryland CLPsych 2015 shared task system. In *Proceedings of the Workshop on Computational Linguistics and Clinical Psychology: From Linguistic Signal to Clinical Reality*, Denver, Colorado, USA, June. North American Chapter of the Association for Computational Linguistics.

Stephanie Rodrigues, Barbara Bokhour, Nora Mueller, Natalie Dell, Princess E Osei-Bonsu, Shibei Zhao, Mark Glickman, Susan V Eisen, and A Rani Elwy. 2014. Impact of stigma on veteran treatment seeking for depression. *American Journal of Psychiatric Rehabilitation*, 17(2):128–146.

Stephanie Rude, Eva-Maria Gortner, and James Pennebaker. 2004. Language use of depressed and depression-vulnerable college students. *Cognition & Emotion*, 18(8):1121–1133.

H. Andrew Schwartz, Johannes Eichstaedt, Margaret L. Kern, Gregory Park, Maarten Sap, David Stillwell, Michal Kosinski, and Lyle Ungar. 2014. Towards assessing changes in degree of depression through facebook. In *Proceedings of the Workshop on Computational Linguistics and Clinical Psychology: From Linguistic Signal to Clinical Reality*, pages 118–125, Baltimore, Maryland, USA, June. Association for Computational Linguistics.

Kathleen Sibelius. 2013. Increasing access to mental health services, April. http://www.whitehouse.gov/blog/2013/04/10/increasing-access-mental-health-services.

Ivan Titov and Ryan McDonald. 2008. Modeling online reviews with multi-grain topic models. In *Proceedings of the 17th international conference on World Wide Web*, pages 111–120. ACM.

Monica Vermani, Madalyn Marcus, and Martin A Katzman. 2011. Rates of detection of mood and anxiety disorders in primary care: a descriptive, cross-sectional study. *The primary care companion to CNS disorders*, 13(2).

Automated morphological analysis of clinical language samples

Kyle Gorman **Steven Bedrick** **Géza Kiss** **Eric Morley**
Rosemary Ingham **Metrah Mohammad** **Katina Papadakis** **Jan P.H. van Santen**

Center for Spoken Language Understanding
Oregon Health & Science University
Portland, OR, USA

Abstract

Quantitative analysis of clinical language samples is a powerful tool for assessing and screening developmental language impairments, but requires extensive manual transcription, annotation, and calculation, resulting in error-prone results and clinical underutilization. We describe a system that performs automated morphological analysis needed to calculate statistics such as the mean length of utterance in morphemes (MLUM), so that these statistics can be computed directly from orthographic transcripts. Estimates of MLUM computed by this system are closely comparable to those produced by manual annotation. Our system can be used in conjunction with other automated annotation techniques, such as maze detection. This work represents an important first step towards increased automation of language sample analysis, and towards attendant benefits of automation, including clinical greater utilization and reduced variability in care delivery.

1 Introduction

Specific language impairment (SLI) is a neurodevelopmental disorder characterized by language delays or deficits in the absence of other developmental or sensory impairments (Tomblin, 2011). A history of specific language impairment is associated with a host of difficulties in adolescence and adulthood, including poorer quality friendships (Durkin and Conti-Ramsden, 2007), a greater risk for psychiatric disturbance (Durkin and Conti-Ramsden, 2010), and diminished educational attainment and occupational opportunities (Conti-Ramsden and Durkin, 2012). SLI is common but remains significantly underdiagnosed; one large-scale study estimates that over 7% of kindergarten-aged monolingual English speaking children have SLI, but found that the parents of most of these children were unaware that their child had a speech or language problem (Tomblin et al., 1997).

Developmental language impairments are normally assessed using standardized tests such as the Clinical Evaluation of Language Fundamentals (CELF), a battery of norm-referenced language tasks such as Recalling Sentences, in which the child repeats a sentence, and Sentence Structure, in which the child points to a picture matching a sentence. However, there has been a recent push to augment norm-referenced tests with language sample analysis (Leadholm and Miller, 1992; Miller and Chapman, 1985), in which a spontaneous language sample collected from a child is used to compute various statistics measuring expressive language abilities.

Natural language processing (NLP) has the potential to open new frontiers in language sample analysis. For instance, some recent work has applied NLP techniques to quantify clinical impressions that once were merely qualitative (e.g., Rouhizadeh et al. 2013, van Santen et al. 2013) and other work has proposed novel computational features for detecting language disorders (e.g., Gabani et al. 2011). In this study, our goal is somewhat sim-

Proceedings of the 2nd Workshop on Computational Linguistics and Clinical Psychology: From Linguistic Signal to Clinical Reality, pages 108–116,
Denver, Colorado, June 5, 2015.

pler: we attempt to apply novel NLP techniques to assist the clinician by automating the computation of firmly established spontaneous language statistics.

Quantitative analysis of language samples is a powerful tool for assessing and screening developmental language impairments. Measures derived from naturalistic language samples are thought to be approximately as sensitive to language impairment as are decontextualized tests like those that make up the CELF (Aram et al., 1993); they may also be less biased against speakers of non-standard dialects (Stockman, 1996). Despite this, language sample analysis is still underutilized in clinical settings, in part due to the daunting amount of manual transcription and annotation required.

Clinicians may avail themselves of software like Systematic Analysis of Transcripts (SALT; Miller and Iglesias 2012), which partially automates the language sample analysis. But this tool (and others like it) require the clinician to provide not only a complete orthographic transcription, but also detailed linguistic annotations using a complex and unforgiving annotation syntax that itself takes significant effort to master. In what follows, we describe a system which automates a key part of this annotation process: the tedious and error-prone annotation of morphological structure.

In the next section, we describe *mean length of utterance in morphemes* (MLUM), a widely used measure of linguistic productivity, and associated morphological annotations needed to compute this measure. We then outline a computational model which uses a cascade of linear classifiers and finite-state automata to generate these morphological annotations; this allows MLUM to be computed directly from an orthographic transcription. Our evaluation demonstrates that this model produces estimates of MLUM which are very similar to those produced by manual annotation. Finally, we outline directions for future research.

2 Mean length of utterance and morphological annotations

Mean length of utterance in morphemes is a widely-used measure of linguistic productivity in children, consisting essentially of the average number of morphemes per utterance. Brown (1973), one of the first users of MLUM, describes it as a simple, face-valid index of language development simply because nearly any linguistic feature newly mastered by the child—be it obligatory morphology, more complex argument structure, or clausal recursion—results in an increase in the average utterance length. MLUM has also proven useful in diagnosing developmental language impairments. For instance, typically-developing children go through a stage where they omit affixes and/or function words which are obligatory in their target language (e.g., Harris and Wexler 1996; Legate and Yang 2007). Children with language impairment are thought to omit obligatory morphemes at a higher rate than their typically-developing peers (Eisenberg et al., 2001; Rice and Wexler, 1996; Rice et al., 1998; Rice et al., 2006), and differences in omission rate can be detected, albeit indirectly, with MLUM.

SALT (Miller and Chapman, 1985) provides specific guidelines for estimating MLUM. These guidelines are concerned both with what utterances and tokens "count" towards MLUM, as well as which tokens are to be considered morphologically complex. The SALT guidelines require that complex words be written by writing the free stem form of the word, followed by a forward-slash (/) and an unambiguous signature representing the suffix. SALT recognizes 13 "suffixes", including the noun plural (`dog/s`), possessive (`mom/z`), preterite/past participle (`walk/ed`), progressive/future (`stroll/ing`), and various enclitics (`I/'m`, `we/'re`, `is/n't`); some SALT suffixes can also be combined (e.g., the plural possessive `boy/s/z`). Each SALT suffix is counted as a single morpheme, as are all stems and simplex words. Irregulars affixes (*felt*), derivational affixes (*un-lock*, *write-r*), and compounds (*break-fast*) are not annotated, and words bearing them are counted as a single morpheme unless these words happen to contain one of the aforementioned SALT suffixes.

In the next section, we propose a computational model which generates SALT-like morphological annotations. Our highest priority is to be faithful to the SALT specification, which has proved sufficient for the creators' well-defined, clinically-oriented aims. We do not claim that our system will generalize to any other linguistic annotation scheme, but only that we have successfully automated SALT-style morphological annotations. We recognize the limitations of the SALT specification: it draws little inspiration from linguistic theory, and furthermore fails to anticipate the possibility of the sort of automation we propose. As it happens, there is a large body of work in natural language processing on automated methods for morphological segmentation and/or analysis, which could easily be applied to this problem. Yet, the vast majority of this literature is concerned with unsupervised learning (i.e., inducing morphological analyses from unlabeled data) rather than the (considerably easier) task of mimicking morphological analyses produced by humans, our goal here. (For one exception, see the papers in Kurimo et al. 2010.) While it would certainly be possible to adapt existing unsupervised morphological analyzers to implement the SALT specification, the experiments presented below demonstrate that simple statistical models, trained on a small amount of data, achieve near-ceiling performance at this task. Given this result, we feel that adapting existing unsupervised systems to this task would be a purely academic exercise.

3 The model

We propose a model to automatically generate SALT-compatible morphological annotations, as follows. First, *word extraction* identifies words which count towards MLUM. Then, *suffix prediction* predicts the most likely set of suffixes for each word. Finally, *stem analysis* maps complex words back to their stem form. These three steps generate all the information necessary to compute MLUM. We now proceed to describe each step in more detail.

3.1 Word extraction

The SALT guidelines excludes any speech which occurs during an incomplete or abandoned utterance, speech in utterances that contain incomprehensible words, and speech during *mazes*—i.e., disfluent intervals, which encompass all incomplete words and fillers—for the purpose of computing MLUM and related statistics. A cascade of regular expressions are used to extract a list of eligible word tokens from individual lines of the orthographic transcript.

3.2 Suffix prediction

Once unannotated word tokens have been extracted, they are input to a cascade of two linear classifiers. The first classifier makes a binary prediction as to whether the token is morphologically simplex or complex. If the token is predicted to be complex, it is input to a second classifier which attempts to predict which combination of the 13 SALT suffixes is present.

Both classifiers are trained with held-out-data using the perceptron learning algorithm and weight averaging (Freund and Schapire, 1999). We report results using four feature sets. The baseline model uses only a bias term. The φ_0 set uses orthographic features inspired by "rare word" features used in part-of-speech tagging (Ratnaparkhi, 1997) and intended to generalize well to out-of-vocabulary words. In addition to bias, φ_0 consists of six orthographic features of the target token (w_i), including three binary features ("w_i contains an apostrophe", "w_i is a sound effect", "w_i is a hyphenated word") and all proper string suffixes of w_i up to three characters in length. The φ_1 feature set adds a nominal attribute, the identity of w_i. Finally, φ_2 also includes four additional nominal features, the identity of the nearest tokens to the left and right ($w_{i-2}, w_{i-1}, w_{i+1}, w_{i+2}$). Four sample feature vectors are shown in Table 1.

3.3 Stem analysis

Many English stems are spelled somewhat differently in free and bound (i.e., bare and inflected) form. For example, stem-final usually changes to *i* in the past tense (e.g., *buried*), and stem-final *e* usually deletes before the progressive (e.g., *bouncing*). Similarly, the SALT suffixes have different spellings depending on context; the noun plural suffix is spelled *es* when affixed to stems ending in stridents (e.g., *mixes*), but as *s* elsewhere. To model these spelling changes triggered by suffixation, we use finite state automata (FSAs), math-

	I'm	looking	for	one	dinosaur
φ_0	*apostrophe* suf1="M" suf2="'M"	suf1="G" suf2="NG" suf3="ING"	suf1="R" suf2="OR"	suf1="E" suf2="NE"	suf1="R" suf2="UR" suf3="AUR"
φ_1	w_i="I'M"	w_i="LOOKING"	w_i="FOR"	w_i="ONE"	w_i="DINOSAUR"
φ_2	*initial* w_i+1="LOOKING" w_i+2="FOR"	*peninitial* w_i-1="I'M" w_i+1="FOR" w_i+2="ONE"	w_i-2="I'M" w_i-1="LOOKING" w_i+1="ONE" w_i+2="PET"	w_i-2="LOOKING" w_i-1="FOR" w_i+1="DINOSAUR" *penultimate*	w_i-2="FOR" w_i-1="ONE" *ultimate*

Table 1: Sample features for the utterance *I'm looking for one dinosaur*; each column represents a separate feature vector.

ematical models widely used in both natural language processing and speech recognition. Finite state automata can be used implement a cascade of context-dependent rewrite rules (e.g., "α goes to β in the context δ __ γ") similar to those used by linguists in writing phonological rules. This makes FSAs particularly well suited for dealing with spelling rules like the ones described above.

This spell-out transducer can also be adapted to recover the stem of a wordform, once morphological analysis has been performed. If I is the input wordform, S is the spell-out transducer, and D is a simple transducer which deletes whatever suffixes are present, then the output-tape symbols of $I \circ S^{-1} \circ D$ contain the original stem.[1] However, there may be multiple output paths for many input wordforms. For instance, a doubled stem-final consonant in the inflected form could either be present in the bare stem (e.g., *guess* → *guessing*) or could be a product of the doubling rule (e.g., *run* → *running*); both are permitted by S^{-1}. To resolve these ambiguities, we employ a simple probabilistic method. Let W be a weighted finite-state acceptor in which each path represents a stem, and the cost of each path is proportional to that stem's frequency.[2] Then, the most likely stem given the input wordform and analysis is given by the output-tape symbols of

$$\text{ShortestPath}(I \circ S^{-1} \circ D \circ W)\,.$$

Both the spell-out transducer and the stemmer were generated using the Thrax grammar-compilation tools (Roark et al., 2012); a full specification of both models is provided in the appendix.

4 Evaluation

We evaluate the model with respect to its ability to mimic human morphological annotations, using three intrinsic measures. *Suffix detection* refers to agreement on whether or not an eligible word is morphologically complex. *Suffix classification* refers to agreement as to which suffix or suffixes are borne by a word which has been correctly classified as morphologically complex by the suffix detector. Finally, *token agreement* refers agreement as to the overall morphological annotation of an eligible word. We also evaluate the model extrinsically, by computing the Pearson product-moment correlation between MLUM computed from manual annotated data to MLUM computed from automated morphological annotations. In all evalu-

[1]An anonymous reviewer asks how this "stemmer" relates to familiar tools such as the Porter (1980) stemmer. The stemmer described here takes morphologically annotated complex words as input and outputs the uninflected ("free") stem. In contrast, the Porter stemmer takes unannotated words as input and outputs a "canonical" form—crucially, not necessarily a real word—to be used in downstream analyses.

[2]To prevent composition failure with out-of-vocabulary stems, the acceptor W is also augmented with additional arcs permitting it to accept, with some small probability, the closure over the vocabulary.

ations, we employ a "leave one child out" cross-validation scheme.

4.1 Data

Our data comes from a large-scale study of autism spectrum disorders and language impairment in children. 110 children from the Portland, OR metropolitan area, between 4–8 years of age, took part in the study: 50 children with autism spectrum disorders (ASD), 43 typically-developing children (TD), and 17 children with specific language impairment (SLI). All participants had full-scale IQ scores of 70 or higher. All participants spoke English as their first language, and produced a mean length of utterance in morphemes (MLUM) of at least 3. During the initial screening, a certified speech-language pathologist verified the absence of speech intelligibility impairments. For more details on this sample, see van Santen et al. 2013.

The ADOS (Lord et al., 2000), a semi-structured autism diagnostic observation, was administered to all children in the current study. These sessions were recorded and used to generate verbatim transcriptions of the child and examiner's speech. Transcriptions were generated using SALT guidelines. Conversational turns were segmented into individual utterances (or "C-units"), each of which consisted of (at most) a main clause and any subordinate clauses modifying it.

4.2 Interannotator agreement

Manual annotation quality was assessed using a stratified sample of the full data set, consisting of randomly-selected utterances per child. These utterances were stripped of their morphological annotations and then re-annotated by two experienced transcribers, neither of whom participated in the initial transcription efforts. The results are shown in Table 2. On all three intrinsic measures, the original and retrospective annotators agreed an overwhelming amount of the time; the K (chance-adjusted agreement) values for the former two indicate "almost perfect" (Landis and Koch, 1977) agreement according to standard qualitative guidelines.

	Anno. 1	Anno. 2
Suffix detection K	.9207	.9529
Suffix classification K	.9135	.9452
Token agreement	.9803	.9869

Table 2: Interannotator agreement statistics for suffix detection, suffix identity, and overall token-level agreement; the K values indicate "almost perfect agreement" (Landis and Koch, 1977) according to qualitative guidelines.

4.3 Results

Table 3 summarizes the intrinsic evaluation results. The baseline system performs poorly both in suffix detection and suffix classification. Increasingly complex feature sets result in significant increases in both detection and classification. Even though most eligible words are not morphologically complex, the full feature set (φ_2) produces a good balance of precision and recall and correctly labels nearly 99% of all eligible word tokens. MLUMs computed using the automated annotations and the full feature set are almost identical to MLUMs derived from manual annotations ($R = .9998$).

This table also shows accuracies for two particularly difficult morphological distinctions, between the noun plural `S` and the 3rd person active indicative suffix `3s` (*seeks*), and between the possessive `'S` and `Z` (the contracted form of *is*), respectively. These distinctions in particular appear to benefit in particular from the contextual features of the φ_2 feature set.

In the above experiments, the data contained manually generated annotations of mazes. These are required for computing measures like MLUM, as speech in mazes is ignored when counting the number of morphemes in an utterance. Like morphological annotations, human annotation of mazes is also tedious and time-consuming. However, some recent work has attempted to automatically generate maze annotations from orthographic transcripts (Morley et al., 2014a), and automatic maze annotation would greatly increase the utility of the larger system described here.

We thus performed a simple "pipeline" evaluation of the morphological annotation system, as

	Baseline	φ_0	φ_1	φ_2
Suffix detection				
Accuracy	.8122	.9667	.9879	.9913
Precision		.8710	.9508	.9610
Recall		.8393	.9451	.9644
F_1		.8549	.9479	.9627
Suffix classification				
Overall accuracy	.1917	.8916	.9689	.9880
S vs. 3S accuracy		.7794	.9478	.9788
'S vs. Z accuracy		.9341	.9469	.9923
Token accuracy	.8267	.9663	.9878	.9899

Table 3: Intrinsic analysis results on suffix detection, suffix classification, and overall token accuracy.

follows. First, maze annotations are automatically generated for each transcript. We then feed the maze-annotated transcripts into the morphological analyzer described above, which is then used to compute MLUM. The maze annotation system used here was originally developed by Qian and Liu (2013) for detecting fillers in Switchboard as an early step in a larger disfluency detection system; Morley et al. (2014a) adapted it for maze detection. This system is trained from a dataset of transcripts with manually-annotated mazes; here we depart from the prior work in training it using a leave-one-child-out strategy. Features used are derived from tokens and automatically generated part-of-speech tags. This system treats maze detection as a sequence labeling task performed using a max-margin Markov network (Taskar et al., 2004); for more details, see Morley et al. 2014a.

We hypothesized that the errors introduced by automated maze annotation would not greatly affect MLUM estimates, as maze detection errors do not necessarily impact MLUM. For example, an utterance like *I went to I go to school* might be bracketed as either `(I went to) I go to school` and `I went to (I go to) school`, but either analysis results in the same MLUM. And in fact, MLUMs computed using the combined maze detection/morphological annotation system are competitive with MLUMs derived from manual annotations ($R = .9991$).

4.4 Discussion

Our results show that the proposed morphological analysis model produces accurate annotations, which then can be used to compute relatively precise estimates of MLUM. Furthermore, automation of other SALT-style annotations (such as maze detection) does not negatively impact automatic MLUM estimates.

We experimented with other feature sets in the hopes of approving accuracy and generalizability. We hypothesized that suffix classification would benefit from part-of-speech features. Since our data was not manually part-of-speech tagged, we extracted these features using an automated tagger similar to the one described in (Collins, 2002).[3] The tagger was trained on a corpus of approximately 150,000 utterances of child-directed speech (Pearl and Sprouse, 2013) annotated with a 39-tag set comparable to the familiar PTB tagset. Addi-

[3]The tagger was tested using the traditional "standard split" of the Wall St. Journal portion of the Penn Treebank, with sections 0–18 for training, sections 19–21 for development, and sections 22–24 for evaluation. The tagger correctly assigned 96.69% of the tags for the evaluation set.

tional POS features were also generated by mapping the 39-tag set down to a smaller set of 11 "universal" tags (Petrov et al., 2012). However, neither set of POS features produced any appreciable gains in performance. We speculate that these features are superfluous given the presence of the φ_2 word context features.

5 Conclusions

We have described a principled and accurate system for automatic calculation of widely-used measures of expressive language ability in children. The system we propose does *not* require extensive manual annotation, nor does it require expensive or difficult-to-use proprietary software, another potential barrier to use of these measures in practice. It is trained using a small amount of annotated data, and could easily be adapted to similar annotation conventions in other languages.

We view this work as a first step towards increasing the use of automation in language assessment and other language specialists. We foresee two benefits to automation in this area. First, it may reduce time spent in manual annotation, increasing the amount of time clinicians spend interacting with patients face to face. Second, increased automation may lead to decreased variability in care delivery, a necessary step towards improving outcomes (Ransom et al., 2008).

One remaining barrier to wider use of language sample analysis is the need for manual transcription, which is time-consuming even when later annotations are generated automatically. Future work will consider whether transcripts derived from automatic speech recognition are capable of producing valid, unbiased estimates of measures like MLUM.

Our group has made progress towards automating other clinically relevant annotations, including grammatical errors (Morley et al., 2014b) and repetitive speech (van Santen et al., 2013), and we are actively studying ways to integrate our various systems into a full suite of automated language sample analysis utilities. More importantly, however, we anticipate collaborating closely with our clinical colleagues to develop new approaches for integrating automated assessment tools into language assessment and treatment workflows—an area in which far too little research has taken place.

Acknowledgments

All experiments were conducted using OpenFst (Allauzen et al., 2007), OpenGrm-Thrax (Roark et al., 2012), and Python 3.4. A demonstration version of the system can be viewed at the following URL: `http://sonny.cslu.ohsu.edu:8080`.

Thanks to the other members of the CSLU autism research group, and to Emily Prud'hommeaux and Mabel Rice.

This material is based upon work supported by the National Institute on Deafness and Other Communication Disorders of the National Institutes of Health under awards R01DC007129 and R01DC012033, and by Autism Speaks under Innovative Technology for Autism Grant 2407. The content is solely the responsibility of the authors and does not necessarily represent the official views of the granting agencies or any other individual.

References

Cyril Allauzen, Michael Riley, Johan Schalkwyk, Wojciech Skut, and Mehryar Mohri. 2007. OpenFst: A general and efficient weighted finite-state transducer library. In *Proceedings of the 9th International Conference on Implementation and Application of Automata*, pages 11–23.

Dorothy M. Aram, Robin Morris, and Nancy E. Hall. 1993. Clinical and research congruence in identifying children with specific language impairment. *Journal of Speech and Hearing Research*, 36(3):580–591.

Roger Brown. 1973. *A first language: The early stages*. Harvard University Press, Cambridge.

Michael Collins. 2002. Discriminative training methods for hidden Markov models: Theory and experiments with perceptron algorithms. In *EMNLP*, pages 1–8.

Gina Conti-Ramsden and Kevin Durkin. 2012. Postschool educational and employment experiences of young people with specific language impairment. *Language, Speech, and Hearing Services in Schools*, 43(4):507–520.

Kevin Durkin and Gina Conti-Ramsden. 2007. Language, social behavior, and the quality of friendships in adolescents with and without a history of specific language impairment. *Child Development*, 78(5):1441–1457.

Kevin Durkin and Gina Conti-Ramsden. 2010. Young people with specific language impairment: A review of social and emotional functioning in adolescence. *Child Language Teaching and Therapy*, 26(2):105–121.

Sarita L. Eisenberg, Tara McGovern Fersko, and Cheryl Lundgren. 2001. The use of MLU for identifying language impairment in preschool children: A review. *American Journal of Speech-Language Pathology*, 10(4):323–342.

Yoav Freund and Robert E. Schapire. 1999. Large margin classification using the perceptron algorithm. *Machine Learning*, 37(3):277–296.

Keyur Gabani, Thamar Solorio, Yang Liu, Khairun-nisa Hassanali, and Christine A. Dollaghan. 2011. Exploring a corpus-based approach for detecting language impairment in monolingual English-speaking children. *Artificial Intelligence in Medicine*, 53(3):161–170.

Tony Harris and Kenneth Wexler. 1996. The optional-infinitive stage in child English: Evidence from negation. In Harald Clahsen, editor, *Generative perspectives on language acquisition: Empirical findings*, pages 1–42. John Benjamins, Amsterdam.

Mikko Kurimo, Sami Virpioja, and Ville T. Turunen. 2010. Proceedings of the Morpho Challenge 2010 workshop. Technical Report TKK-ICS-R37, Aalto University School of Science and Technology.

J. Richard Landis and Gary G. Koch. 1977. The measurement of observer agreement for categorical data. *Biometrics*, 33(1):159–174.

Barbara J. Leadholm and Jon F. Miller. 1992. *Language sample analysis: The Wisconsin guide*. Wisconsin Department of Public Instruction, Madison, WI.

Julie A. Legate and Charles Yang. 2007. Morphosyntactic learning and the development of tense. *Language Acquisition*, 14(3):315–344.

Catherine Lord, Susan Risi, Linda Lambrect, Jr. Edwin H. Cook, Bennett L. Leventhal, Pamela C. DiLavore, Andrew Pickles, and Michael Rutter. 2000. The Autism Diagnostic Observation Schedule-Generic: A standard measure of social and communication deficits associated with the spectrum of autism. *Journal of Autism and Developmental Disorders*, 30(3):205–223.

Jon F. Miller and Robin S. Chapman. 1985. *Systematic Analysis of Language Transcripts*. University of Wisconsin, Madison, WI.

Jon F. Miller and Aquiles Iglesias. 2012. *Systematic Analysis of Language Transcripts, Research Version 2012*. SALT Software, LLC, Middleton, WI.

Eric Morley, Anna Eva Hallin, and Brian Roark. 2014a. Challenges in automating maze detection. In *ACL CLPsych*, pages 69–77.

Eric Morley, Anna Eva Hallin, and Brian Roark. 2014b. Data-driven grammatical error detection in transcripts of children's speech. In *EMNLP*, pages 980–989.

Lisa Pearl and Jon Sprouse. 2013. Syntactic islands and learning biases: Combining experimental syntax and computational modeling to investigate the language acquisition problem. *Language Acquisition*, 20(1):23–68.

Slav Petrov, Dipanjan Das, and Ryan McDonald. 2012. A universal part-of-speech tagset. In *LREC*, pages 2089–2096.

Martin F. Porter. 1980. An algorithm for suffix stripping. *Program*, 14(3):130–137.

Xian Qian and Yang Liu. 2013. Disfluency detection using multi-step stacked learning. In *NAACL-HLT*, pages 820–825.

Elizabeth R. Ransom, Maulik S. Joshi, David B. Nash, and Scott B. Ransom. 2008. *The healthcare quality book: Vision, strategy, and tools*. Health Administration Press, Chicago, 2nd edition.

Adwait Ratnaparkhi. 1997. A maximum entropy model for part-of-speech tagging. In *EMNLP*, pages 133–142.

Mabel L. Rice and Kenneth Wexler. 1996. Towards tense as a clinical marker of Specific Language Impairment in English-speaking children. *Journal of Speech and Hearing Research*, 39(6):1239–1257.

Mabel L. Rice, Kenneth Wexler, and Scott Hershberger. 1998. Tense over time: The longitudinal course of tense acquisition in children with Specific Language Impairment. *Journal of Speech, Language, and Hearing Research*, 41(6):1412–1431.

Mabel L. Rice, Sean M. Redmond, and Lesa Hoffman. 2006. Mean length of utterance in children with specific language impairment and in younger control children shows concurrent validity, stable and parallel growth trajectories. *Journal of Speech, Language, and Hearing Research*, 49(4):793–808.

Brian Roark, Richard Sproat, Cyril Allauzen, Michael Riley, Jeffrey Sorensen, and Terry Tai. 2012. The OpenGrm open-source finite-state grammar software libraries. In *ACL*, pages 61–66.

Masoud Rouhizadeh, Emily Prud'hommeaux, Brian Roark, and Jan van Santen. 2013. Distributional semantic models for the evaluation of disordered speech. In *NAACL-HLT*, pages 709–714.

Ida J. Stockman. 1996. The promises and pitfalls of language sample analysis as an assessment tool for linguistic minority children. *Language, Speech, and Hearing Services in Schools*, 27(4):355–366.

Ben Taskar, Carlos Guestrin, and Daphne Koller. 2004. Max-margin Markov networks. In *NIPS*, pages 25–32.

J. Bruce Tomblin, Nancy L. Records, Paula Buckwalter, Xuyang Zhang, Elaine Smith, and Marlea O'Brien. 1997. Prevalence of specific language impairment in kindergarten children. *Journal of Speech, Language, and Hearing Research*, 6:1245–1260.

J. Bruce Tomblin. 2011. Co-morbidity of autism and SLI: Kinds, kin and complexity. *International Journal of Language and Communication Disorders*, 46(2):127–137.

Jan van Santen, Richard Sproat, and Alison Presmanes Hill. 2013. Quantifying repetitive speech in autism spectrum disorders and language impairment. *Autism Research*, 6(5):372–383.

Similarity Measures for Quantifying Restrictive and Repetitive Behavior in Conversations of Autistic Children

Masoud Rouhizadeh[†], **Richard Sproat**[§], **Jan van Santen**[†]
[†]Center for Spoken Language Understanding, Oregon Health & Science University
[§] Google, Inc.
{rouhizad,vansantj}@ohsu.edu, rws@xoba.com

Abstract

Restrictive and repetitive behavior (RRB) is a core symptom of autism spectrum disorder (ASD) and are manifest in language. Based on this, we expect children with autism to talk about fewer topics, and more repeatedly, during their conversations. We thus hypothesize a higher semantic overlap ratio between dialogue turns in children with ASD compared to those with typical development (TD). Participants of this study include children ages 4-8, 44 with TD and 25 with ASD without language impairment. We apply several semantic similarity metrics to the children's dialogue turns in semi-structured conversations with examiners. We find that children with ASD have significantly more semantically overlapping turns than children with TD, across different turn intervals. These results support our hypothesis, and could provide a convenient and robust ASD-specific behavioral marker.

1 Introduction

Autism spectrum disorder (ASD) is a neurodevelopmental disorder characterized by two broad groups of symptoms: impaired social communication and presence of restrictive and repetitive behavior (RRB) (American Psychiatric Association, 2000; American Psychiatric Association, 2013). RRB comprises both lower-order behaviors such as motor movements and higher-order cognitive behaviors such as circumscribed interests and insistence on sameness. Both of these are manifest in language as well. (Boyd et al., 2012; Szatmari et al., 2006; Turner, 1999; Kanner, 1943). All major ASD diagnostic instruments require the evaluation of RRB (Rutter et al., 2003; Lord et al., 2002; Lord et al., 1994). Individuals with ASD have significantly more RRB, stereotyped phrases, and idiosyncratic utterances in their conversations (Nadig et al., 2010; Capps et al., 1998; Volden and Lord, 1991).

However, such assessments are mostly qualitative, relying on clinical impressions or parental reports. There has been little work on quantitative or automated assessment methods for these behaviors in ASD, possibly due to the significant effort of detailed annotation of conversations that this would entail. Previous research in our group analyzed automatic detection of poor topic maintenance and use of off-topic words (Rouhizadeh et al., 2013; Prud'hommeaux and Rouhizadeh, 2012). We have also explored the different directions of departure from the target topic in ASD (rou, 2014; Prud'hommeaux et al., 2014).

In this paper, we attempt to automatically assess the presence of RRB in language, specifically at the semantic level, in children's conversation with an adult examiner during a semi-structured dialogue. We expect children with ASD to talk about fewer topics more repeatedly during their conversations. Specifically, we hypothesize a significantly higher semantic overlap ratio (SOR) between dialogue turns in children with ASD compared to those with typical development (TD). In order to calculate the SOR at different turn intervals for each child, we apply multiple semantic similarity metrics (weighted by child specificity scores) on every turn

Proceedings of the 2nd Workshop on Computational Linguistics and Clinical Psychology: From Linguistic Signal to Clinical Reality, pages 117–123,
Denver, Colorado, June 5, 2015.

pair in four distance windows. We then compute the SOR for each child by averaging the similarity of every turn pair in the four distance windows. Our analysis indicates that, based on different similarity metrics, the ASD group had a significantly higher SOR than the TD group in most of the distance windows. These results support our hypothesis. Thus, patterns of semantic similarity between child's turns could provide an automated and robust ASD-specific behavioral marker.

In a previous study, van Santen and colleagues (van Santen et al., 2013) reported an automated method for identifying and quantifying two types of repetitive speech in ASD: repetitions of what child him or herself said (*intra-speaker repetitions*) and of what the conversation partner said (*inter-speaker repetitions*, or *echolalia*). The focus of this study was on verbatim repeats of word n-grams at short turn distances. The present study differs in several ways. (1) We focus on intra-child repetitions only. (2) We do so using bag-of-words similarity measures and lexical semantic expansion. (3) We consider short and long turn distance windows. (4) We use frequency weighting, assigning lower weights to frequent words.

2 Participants and data

Participants in this study include 44 children with TD and 25 children with ASD. ASD was diagnosed via clinical consensus according to the DSM-IV-TR criteria (American Psychiatric Association, 2000) and established threshold scores on two diagnostic instruments: the Autism Diagnostic Observation Schedule (ADOS) (Lord et al., 2002); and the Social Communication Questionnaire (Rutter et al., 2003). None of the ASD children in this study met criteria for a language impairment, defined as having a Core Language Score (CLS) on the CELF (Semel et al., 2003) of more than one standard deviation below the mean. The groups were well matched in age (6.41 vs. 5.91 years for the ASD and TD groups, respectively; $p>0.2$), and Nonverbal IQ (114.0 and 118.4; $p>0.25$), but not for nonverbal IQ (108 and 119; $p<0.0025$).

Each participant's ADOS session was recorded and the recordings were transcribed. The examiner and transcribers were unaware of the child's diagnostic status, the study hypothesis, and the computational methods. The automated methods in this paper are applied to these un-annotated raw transcripts.

The ADOS is a widely-used instrument for ASD diagnosis. It consists of a semi-structured series of spontaneous conversations and interactions between a child and a examiner (usually 30 to 60 minutes long) in which the examiner asks questions and provides prompts that serve to bring out verbal and non-verbal behaviors indicative of ASD. The ADOS covers a broad range of conversational topics and activities, including Picture Description, Play, and Wordless Picture Book Description activities. Our expectation is that even though the activities, conversation topics, and actual questions are standardized, ASD children will tend to stick with their own topics of interest to a larger degree than children with TD.

3 Measuring the semantic overlap ratio (SOR)

For each child, we compute the semantic similarity score between every turn pair I and J in the following exponentially increasing distance windows, D:

a) $0<D\leq3$: J is between 1 to 3 turns after I,
b) $3<D\leq9$,
c) $9<D\leq27$,
d) $27<D\leq81$.

Then we compute the child's SOR for a given window D by averaging the similarity scores of turn pairs in D. We explored four semantic similarly measures which we describe in this section.

3.1 Semantic Similarity Measures

We expect ASD children to use more specific terms, relevant to their particular and often idiosyncratic interest due to their restrictive behavior. Therefore, we want our measures to be sensitive to how common or uncommon the words used by an individual child are. To assign lower weights to words used frequently by a large number of children, we apply an inverse document frequency (IDF) term weight using the standard definition of IDF in Information Retrieval (IR) (Manning et al., 2008):

$$idf_w = log\left(\frac{N}{df_w}\right) \quad (1)$$

where N is the total number of participants and df_w is the number of children who used the word w. We also lemmatize our corpus to reduce the sparsity (hence higher IDF weights) caused by inflectional variations of the same lexeme.

3.1.1 Weighted Jaccard Similarity Coefficient

The weighted Jaccard similarity coefficient (Jac) (Jaccard, 1912) is a word overlap measure between a pair of turns I and J defined as the sum of the minimum term frequency of each overlapping word w in I and J weighted by idf_w, and then normalized by the sum of the maximum term frequency of each word in either turn:

$$Jac(I,J)=\frac{\sum_{w\in I\cap J}\min(tf_{w,I},tf_{w,J})\times idf_w}{\sum_{w\in I\cup J}\max(tf_{w,I},tf_{w,J})} \quad (2)$$

where $tf_{w,I}$ is the term frequency of word w in turn I (number of times w occurs in I), and $tf_{w,J}$ is the term frequency of w in J.

3.1.2 Cosine Similarity Score

The cosine similarity score (Cos) is a popular metric in IR to measure the similarity between the two turns I and J via the cosine of the angle between their vectors. We assign IDF weights to term frequencies, and then normalize the turn vectors by their length and the term weights:

$$Cos(I,J)=\frac{\sum_{w\in I\cap J} tf_{w,I}\times tf_{w,J}\times(idf_w)^2}{\sqrt{\sum_{w_i\in I}(tf_{w_i,I}\times idf_{w_i})^2}\times\sqrt{\sum_{w_j\in j}(tf_{w_j,J}\times idf_{w_j})^2}} \quad (3)$$

3.1.3 Relative Frequency Measure

The relative frequency measure (RF) (Hoad and Zobel, 2003) is introduced as an author identity measure for detecting plagiarism at the document level. However, it has been shown to be applicable to the sentence level as well (Metzler et al., 2005). For this measure, we first normalize the differences in the turn lengths, and, second, we measures the similarity of the two turns I and J by the weighted relative frequency of their common words:

$$RF(I,J)=\frac{1}{1+||I|-|J||}\times\sum_{w\in I\cap J}\frac{idf_w}{1+|tf_{w,I}-tf_{w,J}|} \quad (4)$$

3.1.4 Knowledge-Based Similarity Measure

We now generalize our measures that are based on verbatim overlap to non-verbatim overlap. Toward this end, we use a knowledge-based turn similarity measure KBS that integrates verbatim word overlap with lexical relatedness (Mihalcea et al., 2006).

We begin with finding the maximum lexical similarity score $S(w_i, J)$ for each word w_i in turn I with words in turn J using the following formulation:

$$S(w_i,J)=\begin{cases}1\times idf_{w_i} & \text{if } w_i\in J\\ \max_{w_j\in J} LS(w_i,w_j)\times idf_{w_i} & \text{otherwise}\end{cases} \quad (5)$$

where LS is Lin's universal similarity (Lin, 1998).

In other words, if the word w_i is present in J, $S(w_i, J)$ will be 1 multiplied by idf_{w_i}. If not, the most similar word to w_i will be chosen from words in J using Lin's universal similarity and $S(w_i, J)$ will be that maximum score multiplied by idf_{w_i}. The same procedure is applied to the words in J, and finally the similarity between I and J is calculated :

$$KBS(I,J)=\frac{1}{2}\left(\frac{\sum_{w_i\in I}S(w_i,J)}{\sum_{w_i\in I}idf_{w_i}}+\frac{\sum_{w_j\in J}S(w_j,I)}{\sum_{w_j\in J}idf_{w_j}}\right) \quad (6)$$

Lin's universal similarity can only be applied to word pairs with the same part-of-speech (POS). For automatic POS tagging of the ADOS corpus, we trained a multi-class classifier (Yarmohammadi, 2014) from labeled training data from the CHILDES corpus of transcripts of children's conversational speech (MacWhinney, 2000). The classifier uses a discriminative linear model, learning the model parameters with the averaged perceptron algorithm (Collins, 2002). The feature set includes bigrams of surrounding words, a window of size 2 of the next and previous words, and the POS-tag of the previous word. An additional orthographical feature set is used to tag rare and unknown words. This feature set includes prefixes and suffixes of the words (up to 4 characters), and presence of a hyphen, digit, or an uppercase character.

4 Results

As described in Section 3, we use our measures to calculate the similarity scores of all turn pairs for each distance window. Table 1 shows examples of similar turn pairs in the four distance windows based on the Weighted Jaccard Similarity Coefficient score.

We then calculate the SOR of each child in each given distance window by averaging the similarity scores of turn pairs in that window. Finally, we perform a two-tailed Mann-Whitney's U test, which is a non-parametric test of significance that does not assume that scores have a normal distribution. It evaluates the statistical difference between the SOR in ASD and TD children by comparing the medians of the two groups. For each similarity measure we report the medians of SOR in ASD and TD groups (with the group mean rank) as well as the significance test results: Mann-Whitney's U-Value (reported as W), P-Value (p), and the effect size (R).

Table 2 shows that both ASD and TD groups have a greater SOR in shorter distances with more significant difference and higher effect size. We see a decreasing trend in SOR by exponentially increasing the window size and distance. For each analysis, ASD group has a higher SOR than TD and the difference is statistically significant ($p<0.05$) in all short distances (up to $9<D\leq27$) and marginally missed the standard significance levels for the longest window ($p<0.1$ in $27<D\leq81$). We also investigated the effect of distance window on SOR in a different window set. The results are shown in Figure 1 using the KBS measure. We observe the exact same trend in these new windows as our main distance windows. All the differences between SOR in ASD and TD are statistically significant as well ($p<0.05$).

The comparison between various semantic similarity measures also indicates that KBS measure which takes into account lexical similarity in addition to word overlap, have more statistical power

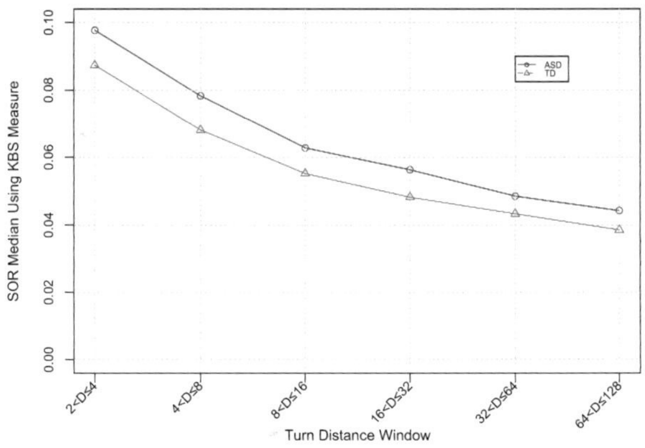

Figure 1: Semantic Overlap Ratio in ASD and TD at different turn distance windows using the KBS measure

to distinguish between ASD and TD groups in the longer windows ($9<D\leq27$ and $27<D\leq81$). This observation is reasonably consistent with our expectations that children may use synonyms and semantically similar words (rather than the exact set of words) within the same topic space especially in the longer distances.

To address the possible confounding effect of verbal IQ, where a small but significant difference between the groups was found, we conducted two additional analyses. In one, we used analysis of covariance, with age, VIQ, and NVIQ as covariates; unlike W, there is no non-parametric equivalent of the analysis of covariance. In the other, we applied an algorithm that iteratively removes data until no significant group difference remains (at $p>0.15$) on age, VIQ, or NVIQ. Both analyses provided results that, while quantitatively different, were qualitatively the same.

5 Conclusions and future work

The results obtained with the methods presented here for measuring the semantic overlap between conversational turns in children with and without ASD in a spontaneous conversation indicate the utility of natural language processing for capturing diagnostically relevant information. The higher ratio of semantic overlap in children with ASD compared with TD children suggests that children with ASD are returning to specific topics more repeatedly. Thus, the findings support our hypothesis.

Window	*Example of turn pairs*
$0<D\leq3$	That is a crab with a humongous tail. Crab with a humongous tail is called a lobster.
$3<D\leq9$	So well, plus I got my and I got my magic carpets. You could use my magic carpet as a blanket.
$9<D\leq27$	Could you please get me some sports action figures? I just really want to play with sports action figures.
$27<D\leq81$	Yeah, just challenge him for one more duel. Alright, but first I challenge you for a duel.

Table 1: Examples of similar turns in four distance windows based on the Weighted Jaccard Similarity Coefficient

Similarity	*Window*	*ASD Mdn* (M Rank)*	*TD Mdn* (M Rank)*	W	p	r
Jac	$0<D\leq3$	.72 (43.68)	.59 (30.07)	333	.006	.33
	$3<D\leq9$	.25 (42.84)	.17 (30.55)	354	.014	.29
	$9<D\leq27$	.14 (42.44)	.09 (30.77)	364	.02	.28
	$27<D\leq81$	.08 (40.32)	.05 (31.98)	417	.09	.2
Cos	$0<D\leq3$	6.0 (45.28)	4.6 (29.16)	293	.001	.39
	$3<D\leq9$	2.2 (41.64)	1.8 (31.23)	384	.038	.25
	$9<D\leq27$	1.3 (42.32)	1.0 (30.84)	367	.022	.28
	$27<D\leq81$	.76 (40.6)	.53 (31.82)	410	.082	.21
RF	$0<D\leq3$	1.8 (44.48)	1.4 (29.61)	313	.003	.36
	$3<D\leq9$	.59 (45.2)	.41 (29.2)	295	.001	.38
	$9<D\leq27$	.31 (42.52)	.23 (30.73)	362	.018	.28
	$27<D\leq81$	.16 (40.68)	.13 (31.77)	408	.077	.21
KBS	$0<D\leq3$	15.0 (43.16)	12.0 (30.36)	346	.01	.31
	$3<D\leq9$	7.7 (41.64)	6.9 (31.23)	384	.038	.25
	$9<D\leq27$	5.9 (42.72)	5.0 (30.61)	357	.016	.29
	$27<D\leq81$	4.7 (43.76)	4.2 (30.02)	331	.006	.33

**ASD and TD SOR Median values are multiplied by* 10^2.

Table 2: Significance Test Results of Semantic Overlap Ratio in ASD and TD groups at different turn distance windows, D

We are proposing a method of enabling measurement of a characteristic of language use in ASD that is currently "known" to be aberrant but is now ascertained only by impressionistic judgments rather than by quantification; and this is performed automatically on easy-to-obtain raw transcriptions of a clinical behavioral observation session (the ADOS) as opposed to requiring labor-intensive expert coding. To the best of our knowledge, this is the first time that verbal repetitiveness in natural language samples has been successfully measured — quantitatively, and automatically.

A major focus of our future work will be to automatically detect the topics introduced by the examiner to the child. The main assumption of this work is that children with ASD return to a set of topics during their conversation, no matter if they or the examiner initiated the topic. Given the high semantic overlap ratio seen here, we expect that children with autism contribute in conversations related to their particular topic of interest, rather than collaborating with the examiner in a dialogue.

A second area to investigate in the future is determining the children's conversation topics, especially the ones that are repeated. We could combine the child specificity scores such as IDF with the highly overlapping lexical items across different turns. We could also use manual annotation and clinical impression to determine if a child has a particular (idiosyncratic) topic of interest . We could then compare these annotations with the findings from our automated measures.

Third, we are also interested in trying additional similarity measures including BLEU (Papineni et al., 2002), ROUGE, (Lin, 2004), and Latent Semantic Analysis (Deerwester et al., 1990) to verify the robustness of our findings even further.

Finally, we plan to apply our methods to the output of Automatic Speech Recognition (ASR) systems to eliminate the transcription process. Measuring semantic similarity on ASR output will be an interesting challenge since it will likely contain word errors especially in children's spontaneous speech.

Acknowledgments

This work was supported in part by NSF grant #BCS-0826654, and NIH NIDCD grants #R01-DC007129 and #1R01DC012033-01. Any opinions, findings, conclusions or recommendations expressed in this publication are those of the authors and do not necessarily reflect the views of the NSF or the NIH.

References

American Psychiatric Association. 2000. *DSM-IV-TR: Diagnostic and Statistical Manual of Mental Disorders*. American Psychiatric Publishing, Washington, DC.

American Psychiatric Association. 2013. *Diagnostic and statistical manual of mental disorders (5th ed.)*. American Psychiatric Publishing, Washington, DC.

Brian A Boyd, Stephen G McDonough, and James W Bodfish. 2012. Evidence-based behavioral interventions for repetitive behaviors in autism. *Journal of autism and developmental disorders*, 42(6):1236–1248.

Lisa Capps, Jennifer Kehres, and Marian Sigman. 1998. Conversational abilities among children with autism and children with developmental delays. *Autism*, 2(4):325–344.

Michael Collins. 2002. Discriminative training methods for hidden markov models: Theory and experiments with perceptron algorithms. In *Proceedings of the ACL-02 conference on Empirical methods in natural language processing-Volume 10*, pages 1–8. Association for Computational Linguistics.

Scott C. Deerwester, Susan T Dumais, Thomas K. Landauer, George W. Furnas, and Richard A. Harshman. 1990. Indexing by latent semantic analysis. *JASIS*, 41(6):391–407.

Timothy C Hoad and Justin Zobel. 2003. Methods for identifying versioned and plagiarized documents. *Journal of the American society for information science and technology*, 54(3):203–215.

Paul Jaccard. 1912. The distribution of the flora in the alpine zone. 1. *New phytologist*, 11(2):37–50.

Leo Kanner. 1943. Autistic disturbances of affective content. *Nervous Child*, 2:217–250.

Dekang Lin. 1998. An information-theoretic definition of similarity. In *ICML*, volume 98, pages 296–304.

Chin-Yew Lin. 2004. Rouge: A package for automatic evaluation of summaries. In *Text Summarization Branches Out: Proceedings of the ACL-04 Workshop*, pages 74–81.

Catherine Lord, Michael Rutter, and Anne LeCouteur. 1994. Autism diagnostic interview-revised: A revised version of a diagnostic interview for caregivers of individuals with possible pervasive developmental disorders. *Journal of Autism and Developmental Disorders*, 24:659–685.

Catherine Lord, Michael Rutter, Pamela DiLavore, and Susan Risi. 2002. *Autism Diagnostic Observation Schedule (ADOS)*. Western Psychological Services, Los Angeles.

Brian MacWhinney. 2000. *The CHILDES project: Tools for analyzing talk*. Lawrence Erlbaum Associates, Mahwah, NJ.

Christopher D. Manning, Prabhakar Raghavan, and Hinrich Schütze. 2008. *Introduction to information retrieval*. Cambridge University Press.

Donald Metzler, Yaniv Bernstein, W Bruce Croft, Alistair Moffat, and Justin Zobel. 2005. Similarity measures for tracking information flow. In *Proceedings of the 14th ACM international conference on Information and knowledge management*, pages 517–524. ACM.

Rada Mihalcea, Courtney Corley, and Carlo Strapparava. 2006. Corpus-based and knowledge-based measures of text semantic similarity. In *AAAI*, volume 6, pages 775–780.

Aparna Nadig, Iris Lee, Leher Singh, Kyle Bosshart, and Sally Ozonoff. 2010. How does the topic of conversation affect verbal exchange and eye gaze? a comparison between typical development and high-functioning autism. *Neuropsychologia*, 48(9):2730–2739.

Kishore Papineni, Salim Roukos, Todd Ward, and Wei-Jing Zhu. 2002. Bleu: a method for automatic evaluation of machine translation. In *Proceedings of the 40th annual meeting on association for computational linguistics*, pages 311–318. Association for Computational Linguistics.

Emily Prud'hommeaux and Masoud Rouhizadeh. 2012. Automatic detection of pragmatic deficits in children with autism. In *WOCCI*, pages 1–6.

Emily Prud'hommeaux, Eric Morley, Masoud Rouhizadeh, Laura Silverman, Jan van Santen, Brian Roark, Richard Sproat, Sarah Kauper, and Rachel DeLaHunta. 2014. Computational analysis of trajectories of linguistic development in autism. In *IEEE Spoken Language Technology Workshop (SLT 2014)*, South Lake Tahoe.

2014. Detecting linguistic idiosyncratic interests in autism using distributional semantic models. *ACL 2014*, page 46.

Masoud Rouhizadeh, Emily Prud'hommeaux, Brian Roark, and Jan van Santen. 2013. Distributional semantic models for the evaluation of disordered language. In *Proceedings of the Conference of the North American Chapter of the Association for Computational Linguistics: Human Language Technologies*.

Michael Rutter, Anthony Bailey, and Catherine Lord. 2003. *Social Communication Questionnaire (SCQ)*. Western Psychological Services, Los Angeles.

Eleanor Semel, Elisabeth Wiig, and Wayne Secord. 2003. *Clinical Evaluation of Language Fundamentals- Fourth Edition*. The Psychological Corporation, San Antonio, TX.

Peter Szatmari, Stelios Georgiades, Susan Bryson, Lonnie Zwaigenbaum, Wendy Roberts, William Mahoney, Jeremy Goldberg, and Lawrence Tuff. 2006. Investigating the structure of the restricted, repetitive behaviours and interests domain of autism. *Journal of Child Psychology and Psychiatry*, 47(6):582–590.

Michelle Turner. 1999. Annotation: Repetitive behaviour in autism: A review of psychological research. *Journal of child psychology and psychiatry*, 40(6):839–849.

Jan van Santen, Richard Sproat, and Alison Presmanes Hill. 2013. Quantifying repetitive speech in autism spectrum disorders and language impairment. *Autism Research*, 6(5):372–383.

Joanne Volden and Catherine Lord. 1991. Neologisms and idiosyncratic language in autistic speakers. *Journal of Autism and Developmental Disorders*, 21:109–130.

Mahsa Yarmohammadi. 2014. Discriminative training with perceptron algorithm for pos tagging task. Technical Report CSLU-2014-001, Center for Spoken Language Understanding, Oregon Health & Science University.

Practical issues in developing semantic frameworks for the analysis of verbal fluency data: A Norwegian data case study

Mark Rosenstein[a], **Peter W. Foltz**[a,b], **Anja Vaskinn**[c,d] **and Brita Elvevåg**[e,f]

[a] Pearson, 4940 Pearl East Circle, Suite 200, Boulder, CO 80301 USA. mbrmbr@acm.org, peter.foltz@pearson.com
[b] Institute of Cognitive Science, University of Colorado, Boulder, CO 80309 USA.
[c] Department of Psychology, University of Oslo, Oslo, Norway.
[d] NORMENT K.G. Jebsen Centre for Psychosis Research, Oslo University Hospital, Oslo, Norway. anja.vaskinn@psykologi.uio.no
[e] Psychiatry Research Group, Department of Clinical Medicine, University of Tromsø, Norway.
[f] Norwegian Centre for Integrated Care and Telemedicine (NST), University Hospital of North Norway, Tromsø, Norway. brita@elvevaag.net

Abstract

Background: Verbal fluency tasks, which require producing as many words in response to a cue in a fixed time, are widely used within clinical neuropsychology and in neuropsychological research. Although semantic word lists can be elicited, typically only the number of words related to the cue is interpreted thus ignoring any structure in the word sequences. Automated language techniques can provide a much needed framework for extracting and charting useful semantic relations in healthy individuals and understanding how cortical disorders disrupt these knowledge structures and the retrieval of information from them.
Methods: One minute, animal category verbal fluency tests from 150 participants consisting of healthy individuals, patients with schizophrenia, and patients with bipolar disorder were transcribed. We discuss the issues involved in building and evaluating semantic frameworks and developing robust features to analyze this data. Specifically we investigate a Latent Semantic Analysis (LSA) semantic space to obtain semantic features, such as pairwise semantic similarity and clusters.
Results and Discussion: An in-depth analysis of the framework is presented, and then results from two measures based on LSA semantic similarity illustrate how these automated techniques provide additional, clinically useful information beyond word list cardinality.

1 Introduction

Language disturbances, especially semantic deficits, constitute one of the hallmark features of severe mental illness such as schizophrenia. Reliably and robustly quantifying these deficits in ways that can support diagnosis, gauge illness severity, determine treatment effectiveness and provide intermediate phenotypes to help further unravel the underlying genetic components of the disease has until recently proven elusive. With the advent of large, corpus-based statistical models of language, it has become possible to investigate techniques that can automatically elucidate and operationalize the semantic structure of elicited language in ways that can further these clinical goals.

Underlying these automated language techniques is an attempt to quantitatively define measures of semantic similarity based on the analysis of large sets of documents. Examples of these techniques include Latent Semantic Analysis (Furnas et al., 1988), Neural Networks and specifically Deep Learning (Hinton, 2006), Topic Models (Blei, Ng, & Jordan, 2003) and Independent Component Analysis (Hyvärinen, Karhunen, & Oja, 2004). Claims for these techniques include progress toward text understanding (Zhang & LeCun, 2015), as a theory of meaning (Landauer, 2007), characterizing the temporal flow of topics in a large set of technical articles (Griffiths & Styvers,

Proceedings of the 2nd Workshop on Computational Linguistics and Clinical Psychology: From Linguistic Signal to Clinical Reality, pages 124–133, Denver, Colorado, June 5, 2015.

2004), and a computational model of vocabulary acquisition (Biemiller et al., 2014).

In this paper, we focus on one of these techniques, Latent Semantic Analysis (LSA; Deerwester et al., 1990) and carefully examine the process of building an LSA semantic space and the resulting issues that arise in applying that space to generate quantitative results for Norwegian verbal fluency test data. The paper provides an in-depth methodological analysis of the approach of applying LSA in order to document the considerations for its effective use in semantic verbal fluency analysis. We provide a rationale for the use of two measures based on semantic similarity that indicate the potential of these automated techniques to provide additional clinically useful information beyond word list cardinality.

1.1 Latent Semantic Analysis

LSA generates semantic representations of words based on an analysis of a large corpus of domain relevant texts. Applying LSA begins when the corpus of texts is reduced to a term by document matrix. The columns of the matrix represent "documents", semantically coherent segments of text (for example a paragraph, or a short encyclopedia article), across all the text in the corpus and the rows represent the union of the words that are present in the corpus. The cell at the *jth* column, *ith* row contains a count of the number of times the *ith* word appears in the *jth* document. Various enhancements to this basic scheme, such as eliding common words (stop words) or applying weighting schemes for cells (see for instance Dumais, 1990) can be used to modify these counts, but for simplicity we will just call the contents of the cells counts. In Norwegian, compound words are concatenated, so for instance water ("vann") buffalo ("bøffel") is written vannbøffel, which simplifies word tokenization for the Norwegian animal words.

A lower dimensional approximation to the term by document matrix is computed using Singular Value Decomposition (SVD) (for details see for instance Berry, Dumais, & O'Brien, 1995). This lower dimensional matrix, or semantic space, distills the semantic relationships of words and contexts, such that the vector representing a document is the sum of its constituent word vectors. The latent semantic structure emerges from the dimension reduction, where semantic similarity between words or documents is computed by taking the cosine between vectors representing the words or the documents. This similarity has been exploited in numerous practical applications, such as information retrieval (Berry & Browne, 2005), essay scoring (Foltz, Laham, & Landauer, 1999) and bioinformatics (for example Homayouni et al., 2005).

LSA has been employed to chart how core cognitive processes are affected by illnesses that disturb cortical function. These include categorizing incoherence in speech during a fairy tale retelling task to distinguish patients with schizophrenia from controls (Elvevåg et al., 2007), as a more informative scoring mechanism for the Wechsler Logical Memory test (a story retelling task) (Dunn et al., 2002; Rosenstein et al., 2014), to distinguish language differences between healthy individuals and individuals with risk of psychosis (Elvevåg et al., 2010; Rosenstein et al., in press) and its use was suggested as an early indicator of Alzheimer's disease derived from analysis of a writer's oeuvre (Garrard et al., 2005). In all of these examples, a substantial amount (a paragraph or larger) of semantically related text was elicited and used in the analysis. Though it is more difficult to obtain semantic measures with shorter quantities of text, in his dissertation Koehn (2003) used LSA to study the degradation of semantic memory in Alzheimer's patients using word lists from verbal fluency tests.

1.2 Verbal Fluency Tests

Verbal Fluency tests, which are also referred to as Word List Generation tests, are one of the more commonly performed neuropsychological tests. They require the participants to produce, in response to a cue, a series of words in a set period of time. In the phonemic or letter fluency test, the cue is unique words that are not proper nouns beginning with a given letter, such as "l" or "s". In the semantic or category fluency task, the cue is unique words related to a category, for instance "animals" or "furniture". In a test to cue affect, the cue is unique words related to an emotional state, such as "happy". The number of correct words generated in these tasks has been shown to be a useful indicator in a number of severe mental illnesses. The verbal fluency test is easy to administer and is relatively easy to score since the scoring rubric typically only requires a count of the correct words produced.

As our concern is with underlying changes in semantics, we limit our investigation to the semantic fluency task. Given that participants are not instructed in any way on the manner in which they should retrieve the words, *a priori* it may be surprising that a tantalizing structure runs through the thread of words from the semantic task. Bousfield and Sedgewick (1944) were the first to report on temporal patterns in participant recall, where recall occurred in fits and starts with the rate of new words decreasing over time, and Bousfield (1953) noted that participants tended to recall groups of semantically similar words. Wixted and Rohrer (1994) provide a review of the research into the structure derived from the timing literature. Based on earlier work in memory search and clustering, such as Pollio (1964), Troyer et al. (1997) posited semantic clustering and switching as two important additional features that could be extracted from word lists produced in the semantic verbal fluency tests.

An obvious difficulty of attempting to reach deeper into the structure of word lists is maintaining objectivity and reliability in detecting these clusters. Beyond the deep philosophical issues of whether to include a dog used in hunting birds ("fuglehund", variously in English a bird dog, pointing dog, or hunting dog) in a cluster containing birds, there is a strong reliability issue in defining cluster boundaries. The appendix of Troyer et al. (1997) defines a set of semantic categories for animals. The difficulty for any fixed list is that the distribution of word frequencies is such that there are many infrequent words (Zipf, 1935) ensuring that it is difficult to obtain comprehensive lists, and even if a partial list is produced the potential combinations that could constitute clusters grows combinatorially.

Pakhomov, Hemmy and Lim (2012), attempted to overcome these concerns by using a lexical database, WordNet (Miller, 1995), a curated word collection that captures hierarchical relations among words for automated analysis of verbal fluency tasks in cognitive decline. Pakhomov and Hemmy (2014) applied LSA to measure cognitive decline in data from the Nun Study, where they proposed using LSA to provide an automated, consistent, generalized measure of cluster boundaries and switching. This contrasts somewhat with Koehn (2003), where the LSA measure was derived from the overall semantic similarity of the word list, and with Nicodemus et al. (2014), where a number of LSA measures were proposed to derive quantitative measures over semantic fluency data in a candidate gene study for schizophrenia. Instead of attempting to define and detect clusters, the measures discussed in Nicodemus et al. (2014) examined the overall coherence (the semantic similarity of all pairs of words in each word list), and coherence in moving windows of fixed word length (sets of 1-3 words). We build on these applications of LSA to verbal fluency data and report on constructing a semantic space for an animal semantic fluency test in Norwegian. We visualize the resulting semantic relations and temporal paths in an effort to understand how better to detect semantic coherence and clusters, and derive useful semantic features.

2 Methods

2.1 Oslo Verbal Fluency Study

Verbal fluency data from 150 participants (50 healthy participants, 75 diagnosed with bipolar disorder and 25 diagnosed with schizophrenia; native Norwegian speakers recruited in the Oslo area) who gave informed consent was analyzed. The participants were asked to generate as many animal words in one minute as possible. The audio data was transcribed. Figure 1 shows a histogram of the list lengths.

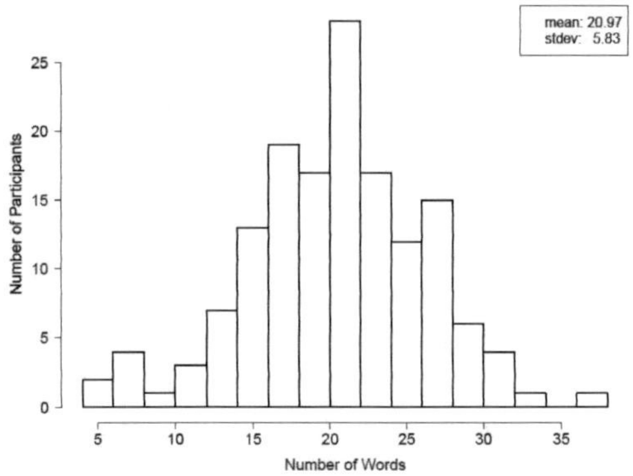

Figure 1: Distribution of word list lengths.

Since one semantic structure of interest is the path of retrieval, we did not remove perservations (repeated words), and 57 participants had at least one repeated word, though no word was repeated more than once by any participant. Nonadjacent perseverations (repeated words) were retained, though non-animal words were discarded, resulting in a total of 3148 words distributed over 269 unique animal words. The mean number of words per participant was 20.97 (5.83), with range from 4 to 38. Table 1 shows the distribution of repeated words by number of participants.

Number of repeated words	1	2	3	4
Number of participants	41	13	2	1

Table 1. Occurrences of perservations in word lists.

Keeping perservations was one aspect of our overall goal to preserve the original intent of the participants as much as practically possible. Overall, we would prefer the semantic space automatically normalize meanings. Participants used different word forms such as "koala" and "koalabjørn" to refer to the same animal. We did not perform lemmatization, and specifically kept both singular and plural forms. The only occasion where we did intervene was when the transcription process added variability due to spelling variants, where we selected the most frequent form. In other cases we preserved the variability except where a form was poorly represented in the corpus, and then the more frequent form was used. All transcripts were checked and corrected for typographical errors. By retaining these differences, the spread of nearly similar meanings can be exploited in the process of determining thresholds for cluster boundaries. Specific modifications of the word lists are discussed as part of developing the semantic space.

2.2 Building the Semantic Space

A semantic space is most effective when it is built from a corpus that captures a wide range of naturally occurring contexts, which produces a space with a robust exposure to the category (e.g. Landauer et al., 1998). Pakhomov and Hemmy (2014) built a space based on Wikipedia articles. We chose a different route due to both the limited animal articles in the Norwegian language version of Wikipedia and also the assumption that a more general source would provide more contexts to build semantic relationships than the encyclopedia model of Wikipedia.

We selected articles from the Norwegian Newspaper Corpus (Norsk aviskorpus), version 0.9 http://www.nb.no/sbfil/tekst/norsk_aviskorpus.zip, which is a component of text resources made available by the National Library of Norway, http://www.nb.no/English/Collection-and-Services/Spraakbanken/Available-resources/Text-Resources.

The newspaper corpus consists of approximately 3.7 million articles, of which we used a subset of 3.6 million articles, excluding approximately 100,000 that were explicitly tagged as "Nynorsk"[1].

There were 269 unique animal words generated in the verbal fluency study. Of these words, two: "gråmeis" and "svintoks" were not contained in any articles and were removed from the word lists. Two additional words "gjerv" and "papegøje" did not appear in the corpus, but alternative spellings "jerv" and "papegøye" were substituted in the word lists. Two other words "måse" and "pandabjørn" had very few representations in the articles, but alternative spellings "måke" and "panda" were well represented, so these substitutions were made. These substitutions resulted in 263 unique animal words for the study. Approximately 620,000 newspaper articles contained one or more occurrences of those 263 animals. Figure 2 shows the frequency of articles containing the words, with the y-axis on a log10 scale. The most frequent word is "ørn" (eagle), due to a popular football team of that name, the next most frequent is "and" (duck), due to contamination from the English connective[2], and the next three are "fisk" (fish), "menneske" (human) and "laks" (salmon). Excluding the tails, the plot is quite linear throughout its range.

For animals appearing in 200 or more articles, a random sample of 200 articles for each animal was added to the space, while for the 114 animals with 200 or fewer articles all the relevant articles were used. Duplicate articles were removed and each article constituted a document for the LSA analy-

[1] There are two versions of the Norwegian language – "Bokmål" and "Nynorsk". Although "Bokmål" is used by the majority in both written and spoken language, they are of equal standing. "Bokmål" is used in the Oslo area where our data was collected, hence our exclusion of the "Nynorsk" articles.

[2] We have experimented using the text categorization technique of Cavnar and Trenkle (1994) on small windows around "and" to separate English "rock and roll" article occurrences from Norwegian "Sprø and med appelsin og koriander" (Crispy duck with orange and coriander), though not implemented for the analysis reported here.

sis. The final space has 286,371 terms and 36,516 articles.

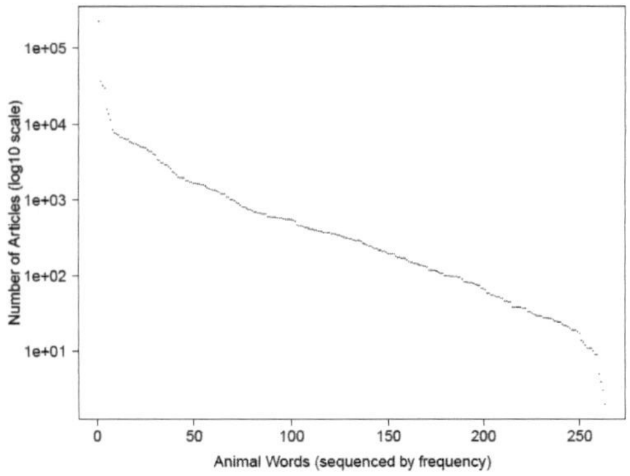

Figure 2. Number of articles per animal word.

We selected 300 dimensions for the reduced dimension space based on experience with other semantic spaces and the observation that usually there is a range of dimensions with approximately similar performance. Often the number of dimensions is chosen to optimize some external performance measure (e.g. Turney & Littman, 2003) and in future work our intention is to explore the choice of dimension. All cosine similarity comparisons were derived from vectors in this 300 dimension space. About half the terms are dates and times, not of much semantic value, but we tend to be conservative in tokenization, so preserve terms such as "Øst-Afrika" (East Africa) and "økomaten" (eco-food), which increases the term count.

With the semantic space in place, we performed a set of validations of the semantic relationships. Table 2 shows the cosine similarity for singular vs. plural forms and for variant spellings (the last four rows) that were produced by the participants and transcribers. The columns include the counts in the newspaper articles (news cnt) and among the participants (part cnt). Table S1 in the Supplemental Materials contains an English/Norwegian translation for the 263 animals. Notice that plural forms are relatively uncommon among participants relative to the frequencies found in the newspaper articles. Most of the plurals have relatively high cosine to their singular form. The variant spellings of the participants follow the newspaper frequencies, except in the case of "tarantella". Of the variant spellings, only the "ponni/ponny" pair has high cosine similarity, so the other variants were converted to the most frequent newspaper form. From the cosine similarities between the singular and plural forms, we expect that a cluster threshold will likely be at or below 0.3, if we want to keep those forms clustered.

sing.	plural	sing news cnt	plur news cnt	sing part cnt	plur part cnt	cos(sing. plur.)
fisk	fisker	32321	7239	36	3	0.582
fugl	fugler	7546	6738	48	1	0.815
geit	geiter	1107	1224	53	2	0.522
gris	griser	4630	3122	54	1	0.351
høne	høner	746	1209	32	2	0.649
insekt	insekter	396	1627	2	1	0.614
katt	katter	5510	4075	132	1	0.740
ku	kyr	3351	3088	87	1	0.571
reke	reker	395	2942	3	1	0.332
rotte	rotter	686	5088	53	1	0.395
var. 1	var. 2					
giraff	sjiraff	118	303	1	111	0.246
lemen	lemmen	371	150	5	1	0.003
ponni	ponny	194	28	2	1	0.742
taran-tell	tarantel-la	341	77	1	3	-0.012

Table 2. Singular and plural forms (top) and spelling variants (bottom 4 rows).

There are a number of additional ways to validate the overall semantic relationships in the space. Figure 3 shows the distribution of cosines taken between all pairs of animal words. The median of this distribution is essentially zero, though due to the long right tail the mean is 0.022 (.117). Of the 34,453 word pairs, only 1098 have a cosine greater than 0.3 and 2174 have a cosine greater than 0.2, so most animals have low similarity.

Another approach is to use hierarchical clustering on the cosine distance matrix among the animals to see one representation of the imposed relationships. We used hierarchical clustering from the statistical programming environment R (R Core Team, 2014).

Figure S1 in the Supplemental Materials (a high resolution version to allow magnified viewing to facilitate examining details), shows the hierarchical clustering. In addition we have labeled a few subtrees with categories, and smaller scale effects can be seen within categories, for instance in barnyard animals, subtrees of horses, hens and livestock naturally arise. Like any projection, hierarchical clustering reveals some relationships, while others require a different projection to be revealed. Using LSA to measure semantic similarity is equivalent to allowing the relationships that emerge from the corpus to constrain semantic similarity. The only free parameter is the cosine similarity threshold to define a cluster[3].

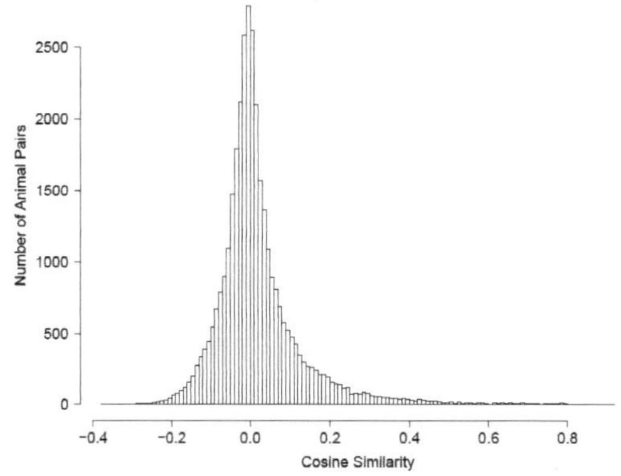

Figure 3. Distribution of animal pair cosines.

2.3 Analysis of Fluency Data

While it is informative to examine the relationships across all the animals, our particular interest is in the sets of animals generated by each participant both in terms of the choices of animals, and the structure of the order of those choices. Figure 4 shows the distribution of cosines for all the word pairs (reiterating Figure 3 but as a density plot), as well as just the sequential pairs in the word lists of participants. While there are still a majority of unrelated pairs, the participants clearly have more structure and higher cosines with a median 0.08 and 25% of the pairs having a cosine exceeding 0.24. So, as expected, there is substantial structure here.

Figures 5 and 6 show the cosine time paths from two participants. The x-axis is the word sequence, and the y-axis is the cosine similarity between each sequential pair of words. The word pair is plotted vertically next to the cosine point. Table S1 in the supplemental materials contains both English and Norwegian forms of the 263 animal words. Both figures indicate that as the threshold for defining a cluster is lowered the size of clusters will increase, while increasing will cause an increase in number of clusters (in the limit each word will be its own cluster).

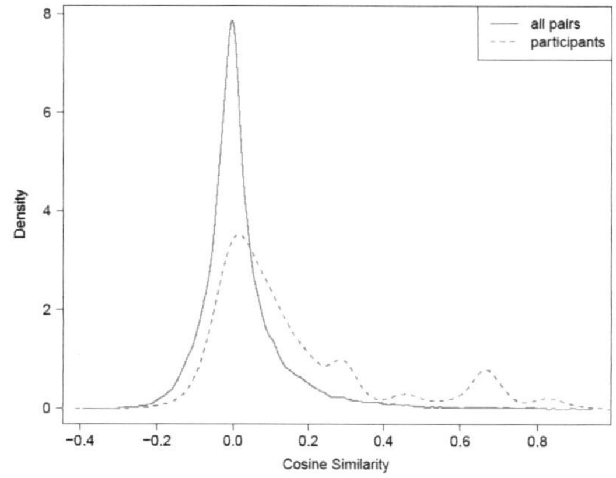

Figure 4. Distribution of all animal pair cosines vs. pairs limited to participants.

In Figure 5, we see potentially 4 clusters. The first peak might be called Africa, the second dogs, the third fish and the last pets. Where the boundaries are located and cluster membership depends on the cosine threshold. We note that the "fuglehund" (bird dog) does cluster with dogs, but not with the bird "papegøye" (parrot), and the overall bird similarity is quite low in this sequence.

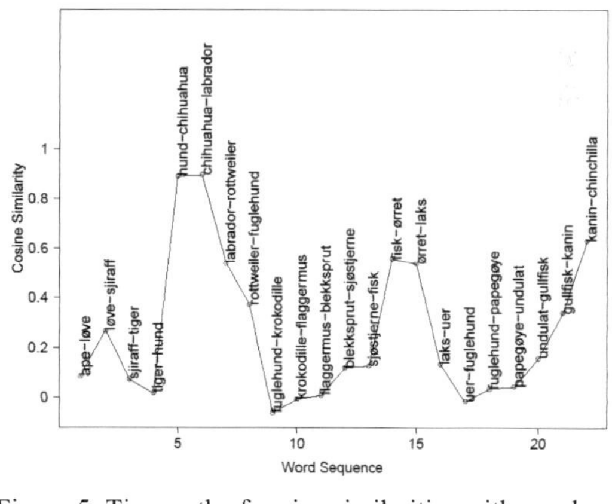

Figure 5. Time path of cosine similarities with word pairs (example 1).

In Figure 6, the sequence begins with four fish, but the cluster likely ends with "hai" (shark) then

[3] The selection of number of dimensions for the space is also a free parameter, but much less directly related to cluster size than this threshold.

"hval" (whale) and a return to fish in the next peak. In addition there is a long low peak of barnyard animals, followed by a pet peak and a small bear peak. How the threshold is set in conjunction with the semantic similarity of the space will greatly influence the shape of clusters.

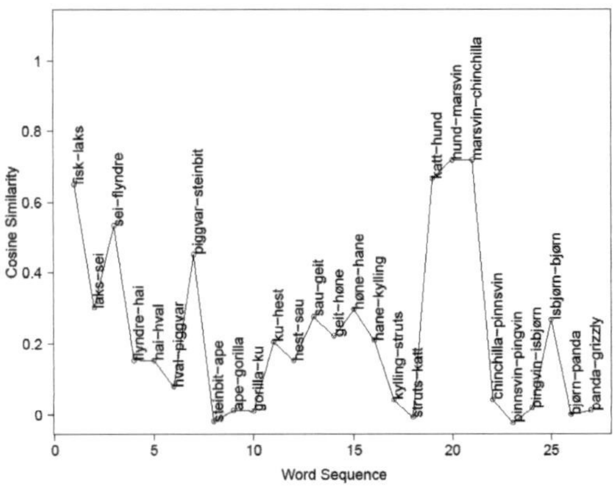

Figure 6. Time path of cosine similarities with word pairs (example 2).

These examples illustrate that clusters may have a good deal of variability, since they can be dependent on single words to delimit the cluster. This implies that distortions of the words "and" and "ørn" due to non-animal meanings and words absent from the corpus such as "gråmeis" and "svintoks" may have disproportionate effects. Investigating measures that are more robust to small changes in single words seems a profitable direction. A measure less affected by single word variability is the area under the temporal curve, which if divided by the number of words is just the mean of the cosine pairs.

Figures 5 and 6 indicate that it would be useful to better understand the relationship between threshold and number of clusters over the participants' data. Figure 7 shows the tradeoff in terms of number of clusters as the threshold for cluster boundary is increased. We see a rapid growth and then a leveling off toward the asymptote. The curve drawn in the figure is a locally weighted regression (Loader, 2013) to help visualize the relationship. Following Pollio (1964) the vertical line is at the 75th percentile of the cosine distribution, and is our first pass at a threshold, though further experimentation is necessary to better understand how to set this value.

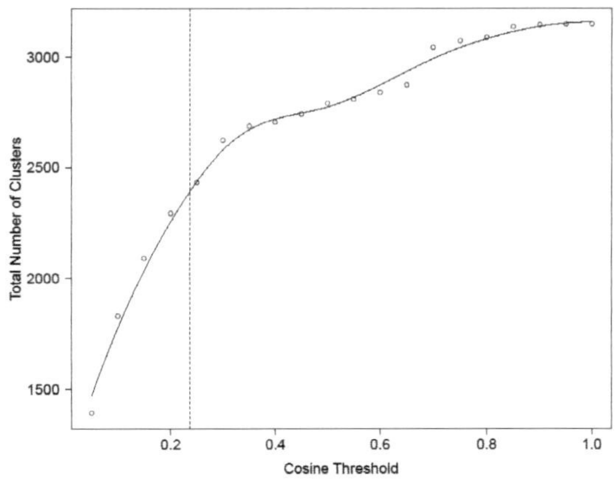

Figure 7. Change in number of clusters as cosine threshold increases.

2.4 Continuous Space Word Representation

To validate this approach, we built a semantic space based on a second automated technique, continuous space word representations (Mikolov, Yih, & Zweig, 2013) with the exact same corpus as the LSA space, utilizing bag-of-words and 300 dimensions, using the word2vec[4] software. We chose this representation since it belongs to the family of statistical vector space representations which use cosine similarity to measure semantic closeness. The mean cosine and cosines using word pairs from the participants were both higher than for the LSA space and well above the mean for 1000 randomly chosen word pairs (mean all animal pairs=0.114 (0.100), for participants=0.275 (0.137), random pairs=0.040 (0.078)).

Figure 8 reprises the first example word list shown for LSA-based semantics in Figure 5, but now using cosine similarity from the new space. The main feature of four peaks remains, but there are differences such as now instead of increasing similarity with on the right (pets), the plot levels off.

To further compare the semantic spaces, we took the correlation between all 263 animal pairs in the two spaces and the subset of pairs generated by the participants. For all pairs the correlation was 0.505 and for the participant pairs the correlation was 0.727, with 95% confidence interval (0.709,

[4] http://code.google.com/p/word2vec/

0.743). This is a quite interesting result in that pairs humans generate have higher similarity, but also that both models capture more similar semantic patterns over the human generated pairs. This result increases our confidence that these models are capturing critical aspects of human semantic organization.

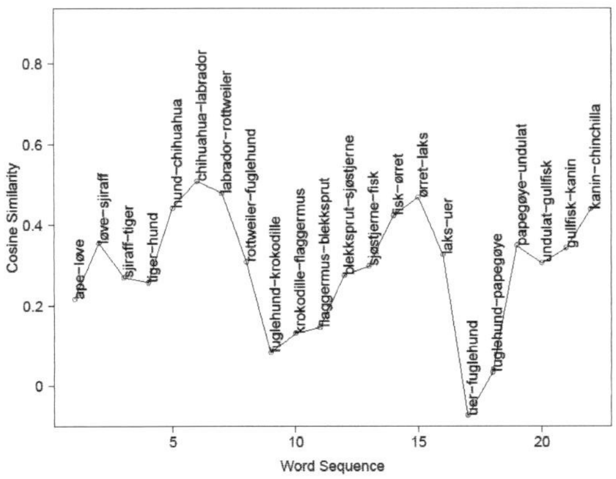

Figure 8. Time path of cosine similarities using continuous space model with word pairs (example 1).

2.5 Differences in Diagnostic Groups

The primary purpose of developing this semantic framework is to provide the basis for much needed tools to measure how semantic structures are affected by cortical disorders. Utilizing the LSA space and threshold from Section 2.3, we can now begin that process. We compute three measures on the data, the mean number of words per diagnostic group, the mean cosine, and a cluster measure, the cluster fraction which is the number of clusters divided by the number of words. Since the number of clusters is limited by the number of words, we need a measure that factors out the number of words, and dividing by the number of words is a way to achieve that aim. Table 3 shows the three measures and their standard deviations, as well as the number of participants for the three groups, control (CNTL), bipolar disorder (BD) and schizophrenia (SZ).

All three measures are significantly different among the groups: number of words ($F[2,147]$ = 13.117, p = 5.73e-6), mean cosine ($F[2,147]$ = 3.398, p = .036), and cluster fraction ($F[2,147]$ = 3.190, p = 0.044). The two new semantic features are only moderately correlated to number of words, mean cos, cor = 0.301 and cluster fraction, cor = -0.254, indicating both provide additional information beyond the number of words. The control group results are consistent with normative word count results reported by Egeland et al. (2006), where in their Table 5 they report a mean animal word list length of 23.5 (5.7) for 201 participants. Unfortunately, they did not separately report animal counts for their groups with schizophrenia or depression.

Group	n	num words	mean cos	cluster frac
CNTL	50	23.92(4.750)	0.172(0.0597)	0.736(0.0994)
BD	75	20.12(5.273)	0.151(0.0589)	0.778(0.103)
SZ	25	17.64(6.867)	0.137(0.0572)	0.794(0.131)

Table 3. Mean(sd) semantic features by group.

The direction of change is consistent among the three measures, number of words decreases from control to bipolar disease to schizophrenia, semantic coherence between pairs of words also drops in that order, and cluster fraction, which increases as pairwise semantic coherence decreases moves in the expected opposite direction to the other two measures.

3 Discussion

The aim of this paper is to illustrate a semantic framework that can provide tools for measuring how semantic structure is affected by cortical disorders. The approach illustrates that effective semantic representations can be developed through automated language models such as LSA. While it is possible to treat automated language models as black boxes, we have attempted to show that there are many ways these spaces can be probed to ensure that they provide useful semantic relations that correspond to human results and provide potentially clinically useful applications.

From comparing the semantic similarity of singular to plural forms or visualizing the semantic path of verbal fluency word lists, we gain confidence that the mathematical models behind the scenes matches our understanding. When we compared LSA to a continuous space model, we observed strong overlap in the semantic relations increasing our confidence in this enterprise. Delegating the responsibility to determine semantic similarity to an automated method, captures a consensus view of semantics based on the corpus used in building the semantic relationships. This approach can help reduce variability due to human judgements, making it easier to detect important patterns in the data. Individual differences will continue to make it difficult to detect diagnostic group differences, but by having multiple classes of semantic features we improve the chances of capturing those group differences. Our next steps are to use this knowledge to continue to build robust semantic features and attempt to operationalize those features with fluency data as well as with other tasks. The overall framework provides a means to continue work to better understand how to use semantics to build robust features, and apply it to data.

Acknowledgments

We wish to thank Kjetil Sundet, Carmen Simonsen and Ole A. Andreassen from the NORMENT KG Jebsen Centre for Psychosis Research at Oslo University Hospital in Norway for recruitment and neuropsychological assessment of participants. This research was supported in part by the Northern Norwegian Regional Health Authority, Helse Nord RHF. Brita Elvevåg was also funded by the Northern Norwegian Regional Health Authority. Peter Foltz and Mark Rosenstein are employees of Pearson, which partially supported their work as part of their employment. The funders had no role in study design, data collection and analysis, decision to publish, or preparation of the manuscript.

References

Michael W. Berry, & Murray Browne. (2005). *Understanding Search Engines: Mathematical Modeling and Text Retrieval*. Philadelphia, PA: SIAM Press.

Michael W. Berry, Susan T. Dumais, & G. W. O'Brien. (1995). Using linear algebra for intelligent information retrieval. *SIAM review*, 37(4), 573-595.

Andrew Biemiller, Mark Rosenstein, Randall. Sparks, Thomas K Landauer, & Peter W. Foltz. (2014). Models of vocabulary acquisition: Direct tests and text-derived simulations of vocabulary growth. *Scientific Studies of Reading*, 18(2), 130-154.

David M. Blei, Andrew Y. Ng, & Michael I. Jordan. (2003). Latent dirichlet allocation. *The Journal of Machine Learning Research*, 3, 993-1022.

W. A. Bousfield. (1953). The occurrence of clustering in the recall of randomly arranged associates. *The Journal of General Psychology*, 49(2), 229-240.

W. A. Bousfield, & H. W. Sedgewick. (1944). An analysis of sequences of restricted associative responses. *Journal of General Psychology*, 30, 149-165.

William B. Cavnar, & John M. Trenkle. (1994). N-Gram-Based Text Categorization. Proceedings of SDAIR-94, *3rd Annual Symposium on Document Analysis and Information Retrieval*, 161–175.

Scott C. Deerwester, Susan T. Dumais, George W. Furnas, Thomas K Landauer, & Richard A. Harshman. (1990). Indexing by latent semantic analysis. *JAsIs*, 41(6), 391-407.

Susan T. Dumais. (1990). Enhancing performance in latent semantic (LSI) indexing. *Behavior Research Methods, Instruments and Computers*, 23(2), 229–236.

John C. Dunn, Osvaldo P. Almeida, Lee Barclay, Anna Waterreus, & Leon Flicker. (2002). Latent semantic analysis: A new method to measure prose recall. *Journal of Clinical and Experimental Neuropsychology*, 24(1), 26-35.

Jens Egeland, Nils I. Landrø, Evelin Tjemsland, & Kjersti Walbækken. (2006). Norwegian norms and factor-structure of phonemic and semantic word list generation. *The Clinical Neuropsychologist*, 20(4), 716-728.

Brita Elvevåg, Peter W. Foltz, Daniel R. Weinberger, & Terry E. Goldberg. (2007). Quantifying incoherence in speech: An automated methodology and novel application to schizophrenia. *Schizophrenia Research*, 93, 304-316.

Brita Elvevåg, Peter W. Foltz, Mark Rosenstein, & Lynn E. DeLisi. (2010). An automated method to analyze language use in patients with schizophrenia and their first-degree relatives. *Journal of Neurolinguistics*, 23(3), 270-284.

Peter W. Foltz, Darrell Laham, & Thomas K Landauer. (1999). Automated essay scoring: Applications to educational technology. World Conference on *Educational Multimedia, Hypermedia and Telecommunications.* (1999), 1, 939-944.

George W. Furnas, Scott Deerwester, Susan T. Dumais, Thomas K Landauer, Richard A. Harshman, Lynn A. Streeter, & Karen E. Lochbaum. (1988). Information retrieval using a singular value decomposition model of latent semantic structure. Proceedings of the 11th annual international ACM SIGIR conference on *Research and development in information retrieval*, 465-480. ACM.

Peter Garrard, Lisa M. Maloney, John R. Hodges, & Karalyn Patterson. (2005). The effects of very early Alzheimer's disease on the characteristics of writing by a renowned author. *Brain*, 128(2), 250-260.

Thomas L. Griffiths, & Mark Steyvers. (2004). Finding scientific topics. *Proceedings of the National Academy of Sciences*, 101(suppl 1), 5228-5235.

Geoffrey Hinton, Simon Osindero, & Yee W. Teh. (2006). A fast learning algorithm for deep belief nets. *Neural Computation*, 18(7), 1527-1554.

Ramin Homayouni, Kevin Heinrich, Lai Wei, & Michael W. Berry. (2005). Gene clustering by latent semantic indexing of MEDLINE abstracts. *Bioinformatics*, 21(1), 104-115.

Aapo Hyvärinen, Juha Karhunen, & Erkki Oja. (2004). *Independent component analysis*. New York: John Wiley & Sons.

Henry C. Koehn. (2003). Latent semantic analysis of Alzheimer's disease patients' speech as an indicator of semantic network integrity. *Dissertation Abstracts International*, 65-09, Section: B, 4891.

Thomas K Landauer. (2007). LSA as a theory of meaning. In Landauer, T. K, McNamara, D. S., Dennis, S., & Kintsch, W. (Eds.). *Handbook of Latent Semantic Analysis*. (3-34). Mahway, NJ: Lawrence Erlbaum Associates.

Thomas K. Landauer, Peter W. Foltz, & Darrell Laham. (1998). Introduction to Latent Semantic Analysis. *Discourse Processes*, 25, 259-284.

Catherine Loader. (2013). locfit: Local Regression, Likelihood and Density Estimation. R package version 1.5-9.1. http://CRAN.R-project.org/package=locfit.

Tomas Mikolov, Wen-tau Yih, & Geoffrey Zweig. (2013). Linguistic Regularities in Continuous Space Word Representations. *HLT-NAACL*, 746-751.

George A. Miller. (1995). WordNet: a lexical database for English. *Communications of the ACM*, 38(11), 39-41.

Kristin K. Nicodemus, Brita Elvevåg, Peter W. Foltz, Mark Rosenstein, Catherine Diaz-Asper, & Daniel R. Weinberger. (2014). Category fluency, latent semantic analysis and schizophrenia: a candidate gene approach. *Cortex*, 55, 182-191.

Serguei V. Pakhomov, Laura S. Hemmy, & Kelvin O. Lim. (2012). Automated semantic indices related to cognitive function and rate of cognitive decline. *Neuropsychologia*, 50(9), 2165-2175.

Serguei V. Pakhomov, & Laura S. Hemmy. (2014). A computational linguistic measure of clustering behavior on semantic verbal fluency task predicts risk of future dementia in the Nun Study. *Cortex*, 55, 97-106.

Howard R. Pollio. (1964). Composition of associative clusters. *Journal of Experimental Psychology*, 67(3), 199.

R Core Team (2014). *R: A language and environment for statistical computing*. R Foundation for Statistical Computing, Vienna, Austria. URL http://www.R-project.org/.

Mark Rosenstein, Catherine Diaz-Asper, Peter W. Foltz, & Brita Elvevåg. (2014). A computational language approach to modeling prose recall in schizophrenia. *Cortex*, 55, 148-166.

Mark Rosenstein, Peter W. Foltz, Lynn E. DeLisi, & Brita Elvevåg. (in press). Language as a biomarker in those at high-risk for psychosis. *Schizophrenia Research.*

Angela K. Troyer, Morris Moscovitch, & Gordon Winocur. (1997). Clustering and switching as two components of verbal fluency: evidence from younger and older healthy adults. *Neuropsychology*, 11(1), 138.

Peter D. Turney, & Michael L. Littman.(2003). Measuring praise and criticism: inference of semantic orientation from association. *ACM Transactions on Information Systems (TOIS)*, 21(4), 315-346.

John T. Wixted, & Doug Rohrer. (1994). Analyzing the dynamics of free recall: An integrative review of the empirical literature. *Psychonomic Bulletin & Review*, 1(1), 89-106.

Xiang Zhang, & Yann LeCun. (2015). Text understanding from scratch. arXiv:1502.01710v1.

George K. Zipf. *The Psychobiology of Language*. (1935). Boston, MA: Houghton Mifflin.

A Computer Program for Tracking the Evolution of a Psychotherapy Treatment

Bernard Maskit
Mathematics Department
Stony Brook University
Stony Brook NY 11794-3651
USA
daap@optonline.net

Wilma Bucci
Derner Institute
Adelphi University
Garden City NY 11530 USA
wbucci@optonline.net

Sean Murphy
New York Psychoanalytic Society
and Institute
247 East 82 Street
New York NY 10028, USA
smurphy1@gmail.com

Abstract

Describing troubling events and images and reflecting on their emotional meanings are central components of most psychotherapies. The computer system described here tracks the occurrence and intensity of narration or imagery within transcribed therapy sessions and over the course of treatments; it likewise tracks the extent to which language denoting appraisal and logical thought occurs. The Discourse Attributes Analysis Program (DAAP) is a computer text analysis system that uses several dictionaries, including the Weighted Referential Activity Dictionary (WRAD), designed to detect verbal communication of emotional images and events, and the Reflection Dictionary (REF), designed to detect verbal communication denoting cognitive appraisal, as well as other dictionaries. For each dictionary and each turn of speech, DAAP uses a moving weighted average of dictionary weights, together with a fold-over procedure, to produce a smooth density function that graphically illustrates the rise and fall of each underlying psychological variable. These density functions are then used to produce several new measures, including measures of the vividness of descriptions of images or events, and a measure of the extent to which descriptions of events or images and reflection on their meaning occur separately.

1 Introduction

In most forms of therapy, the treatment process includes two major phases of discourse: (1) the client talks about his or her concerns or problems and describes incidents related to these concerns, and (2) the client, perhaps with the help of the therapist, thinks about these concerns and evaluates the significance of the described incidents (Bucci, 2013). These phases are likely to be repeated in different contexts and with different contents. Some versions of psychodynamic therapy include reports of memories and dreams, as well as current interactions and interpretations of these. Some types of Cognitive-Behavioral Therapy include 'experiments' and other forms of 'homework' outside the treatment situation, and descriptions and evaluations of these critical events in the session. Some exposure therapies require that the client tell and retell the story of the trauma. Different treatments have different mixes of these two crucial phases.

These two styles of discourse have been termed *Symbolizing* and *Reorganizing* by Bucci (1997) and defined within the framework of her general theory of the referential process as this plays out in psychotherapy. According to this theory, an emotion schema is first aroused (this phase will not be discussed here); then communicated in the form of an image or narrative in the Symbolizing phase. The meaning of this image or story is then reflected on in the Reorganizing phase.

Much also occurs in a therapy session that lies outside these two modes of discourse; the client sometimes talks in general terms, sometimes is disfluent, and sometimes discusses matters outside the problem areas. In this paper, we describe a computer system designed to read texts, including transcriptions of therapy sessions, and track the extent

Proceedings of the 2nd Workshop on Computational Linguistics and Clinical Psychology: From Linguistic Signal to Clinical Reality, pages 134–145,
Denver, Colorado, June 5, 2015. ©2015 Association for Computational Linguistics

to which the speaker or writer is engaged in either of these two major phases or in some other mode.

The key components of our system are the Discourse Attributes Analysis Program (DAAP); the empirically derived Weighted Referential Activity Dictionary (WRAD) (Bucci and Maskit, 2006), which measures the extent to which the speaker or writer is in symbolizing mode; and the conceptually derived unweighted Reflection dictionary (REF), which measures the extent to which the speaker or writer is in reorganizing mode; in this paper we focus on these measures and measures derived from them. The system also includes other dictionaries, including disfluency and affect. These dictionaries can be used to help distinguish different phases of discourse (Kingsley, 2009), and also as measures of session effectiveness (Bucci and Maskit, 2007; Mariani et al., 2013; Andrei, 2011)[1].

According to Bucci (1997), Referential Activity (RA) is a psycholinguistic variable that concerns the extent to which language can capture a speaker's bodily, sensory and affective experience in such a way as to evoke corresponding experience in the listener. This communication generally takes the form of narratives or descriptions of imagery, and is the central indicator of the Symbolizing phase. The Weighted Referential Activity Dictionary (WRAD), which was designed to model RA, will be described in more detail below.

The Discourse Attributes Analysis Program (DAAP) is a modern text analysis program that produces, for each weighted or unweighted dictionary, and for each turn of speech or other user-defined segment a smoothly varying *density function* that tracks the rise and fall of the underlying psychological variable that the dictionary is designed to represent. DAAP uses the WRAD density function to derive a measure of average vividness while in symbolizing mode, and a measure of the extent of discourse spent in the symbolizing mode; DAAP also produces a measure of the extent to which a speaker's language is simultaneously in both symbolizing and reorganizing modes; there is evidence that a client's separation of these two modes of speech is related to session or treatment effectiveness.

[1]This system is publicly available for non-commercial use; it can be downloaded from ww.thereferentialprocess.org/the-discourse-attributes-analysis-program-daap.

There are several computer programs that have been used for the study of the content of psychotherapy sessions. Earlier programs, such as the General Inquirer (Stone et al. , 1966), as well as more recent comprehensive programs such as the LIWC of Pennebaker et al. (2001), use counts of words within user-defined segments, such as turns of speech, that match words in dictionaries defined by particular grammatical or psychological categories. Mergenthaler's Text Analysis System (1996) uses artificial segmentation into word blocks of approximately 150 words each, which enables some differentiation of different text modes. However this segmentation does not correspond to turns of speech or boundaries of meaning units. Some modern systems, as for example Salvatore et al. (2012), Imel et al. (2014) or Werbart et al. (2011) use topic models, Latent Semantic Analysis and/or other machine learning techniques to form their categories. Such programs are primarily concerned with the contents of discourse; some of these start by eliminating function words.

1.1 The Referential Process as a Common Mechanism in Talking Cures

Bucci (2013) argues that the sequence of Symbolizing and Reorganizing, characterized as the referential process, constitutes a common factor that occurs in different forms in a wide range of psychotherapies practiced today. In all these treatments, effectiveness of treatment depends on communicating emotional experiences in specific and concrete language. Such language has been shown by Bucci and Maskit (2007) to be associated with effective therapeutic work in psychodynamic treatment. In their extensive and critical review of process-outcome research, appearing in the current Handbook of Psychotherapy and Behavior Change, which provides the standard reference for the field of psychotherapy research, Crits-Cristoph, et al. (2013) have provided evidence that arousal of emotional experience, for example through retelling narratives of central traumatic events, is likely to be an essential ingredient in achieving positive outcomes in exposure treatments. They have also shown that concrete techniques, such as asking for specific examples of beliefs, also lead to better outcome in cognitive therapy, while abstract techniques were unrelated to subsequent improvement. Several studies reviewed by

Crits-Cristoph et al. (2013), have provided evidence that gains in self-understanding lead to improvements in symptoms in psychodynamic therapy. Reorganizing also occurs in the various forms of cognitive behavioral, schema and exposure treatments, in processes characterized as reappraisal, cognitive restructuring and development of techniques of self-regulation.

2 Dictionaries

The DAAP system uses several dictionaries to locate different phases of discourse. We are concerned here only with the Weighted Referential Activity Dictionary (WRAD), as a measure of the extent to which the speaker is in the Symbolizing phase, and the Reflection dictionary (REF), as a measure of the extent to which the speaker is in the Reorganizing phase.

2.1 Referential Activity

Variation in RA is interpreted as indicating a speaker's or writer's degree of emotional engagement or immersion in an experience as represented in language (Bucci, 1997). Such engagement is indicated by qualities of language ranging widely across divergent contents. A novelist may write about chasing the white whale, life in an English village in the early nineteenth century, or experiences in the Spanish Civil War with equivalent degrees of engagement; clients may describe a similarly wide range of experiences. The challenge in developing a lexical measure of engagement in experience was in capturing features of language that are dependent on style and essentially independent of content. Bucci and colleagues began development of the RA measure by turning to the principles of language style as given by Strunk and White, in particular their sixteenth principle of composition, which states: "Use definite, specific, concrete language." (1972) (pp. 16–18). Based on the features specified in this principle, four scales were developed: Specificity (quantity of detail), Clarity (organization and focus) Concreteness (degree of reference to sensory and other bodily experience) and Imagery (degree to which language evokes imagery). Definitions of the scales and procedures for rating them are outlined in a manual (Bucci et al. , 1992; Bucci and McKay, 2014). Scores for the four attributes are averaged to yield an overall RA measure for texts or text segments. The manual provides some explicit features of the several dimensions, but the scoring is based primarily on intuitive judgments. As for most linguistic processing, speakers of a language have more implicit knowledge concerning language style and its effects than they are able to state in explicit terms. Scorers achieve acceptable reliability levels by reading the manual and brief training with practice segments.

The RA scales have been applied to many types of texts, including brief monologues, early memories, and Thematic Apperception Test (TAT) protocols as well as transcripts of therapy sessions, in populations varying on demographic and clinical dimensions. In a meta-analysis of 23 studies, Samstag (1996) found significant relationships, with moderate to strong effect size, between RA scales and other indicators of capacity to connect cognitive, and emotional experience to language. While the scales are reliably scored with relatively brief training, computerized procedures are needed to enable assessment of RA in large sample and longitudinal studies, and micro-analytic tracking of fluctuation in RA within various forms of communicative discourse. Traditional methods of computerized language analysis depend on construction of word lists representing specified contents and concepts. For the RA dimension, a different approach to modeling the scales was used.

A first computer model of Referential Activity, called CRA, was empirically derived by Mergenthaler and Bucci (1999) using a set of transcriptions of spoken language that had been scored for RA. The model consisted of two dictionaries; one made up of words that are used significantly more often in high RA speech and the other of words used significantly more often in low RA speech. These were used as a measure of RA with the Text Analysis System (TAS) of Mergenthaler (1996), which segments each text into word blocks of approximately 150 words each, and then computes a mean CRA score for each such word block (High RA words minus Low RA words divided by the total number of words).

The dictionary currently in use, the Weighted Referential Activity Dictionary (WRAD), was also empirically derived from a set of transcriptions of spoken language that had been scored for RA (Bucci and Maskit, 2006). Weighted referential activity dictionaries have also been constructed in Spanish (Roussos and O'Connell, 2005), and Italian (Mariani et al., 2013). The WRAD contains approximately 700 single-word items, including many very frequent function words; thus WRAD covers roughly 75–85% of spoken language. Each item in the WRAD has a weight, ranging from -1 to $+1$, that was empirically derived so as to model that item's usage in segments at different RA levels. For example, an item with weight -1 is used much more often in text segments having RA scores in the range of 0 to 2.75, an item with weight $+1$ is used much more often in text segments having RA scores in the range of 7.25 to 10. As described in Bucci and Maskit (2006), the algorithm used to make the WRAD uses different definitions of the term 'much more often' to construct different dictionaries; the final one is chosen by maximizing the correlation with judge's scores of RA on a separate set of texts.

As shown in Bucci and Maskit (2006), the WRAD and CRA were tested on a set of 113 text segments that had been scored for RA, and that had not been used in the construction of either dictionary. For this test set, the WRAD/RA correlation was .47; the CRA/RA correlation was .31. As the coverage of a dictionary could be important for interpreting the corresponding density function, we note that the CRA coverage of this material was .50, while the WRAD coverage was .83. To the best of the authors' knowledge, there are no other computer measures of RA to test the WRAD against.

Since the contents of the WRAD are based on the scales, which are intuitively scored, the weights are generally independent of linguistic or grammatical category and relate to language style in ways that are generally not explicitly understood. Thus general content or grammatical categories, such as are applied in the LIWC and other text analysis systems, could not be used in making the WRAD. For example, 'in' and 'inside' might be grouped together in typical categorical systems; however the WRAD weight of the word 'in' is $+1$, signifying that people generally use this word far more often in symbolizing mode than otherwise; the weight of the word 'inside' is -1, signifying that people generally use this word far less often in symbolizing mode than otherwise. Similarly, the words 'and', 'was', 'she' and 'on' each have the highest possible WRAD weight of $+1$, while the words 'also', 'is', 'it' and 'off', which appear semantically related to these four items respectively, have very low WRAD weights ('it' has weight $-.875$, the others have the lowest possible weight of -1). The content words in the dictionary include 'mother' and 'class', which have WRAD weight $+1$, as well as 'family' and 'money', which have WRAD weight -1.

Post-hoc examination of the lexical contents of the WRAD suggests that many frequent words with high WRAD weights are those with the types of functions required for telling stories. The five most frequent words with weights of +1 are the conjunction 'and', the definite article 'the', the past tense verb 'was', the spatial preposition 'in', and the personal pronoun 'she'; these are items with the types of pointing and connecting functions that are likely to be used in describing episodes — to locate the objects of discourse in place and time, and to join together or relate objects or ideas — as well as past tense verbs that serve as indicators of memory retrieval, and third person singular animate pronouns that are used to refer to specific other people figuring in an episode. The most frequent words with low WRAD weights are associated with subjective focus ('I') rather than pointing to objects and describing events, present rather than past tense ('is'), general and abstract usage ('it' and 'that') and disfluency indicated by the filled pause term ('mm') (Bucci et al., 2015). Other factors contributing to the contents of the WRAD are now being studied by Murphy et al. (2015).

2.2 Reflection

The Reflection dictionary (REF) is an unweighted list of over 1400 words that relate to reflection or logical thought. These include logic terms ('if', 'but'); words referring to cognitive functions ('think', 'plan'), or entities ('cause', 'belief'); problems of failure of cognitive or logical functions ('confuse', 'confound'); complex verbal communicative functions ('comment', 'argue'); and features of mental functioning ('creative', 'logical').

The REF dictionary was formed by having three judges, using a definition of the Reflection category, independently rate words from a large set of texts, including the texts used to make and test the WRAD.

For each word, if all three judges agreed on its inclusion, it was added to the REF dictionary. If two of the three agreed on inclusion, the word was given to a fourth judge, and included in the dictionary if the fourth judge agreed.

3 The Discourse Attributes Analysis Program (DAAP)

The DAAP system operates on the assumption that each dictionary represents an underlying psychological process that varies over time. For each dictionary and each turn of speech DAAP produces a smoothly varying *density function* that models the underlying psychological variable. DAAP uses these density functions to produce several derived measures; the density functions and some derived measures will be described and illustrated below.

The WRAD weights are given as lying between -1 and $+1$, with a *neutral value* of 0, corresponding to the RA scale score neutral value of 5. As is usual for a text analysis system, DAAP assigns the weight 0 to a word that is not in a dictionary; a word that is in an unweighted dictionary is assigned the weight $+1$; a word that is in a weighted dictionary is assigned its dictionary weight. As negative values are sometimes difficult to interpret for psychological variables, the WRAD dictionary scores are linearly transformed so as to lie between 0 and 1, with neutral value at .5. With this transformation, the DAAP density functions are all non-negative and have values between 0 and $+1$.

In what follows, the WRAD neutral value of .5 is used as a dividing line between segments of discourse that are considered to be high in RA and those that are considered to be low. This division enables DAAP to segment text into contiguous sets of words for which the WRAD density function is either high or low; that is, greater than or less than this neutral value.

3.1 Ordinary Text Analysis Functions

Session material is usually transcribed with markers indicating changes in speaker. DAAP permits but does not require this or other segmentation markers and treats each such marker as indicating a new turn of speech, thus allowing for different definitions of 'turn of speech'. For example, pauses of a certain length or longer might be viewed as indicating a new turn of speech, even if no change of speaker has actually occurred; or certain interjections, such as 'umhm', might be viewed as not indicating a change of speaker. For qualitative analysis of content spoken at interesting points as indicated by the graphs of the density functions, DAAP produces a marked text; this reproduces the original text file with markers inserted every 50 words.

3.2 The Density Function

For each dictionary and each turn of speech, DAAP constructs a *density function*, which has a non-negative value at each word in the turn of speech. This construction starts with a moving weighted average of the dictionary weights, where the weighting function is an exponential closely related to the normal curve. This weighting function is equal to zero for all values outside the range, $-99 \leq x \leq +99$. Except for the first and last 99 words of each turn of speech, the density function is equal to this moving weighted average. Special adjustments using a fold-over technique are made for the first and last 99 words. These adjustments have the consequence that the mean of the density function is equal to the mean of the dictionary weights. Precise definitions of the density function and the measures outlined below are given in the appendix.

Most therapy sessions have a total of between 5,000 and 7,000 words. For each dictionary, the density function appears as a visually smooth curve with discontinuities at each change of speaker. (As explained in the appendix, one can regard the density function as being defined at every real number so that it is a mathematically smooth function for every turn of speech.) The segments where the WRAD density function lies above the neutral value of .5 are easily located, and the text corresponding to these segments can be located in the marked text.

We illustrate the density function and the derived measures with graphs of the WRAD and REF density functions of Session 4 from a treatment carried out by Carl Rogers at the research program in psychotherapy of the University of Chicago; the client is known as Miss Vib (Rogers and Kinget, 1965). The treatment was regarded as highly successful, and this session was considered a pivotal session. Rogers and Kinget say that during Session 4 "the inner disorganization that characterizes this phase of the process reaches its climax" leading then to a shift into an evaluation mode in Session 5. In both these figures, the client data appears as the thinner black line; the therapist data appears as the thicker black line.

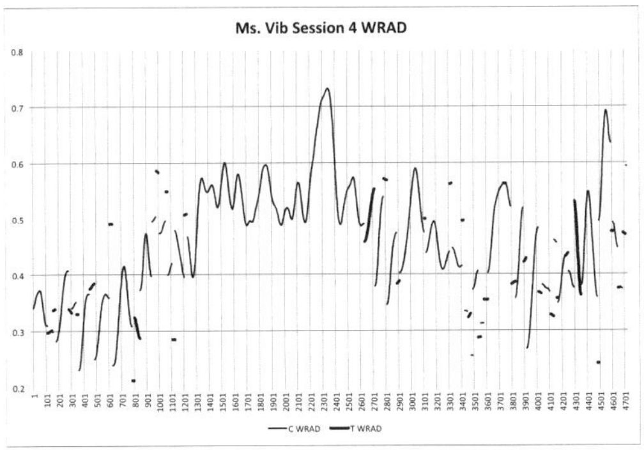

Figure 1: Client and therapist WRAD density.

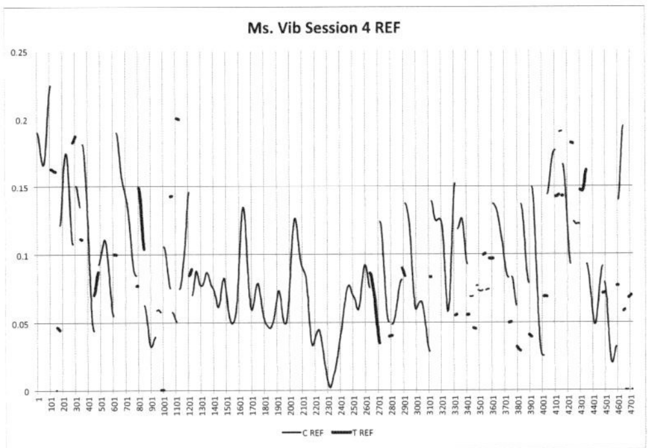

Figure 2: Client and therapist REF density.

The session opens with the client expressing her concern that she is not accomplishing much in the treatment, she wonders whether she should be doing something different, she's not sure what she should talk about. She feels she was functioning well several years ago; she doesn't know what is blocking her now in her life. The conversational pattern of relatively brief utterances by the client and responses by the therapist is characteristic of the treatment and continues until about word 1200; the therapist reflects the client's ideas, with some shifts in language. Following these interactions, Miss Vib begins a turn of speech of approximately 1400 words, lasting from about word 1200 to about word 2600; this is the longest uninterrupted utterance in this treatment.

In this segment, which reaches a WRAD peak of .73, as shown in Figure 1, the client tells how she had accepted a fellowship for graduate training without realizing what the fellowship required; then tells a detailed and vivid story of how she had to push herself through a project that she did not want to do, that she did not believe in, and that required work with a population and in a setting that was frightening for her. She is deeply immersed in the description and it is highly evocative for the reader.

During the same period, the Reflection (REF) measure is very low, as shown in Figure 2. As WRAD declines following the extended speech segment, REF increases; the graphs of the WRAD and REF density functions are close to mirror images of one another. This configuration, indicating separation of the Symbolizing and Reorganizing phases, is a major marker of the referential process. Miss Vib tells a pivotal story, and then reflects on it, leading to development of new emotional meanings.

3.3 Derived Functions

The *covariation* between two variables is a measure of the degree to which the variables are simultaneously high and low. Mathematically it is exactly the same as the (Pearson) correlation coefficient between the corresponding density functions. As the values of a density function at nearby words are not statistically independent, we call this operation *covariation* rather than correlation. The covariation of REF and WRAD is an indicator of the extent to which the speaker is separating the functions of symbolizing and reorganizing; we expect this measure to be mainly negative and to be more negative in more effective sessions and treatments (see Sec. 4.2). The REF-WRAD covariation for the 1405 words in the client's extended turn of speech shown above is -.76; for the session as a whole the covariation is -.56.

The *High WRAD Proportion (HWP)* is computed for each turn of speech, or for any user-defined set of turns of speech, as the proportion of words for which the WRAD density function lies above its neutral value of .5. It is used as an indicator of the proportion of time in a session that the client is in symbolizing mode. We expect this measure to be high for client speech in effective sessions, and at least not to decrease over time in successful treatments (see Sec. 4.2).

The *Mean High WRAD (MHW)* is the mean of the difference between the WRAD density function and the WRAD neutral value of .5, when this difference is positive. That is, MHW is computed by considering only those words for which the WRAD density function is greater than its neutral value of .5. It is used as an indicator of the intensity or vividness of language when the speaker is in symbolizing mode, and is independent of the number of words in the turn of speech or other text segment(s) under consideration. As with HWP, we expect this measure for client speech to be relatively high in more effective sessions and to be at a generally high level in successful treatments (see Sec. 4.2).

The figures above illustrate the power of the density functions to identify pivotal moments of a session. For the long turn of speech discussed above, Mean WRAD (MWRAD) = .55, HWP = .79, MHW = .07 and Mean REF = .07. For this session as a whole, the client Mean WRAD = .47, HWP = .40, MHW = .07 and Mean REF = .09.

4 Related Research

4.1 Evidence for Construct Validity

A relationship between WRAD and narrativity was established by Nelson et al. (2008), who used a set of 55 narratives from high school students talking about their most stressful time. They found a high (Spearman) correlation ($\rho = .69$, $p < .01$) between Mean WRAD and a measure of narrativity given by a count of temporal sequences (Labov, 1997).

Using a data set provided by Addis et al. (2008), Maskit et al. (2015) found a relationship for both MWRAD and HWP with a measure of episodic memory given by the proportion of 'internal' to total 'details'; the measures were applied to a set of responses by 32 participants to prompts for 8 past and 8 future personal (episodic) events. The responses were recorded, transcribed and separated into details by Addis et al. (2008). A detail was considered to be internal if it was a specific fact concerning the main event being described, and was considered to be external if it was general rather than specific, or it concerned an event other than the main event or was a repetition. For the 32 subjects, high (Pearson) correlations were found between this measure of episodic memory and HWP ($r = .68$, $p < .01$) and with MWRAD ($r = .58$, $p < .01$).

A set of 70 segments taken from psychoanalytic sessions were rated by judges on a scale of 1 to 7 for location in each of the phases: Arousal, Symbolizing and Reorganizing. For the symbolizing phase, high (Pearson) correlations were found between those ratings and MWRAD ($r = .56$, $p < .01$), HWP ($r = .58$, $p < .01$) and MHW ($r = .55$, $p < .01$); a high negative correlation with REF ($r = -.27$, $p = .02$) was also found. For the reorganizing phase, a high positive correlation with REF ($r = .42$, $p < .01$), and high negative correlations with MWRAD ($r = -.60$, $p < .01$), HWP ($r = -.60, p < .01$) and MHW ($r = -.52, p < .01$) were also found (Kingsley, 2009).

Murphy (2015) presents three studies showing that WRAD scores tend, on average, to be substantially higher when participants are asked to discuss stories, events, or other scenarios such as dreams in comparison to other speech contexts ($1.5 \leq d \leq 3.5$). These studies also show that WRAD scores have moderate temporal stability over a six week period for the same task ($.33 \leq r \leq .61$).

4.2 Applications to Psychotherapy

In a study of 16 sessions from a long term psychoanalysis, Bucci and Maskit (2007) found high (Pearson) correlations between a measure of session effectiveness based on clinical judgments (Freedman et al., 2003) and DAAP measures; these include the negative REF-WRAD covariation ($r = .70$, $p < .01$), and MWRAD ($r = .54$, $p < .05$). These suggest that in the more effective sessions, the client had more separation of symbolizing and reorganizing discourse, and was more vivid while in symbolizing mode.

Using the Italian version of this system, Mariani et al. (2013) used Spearman correlations to examine the client speech for entire sessions of three successful psychotherapies. They found as expected that HWP increased over time; that is, the client spent an increasing proportion of time in symbolizing mode [($N = 10$, $\rho = .79$, $p < .01$), ($N = 33$, $\rho = .43$, $p < .01$), ($N = 23$, $\rho = .33$, $p = .07$)]; the overall Mean WRAD (MWRAD) also increased over time for all three treatments, [($N = 10$, $\rho = .60$, $p < .05$), ($N = 33$, $\rho = .50$, $p < .01$), ($N = 23$, $\rho = .36$, $p < .05$)], and the REF-WRAD covariation decreased over time; that is, the client on average had more separation of the functions of symbolizing and reorganizing, [($N = 10$, $\rho = -.48$, $p = .08$), ($N = 33$, $\rho = -.49$, $p < .01$), ($N = 23$, $\rho = -.44$, $p < .05$)].

Andrei (2011) studied 15 sessions of a successful psychotherapy treatment (as measured by standard client self-report measures). Using Spearman correlations for client speech only and for sessions as a whole, she found predicted increases in MHW ($\rho = .52$, $p < .05$); MWRAD ($\rho = .37$) and the HWP ($\rho = .35$).

In a study of 14 sets of candidate treatment notes from the New York Psychoanalytic Society and Institute Treatment Center, high (Pearson) correlations were found between a measure of treatment effectiveness (found by comparisons of client functioning between beginning and end of treatment) and both MHW ($r = .73$, $p < .01$) and MWRAD ($r = .70$, $p < .01$), for the treatment notes as a whole (Bucci et al. , 2012).

5 Limitations and Future Research

The system presented here for the study of psychotherapy process is based on Bucci's theory of the referential process (1997). We are concerned with measurements for two of the three phases of this process, Symbolizing and Reorganizing. The WRAD, which was designed as a measure of the Symbolizing phase has been extensively validated and has been favorably compared with the only other known measure of this psycholinguistic style, the CRA. WRAD's correlation to the scales might be improved by including some number of less frequently used words, as was done with the Italian WRAD (Mariani et al., 2013), and/or by enlarging the number of text segments scored for RA on which the measure is based and using some machine learning techniques.

The Reflection dictionary, used to mark the Reorganizing phase, is unweighted and theoretically based. Our current information concerning the REF-WRAD covariation suggests that, just as people use different function words to different extents when speaking at different levels of the Symbolizing phase, so they may also use different function words to different extents for different aspects of the Reorganizing phase. To the best of the authors' knowledge, no weighted reorganizing dictionary or set of dictionaries based on these ideas has as yet been developed.

We have not here addressed the Arousal phase of the referential process, in part due to limitations of space, and in part because this phase is sometimes marked by silence, variation in speech rate and acoustic features rather than lexical items. The system described here, based on word count, includes a Disfluency measure, which can to some extent be used to mark the Arousal phase. We are currently developing a Variable Time DAAP (VTDAAP) that uses sound recordings to provide acoustic data, such as changes in pitch and intensity as well as pausing and speech rate. VTDAAP produces data for which the independent variable is time rather than word count. A first version of this program has been tested and is currently being revised; we expect it to be publicly available in early 2016.

A major feature of the DAAP system is the production of density functions. These depend on the values of the parameters used for the weighting function, as described in the appendix. These parameters were chosen so as to make the graphs of the WRAD and REF density functions for psychotherapy sessions reasonably smooth and readable. Changes in these parameters would produce changes in the derived functions described above; as there are, however, no other measures of the variables these measures are meant to model, we have no standard against which to measure the effect of changing the weighting function parameters.

Several new studies are currently under way relating WRAD to narrativity and Episodic Memory; these use a new version of DAAP that produces density functions based on user-defined segmentation.[2]

[2]We expect this version of DAAP to be publicly available in 2016.

References

Donna Rose Addis, Alana T. Wong and Daniel L. Schacter. 2008. Age-Related Changes in the Episodic Simulation of Future Events. *Psychological Science*,19(1):33–41.

Claudia G. Andrei. 2011. A multi-perspective analysis of a psychodynamic treatment. Doctoral dissertation retrieved from ProQuest (AAT 3491569).

David Arvidsson, Sverker Sikström and Andrzej Werbart. 2011. Changes in self and object representations following psychotherapy measured by a theory-free, computational, semantic space method. *Psychotherapy Research* 21(4):430–446.

Wilma Bucci. 1997. *Psychoanalysis and Cognitive Science: A multiple code theory.* Guilford Press, New York NY

Wilma Bucci. 2002. The Referential Process, Consciousness, and the Sense of Self. *Psychoanalytic Inquiry*, 22:766–793.

Wilma Bucci. 2013. The referential process as a common factor across treatment modalities. *Research in Psychotherapy: Psychopathology, Process and Outcome*, 16:16–23.

Wilma Bucci, Rachel Kabasakalian and the RA Research Group. 1992. *Instructions for scoring Referential Activity (RA) in transcripts of spoken narrative texts.* Ulm, Germany, Ulmer Textbank.

Wilma Bucci, Rachel Kabasakalian and the RA Research Group. 2004. *Instructions for scoring Referential Activity (RA) in transcripts of spoken narrative texts.*

Wilma Bucci and Bernard Maskit. 2006. A weighted dictionary for Referential Activity. In James. G. Shanahan, Yan Qu and Janyce Wiebe (Eds.) *Computing Attitude and Affect in Text.* Springer, Dordrecht, The Netherlands; 49–60.

Wilma Bucci and Bernard Maskit. 2007. Beneath the surface of the therapeutic interaction; The psychoanalytic method in modern dress. *Journal American Psychoanalytic Assn.*, 55, 1355–1397. doi:10.1177/00030651070550O412.

Wilma Bucci, Bernard Maskit and Leon Hoffman. 2012. Objective Measures of Subjective Experience; The use of Therapist Notes in Process-Outcome Research. *Psychodynamic Psychiatry*, 40(2):303–340.

Wilma Bucci, Bernard Maskit and Sean Murphy. 2015. Connecting emotions and words: the referential process. *Phenomonology and the Cognitive Sciences*, doi:10.1007/s11097-015-9417-z.

Wilma Bucci and Rachel K. McKay. 2014. Manual for Scoring RA Scales. figshare http://dx.doi.org/10.6084/m9.figshare.962956.

Paul Crits-Christoph, Mary Beth C. G. Gibbons and Dahlia Mukherjee. 2013. Psychotherapy Process-Outcome Research. In Michael J. Lambert. *Bergin and Garfields's Handbook of Psychotherapy and Behavior Change*, Sixth Edition. (pp. 298–340) Hoboken NJ: John Wiley and Sons, Inc.

General Inquirer. www.wjh.harvard.edu.

Norbert Freedman, Richard Lasky and Marvin Hurvich. 2003. Two pathways torwards knowing psychoanalytic process. In M. Leuzinger-Bohleber, A.U. Dreher and J. Canestri (eds.) *Pluralism and unity: Methods of reserach in psychoanalysis*, International Psychoanalytical Association, pp. 207–221.

Zac E. Imel, Mark Steyvers and David C. Atkins. 2014. Computational Psychotherapy Research: Scaling up the Evaluation of Patient-Provider Interactions. *Psychotherapy*, Advance online publication. http://dx.doi.org/10.1037/a0036841.

George Kingsley. 2009. The clinical validation of measures of the Referential Process. Retrieved from Dissertations & Theses Adelphi University. (Publication No. AAT 3377938)

W. Labov. 1997. Some further steps in narrative analysis. *Journal of Narrtive and Life History*,7: 395–415.

Rachele Mariani, Bernard Maskit, Wilma Bucci and Alessandra DeCoro. 2013. Linguistic measures of the referential process in psychodynamic treatment: The English and Italian versions. *Psychotherapy Research.*, 23(4):430–447; doi:10.1080/10503307.2013.794399

Bernard Maskit. 2014. The Discourse Attributes Analysis Program (DAAP) Operating Instructions. figshare. http://dx.doi.org/10.6084/m9.figshare.947740.

Bernard Maskit, Wilma Bucci and Sean Murphy. 2015 Computer Based Measures of Referential Activity and their Use as Measures of Episodic Memory. www.thereferentialprocess.org/theory/episodic-memory-and-referential-activity.

Erhard Mergenthaler. 1996. Emotion-Abstraction patterns in Verbatim Protocols: A new way of describing psychotherapeutic processes. *Journal of Consulting and Clinical Psychology*, 64:1306–1315.

Erhard Mergenthaler and Wilma Bucci. 1999. Linking verbal and nonverbal representations: Computer analysis of Referential Activity. *British J. of Medical Psychology*, 72:339–354.

Sean Murphy. 2015. Measuring the Details that Matter: The Validity and Psychometric Properties of the Weighted Referential Activity Dictionary. (Under Review)

Sean Murphy, Wilma Bucci and Bernard Maskit. 2015. Putting Feelings into Words: Cross-Linguistic Markers of the Referential Process. This Volume.

Kristin L. Nelson, Damian J. Moskovitz and Hans Steiner. 2008. Narration and Vividness as Measures of Event-Specificity in Autobiographical Memory. *Discourse Processes*, 45:195–209.

J. W. Pennebaker, M. E. Francis and R. J. Booth. 2001. *Linguistic Inquiry and Word Count (LIWC): LIWC2001.* Mahwah, NJ, Lawrence Erlbaum Associates.

Carl R. Rogers and M. G. Kinget. 1965. *Psychothérapie et relations humaines. Théorie et pratique de la thérapie non-directive.* Ed. Nauwelairts Louvain

Andres J. Roussos and M. O'Connell. Construcción de un diccionario ponderado en español para medir la Actividad Referencial. *Revista del Instituto de Investigaciones de la Facultad de Psicologa. UBA*, 10(2):99–119.

Sergio Salvatore, Alessandro Gennaro, Andrea F. Auletta, Marco Tonti and Mariangella Nitti. 2012. Automated method of content analysis: A device for psychotherapy process research *Psychotherapy Research*, 22(3):256–273.

Nicholas Samstag. 1996. A meta-analysis of referential activity. (Doctoral Dissertation) Retrieved from ProQuest (9705478).

P. J. Stone, D. C. Dunphy, M. S. Smith and D. M. Ogilvie. 1966. *The general inquirer: A Computer approach to content analysis.* Cambridge MA and London, The MIT Press.

W. Strunk Jr. and E. B. White. 1972. *The elements of style.* The Macmillan Company.

6 Appendix: The Density Function and Associated Measures

In this appendix we give precise definitions of the density function and the DAAP measures derived from it. The density function is constructed in two steps; the first is a moving weighted average of the dictionary weights using an exponential function related to the normal curve as the weighting function. It is a general statement that the mean of a moving weighted average is equal to the mean of the original function; however, the moving weighted average may have non-zero values at points where the original function is not defined. That is, if we are looking at dictionary values defined for the points, $0, \dots, N$, and the weighting function is different from 0 for the points $-m < x < +m$, then the moving weighted average may have non-zero values at the points $-m+1 \leq x \leq N+m-1$. The second step in the construction of the density function is a *fold-over* procedure that adjusts the values of the moving weighted average to take these 'extra' values into account. After the second step is accomplished, the density function is defined exactly for the words $0, \dots, N$, and its mean is equal to the mean of the original function.

The *Weighting Function* for the moving weighted average is defined in terms of two parameters: a 'pointedness' parameter q, and a 'support' parameter m. We start with the function W_0, which is zero for all x outside the range $-m < x < +m$. Inside this range

$$W_0(x) = \exp(-qm^2 \frac{m^2 + x^2}{(m^2 - x^2)^2}). \qquad (1)$$

Let $S = \sum_{x=-m+1}^{m-1} W_0(x)$. Then the weighting function $W(x) = W_0(x)/S$.

This weighting function has the following properties:

- $\sum W(x) = 1$.
- W is centered at 0, where it attains its maximum; its graph is symmetric with respect to the y-axis. (It is an even function.)
- W is strictly increasing from $-m$ to 0 and strictly decreasing from 0 to m.

- W is equal to zero for all x outside the range $-m < x < +m$.

For most purposes used here, the values of q and m are taken to be $q = 2$ and $m = 100$. We assume below that these are the values of q and m.

Using the same formula, we could have defined W_0 for all real numbers x, where it is positive exactly in the range $-m < x < m$, and then replaced the sum S by the corresponding integral. In this way W would be defined for all x, would have the properties listed above, and would also have derivatives of all orders at all points.

Let R denote some dictionary function defined on the set of words numbered from 0 to N, where $R(x) \geq 0$ for all x in this range. We also set $R(x) = 0$ for x outside this range. The first approximation to the R density function is the moving weighted average (convolution product)

$$C_R(x) = \sum_{y=-m+1}^{m-1} R(y-x)W(y). \qquad (2)$$

This is a finite sum for every x, and is equal to zero for all x outside the range $-100 < x < N + 100$. As remarked above, the mean of C_R, taken inside this range, is equal to the mean of R in the range $0 \leq x \leq N$. As it is difficult to assign a meaning to the value of C_R outside the range $0 \leq x \leq N$, some adjustments are needed to account for these values. The adjustments described below are equivalent to the idea that we "fold over" the x-axis, along with the graph of C_R at the points $x = -1/2$ and $x = N + 1/2$; then add these folded over values to the original values of C_R; and repeat this process as often as necessary.

As a particular example, assume that $N = 300$. Then C_R is defined and non-negative for the points, $-99 \leq x \leq 399$. For this example, we can write down the density function D_R as follows:

$$\begin{aligned}
D_R(0) &= C_R(0) + C_R(-1),\\
D_R(1) &= C_R(1) + C_R(-2), \ldots,\\
D_R(100) &= C_R(100), \ldots,\\
D_R(200) &= C_R(200), \ldots,\\
D_R(299) &= C_R(299) + C_R(302),\\
D_R(300) &= C_R(300) + C_R(301).
\end{aligned}$$

To make this process precise, we first define the auxiliary function $\widetilde{C}(R)$, by introducing the reflections: $r_1(x) = -x - 1$, which is reflection about the point $x = -1/2$, and $r_2(x) = -x + 2N + 1$, which is reflection about the point $x = N + 1/2$. We consider the group of motions G of the real line generated by r_1 and r_2, and define the auxiliary function $\widetilde{C}_R$ by

$$\widetilde{C}_R(x) = \sum_{g \in G} C_R(g(x)). \qquad (3)$$

This is a finite sum for every integer x. This function $\widetilde{C}_R$ is invariant under the group G; that is, for every x and for every $g \in G$, $\widetilde{C}_R(x) = \widetilde{C}_R(g(x))$.

Finally, the density function D_R is defined by $D_R(x) = \widetilde{C}_R(x)$ for $0 \leq x \leq N$, and $D_R(x) = 0$ for x outside this range. With this definition, the mean of the density function D_R is equal to the mean of the dictionary values, R; that is $\sum_{x=0}^{N} D_R(x) = \sum_{x=0}^{N} R(x)$.

Let D_W be the density function for WRAD; once this density function has been defined, it is easy to describe the High WRAD Proportion (HWP) and the Mean High WRAD (MHW).

Let V be the set of all integers x in the range $0 \leq x \leq N$ for which $D_W(x) > .5$, and let Z be the number of points in V; so that $0 \leq Z \leq N + 1$. Then

$$HWP = Z/(N+1), \qquad (4)$$

and

$$MHW = \sum_{x \in V} (D(x) - .5)/Z. \qquad (5)$$

The covariation $C(D_1, D_2)$ between two distinct density functions, D_1 and D_2, both defined on the same set of words labeled $0, \ldots, N$, is then defined exactly as the Pearson correlation coefficient (provided both densities are not constant):

$$C(D_1, D_2) = \frac{\sum_{x=0}^{N} (D_1(x) - M_1)(D_2(x) - M_2)}{\sqrt{V_1 V_2)}},$$

where M_1, respectively M_2, is the mean of D_1, respectively D_2, and V_1, respectively V_2, is the variance of D_1, respectively D_2.

The graph of the density function D for each turn of speech appears as a smooth curve. This can be explained by the underlying mathematical theory, which uses the continuous version of the weighting function W. Here, the dictionary values $R(x)$ are extended so as to be defined for all x in the range $-1/2 \leq x < N + 1/2$, by requiring that, for each integer n, where we already have $R(n)$ defined, we set $R(x) = R(n)$ for all x in the interval $n - 1/2 \leq x < n + 1/2$. Then the moving weighted average $C_R(x)$ is defined as in equation 2, replacing the sum by an integral. The definitions of $\widetilde{C}_R$ and D_R then follow exactly as above. One can use this continuous definition of the density function to define MHW, HWP and the covariations by appropriate modifications of the above formulae; that is, by replacing sums with integrals, and by replacing counts of words by sums of lengths of intervals.

Author Index